Seven Reasons Why
God Created
Marriage

JAMES FORD

Seven Reasons Why God Created Marriage

MOODY PUBLISHERS
CHICAGO

All Web sites listed herein are accurate at the time of publication, but may change in the future or cease to exist. The listing of Web site references and resources does not imply publisher endorsement of the site's entire contents. Groups, corporations, and organizations are listed for informational purposes, and listing does not imply publisher endorsement of their activities.

Editor: Kathryn Hall
Interior Design: Ragont Design
Cover Design: Brand Navigation, LLC
Cover Image: Dreamstime

This book is printed on acid free recycled paper containing 30% PCW (Post Consumer Waste) and manufactured in the United States of America by Versa Press.

Library of Congress Cataloging-in-Publication Data

Ford, James
    Seven reasons why God created marriage / James Ford.
       p. cm.
    Includes bibliographical references.
    ISBN 978-0-8024-2262-0
    1. Marriage—Biblical teaching. 2. Marriage—Religious aspects—Christianity. I. Title.

BS680.M35F67 2009
234'.165—dc22
                                                              2009016063

3 5 7 9 10 8 6 4

Printed in the United States of America

This book is dedicated to the Lord Jesus Christ who not only saved our souls but saved our marriage. His precepts and power enabled us to go from barely surviving to being blessed and thriving from the application of His seven reasons for creating marriage. I also dedicate this book to my lovely wife, Leslie Ann Ford. She is still my 12th rose, my faithful friend, dutiful wife, loving mother, extraordinary grandmother, and the sole object of my affections. The Lord has been very good to me. Bless His holy name.

Contents

Preface

"So do not be foolish,
but understand what the will of the Lord is."
—EPHESIANS 5:17 NRSV

This Scripture issues a warning to which we must wisely take heed, particularly if we want to avoid the pitfalls of marriage. I realize that it contains a sobering message, but it is also one worth taking the time to understand in the light of God's Word. It is only after we gain some understanding that we can then expect it to add meaning to our lives.

Throughout *Seven Reasons Why God Created Marriage* we will discover that we must begin with the right perspective *on* life in order to get the right results *out of* life. In order to be a good partner in marriage, we must first find out God's will for us as individuals. Above all, God's perspective is the one to follow if we desire to be successful in our undertakings.

Why then do we have so much difficulty in pursuing God's will? I contend that it is because we don't first seek God before setting out on our journey to find a mate, marry, and begin a family. If more people would do these things with God's reasons in mind, there would be many more successful marriages and fewer that end in defeat.

The purpose of this book is to help you understand God's will for your marriage by explaining how a godly marriage should function. It will provide practical counsel with a biblical perspective concerning marriage and show how this can transform your relationship. You see, when you invite God to be a part of resolving the problems you may be experiencing, God will bring the balance that your marriage needs. I also want to encourage single people who are contemplating marriage to carefully examine the guidance that I offer so they can refrain from entering marriage wearing "rose-colored glasses" and therefore avoid the common mistakes to which so many fall prey.

After reading *Seven Reasons Why God Created Marriage*, I pray that you would view marriage overall as God sees marriage—as a pattern of the holy Trinity. God instituted marriage for specific reasons—namely, partnership, procreation, perfection, pleasure, purity, and finally, to be a picture of Christ and His bride. These reasons are contained in the Bible and presented in this book with an explanation of how, collectively, they make up the pattern of the Trinity of God.

Just as it is God's desire for you to prosper and be in good health, it is His will for you to know His reasons for why He created marriage. But it is your responsibility to learn them and to make it a personal goal to apply them in your relationship. It is never too late to begin. Now is the time to get an understanding from God's Word about this thing called marriage.

Prologue

Marriage has been likened to flies on a screen door: Those that are on the outside are trying to get in, and those that are on the inside are trying to get out. The point is that the first step toward having a sound marriage is the understanding that if one person in the relationship is not in a good marriage, then neither partner is in a good marriage.

Marriage is a partnership and both partners have an equal responsibility toward each other. They each deserve to experience a true partnership, to have an opportunity for personal improvement, to be involved in the decision whether or not to produce offspring, to find pleasure in each other, and to share in a pure and wholesome relationship. And, above all of this, marriage partners have the opportunity to benefit from making their marriages a picture of Christ and His bride, the church.

The Bible has much to say on such an important subject as what marriage is all about. But first let me give you some insight into how people misunderstand what they are getting into when they decide on a marriage partner. For example, consider the following vignette. It makes a profound point about the misguided approach that many take when it comes to choosing a mate.

Two women were having a conversation. One of them said to the other, "You've been married and widowed four times. I know that each time a husband died you remarried, but what I don't understand is how you chose them. Your first husband was a banker, next you married an actor, then you married a preacher, and finally you married a funeral director. This really makes no sense to me."

Her girlfriend replied, "It makes plenty of sense to me."

Her friend responded, "You are probably the only one that it makes sense to! If you ask me, you took a step down each time you said 'I do.' Please explain it to me."

Her friend answered, "I have had four husbands: one for the money, two for the show, three to get ready, and four to go."

Now, you may find this story funny, but there was a meaning to this woman's madness. As crazy as it may seem, her choices were not random; rather, they were extremely misguided. I think we would agree that her explanation was highly superficial. Sadly, many people get married for reasons that are equally superficial. Although God has seven distinct reasons for marriage, a shallow relationship doesn't focus on doing it God's way.

Consequently, many marriages are in trouble because the partners chose each other for the wrong reasons. They don't realize that God has some very specific reasons for why He created marriage. And their lack of knowledge causes some serious pain. Some marry based on physical attractiveness. They do not understand that looks can attract you, but looks cannot keep you. You cannot live off physical beauty and other material trappings. There are men who married women who were capable of stopping traffic and making other men forget where they were going. However, many of these husbands would privately confess that they actually married "breathing mannequins." In other words, beneath the beauty there is no substance.

On the other hand, many women are married to men who look so good that they are practically indescribable. They were so caught up in choosing a mate based on his looks that they overlooked the fact that "Mr. Wonderful" had never been introduced to a complete sentence or an intelligent conversation.

The moral of this story is that attempting to develop a strong relationship based on physical attributes is like building a house on sand—it won't last. As many can attest, trying to maintain a lasting bond founded on physical attraction is no way to build a meaningful marriage.

Other people get married because of sex: Either they are having it and shouldn't be, or they are very anxious to get to it. However, sex alone will only make you think you have something that you really don't have. It will make you think that you are in love when you are really in lust. Unfortunately, sex has been used to mask a multitude of faults.

There are other reasons that our marriages erode but I think this covers enough areas for you to get the idea. Marriage must be built on a firm foundation. How do you build a strong marriage? First of all, you must understand the reasons God created marriage. God has a purpose for everything He does so it should not be a surprise that God has a purpose for marriage. That's one of the things most people don't consider before marriage. There are not many who sit down together and try to find out what God has to say about marriage; they don't consider that He has a reason for marriage. I believe that God has seven reasons for marriage, and I will attempt to make them clear to you in this book.

I understand what Paul was talking about when he said it would be better if we do not marry (1 Corinthians 7:8). In fact, most people are not ready to marry because they don't have a clue about what they are getting themselves into. If you are not whole within yourself, taking on the additional responsibility of loving and caring for someone else is probably not a good idea for you. The first order of business is to make sure you have developed a personal relationship with Christ before you even think about getting married. For those who have already taken the plunge, press the pause button for a moment and purpose in your heart that you want to improve your marriage. Then read this book with a renewed dedication and focus to do just that.

Marriage is a serious commitment and all too often it is not taken seriously. But thanks to God it is never too late for you to come to Him, acknowledge and confess your shortcomings, determine to make your marriage line up with His reasons for it, repent of your mistakes, and then move on with a new determination to love and honor God, your spouse, and yourself. Moreover, it would be well worth your time to get involved with a marriage ministry class that teaches the importance of knowing and applying God's seven reasons for creating marriage to get a clear vision of what marriage means to God and therefore what it can and should mean to you.

Once, for an illustration, I asked ten couples to look around the room at each other. I then told them that according to statistics, seven of the couples would not have married the person they were with if they could do it over. Why is that? Too often people marry with the wrong criteria and expectations.

When couples come to me for counseling I proceed to guide them in what the Word of God says about their relationship. I point them to the Trinity to help them see the pattern God has set for marriage. I tell them about the principles God has established for the purpose of making marriages successful. For those who believe that following the instruction of God's Word will improve their marriage, they will benefit greatly from the insights that are highlighted throughout this book. As married believers, we must be willing to search the Word of God to find the principles that we need to know and apply them to our relationships. God's Word holds the key to a successful marriage.

Moreover, for married couples who desire to evaluate their marriage so they can take the proper steps to make it all that God desires it to be, I often lead marriage workshops and retreats. During those events, I ask the couples to complete a profile that enables an assessment of the various aspects of their marriages. After having the two spouses exchange their profiles, many husbands and wives wonder if they are talking about the same relationship. This is because their personal opinions of what is happening in their relationship are so far apart that it makes them wonder if perhaps they have someone else's profile by mistake.

If you are anticipating marriage or are already married, you need to use *Seven Reasons Why God Created Marriage* as a guide to discovering the entire scope of marriage as only God's Word can provide it for you.

Introduction

It was on what is commonly called the longest night of the year—Christmas Eve. Our three children, James, Nathaniel, and Jonathan, were having great difficulty falling asleep. I could hear their hushed whispering and futile efforts to try to contain their enthusiasm and excitement. My difficulty was due to the bike that I was attempting to assemble. It was an English Racer that the store would have assembled for an additional twenty dollars. After struggling with it for four hours, I vowed never to be so thrifty again.

With nerves completely frazzled and patience entirely spent, I finally completed my task at approximately 3:00 a.m. The mere twenty dollars I had saved was not worth the eight hours I spent putting the bike together (I get mad every time I think about it)! But proud of my accomplishment, I yawned, stretched, and looked over my handiwork only to discover that I had four pieces of bicycle left over. My first thought was, why do they put extra pieces in these boxes? I soon found out that they were not extra pieces when I tried to ride the bike and it wouldn't move.

My loud shout of "Help me, Lord Jesus!" brought my wife running to me. As she wiped sleep from her eyes, there was obvious concern on her face along with the question "What's wrong?" on her lips. "I've been at this eight hours. I thought I had completed it, but I've got four extra pieces and the bike doesn't work," I explained in anguish. She then asked me a deeply profound question, "Did you follow the directions that they gave you in the manual for assembly?" I immediately gave the male ego answer, "I don't need the manual. I know how to put a bike together." After three more hours of disassembling the bike and then following the manual to put it together again, I had a working bicycle—and no pieces left over.

The next morning, my stock went up dramatically with my oldest son, James, as he rode on his new bike. I learned a valuable lesson that night. The manufacturer designed the bike and put all the pieces for assembly in the box along with the manual. This had been done so that I could have guidance in assembling it and fun watching my son riding it once every part had been put in its proper place.

What happened with putting together that bike is happening in too many marriages today. God has allowed us to have leftover pieces because we haven't consulted the Manual, the Word of God, for assembling a marriage properly. In fact, the failure to use the "extra pieces" He has provided for us has contributed to an almost 50 percent divorce rate in America— even among Christian marriages. Yet, when we take the time to first consult the Manual, we find that God has given us all the pieces to properly put marriage together.

In actuality, those "pieces" are God's reasons for why He created marriage and each one is necessary to a marriage that is truly whole and not lacking any good thing. To be specific, marriage was created for the partners to share the following with each other: the pattern of the Trinity, partnership, perfecting, procreation, pleasure, purity, and the picture of Christ.

Before you can understand these seven reasons for marriage, you need to know who God is. And to do this, you have to recognize that when we speak of God we are speaking of the Trinity. My hope is that you'll be as excited as I was to discover that God's reasons for marriage all have a direct relationship to God's makeup. Each of them is vital to assembling your marriage according to God's blueprint. I pray that your heart's desire is to improve your relationship with your spouse. If so, you must be willing to disassemble your marriage and reassemble it to reflect all God's reasons. When you do, your marriage will begin to grow stronger.

I'm sure that for some these ideas are not altogether associated with being married. Before tackling any subject that is worth knowing about, I am a firm believer in getting a grasp of all the essential parts of that topic in my attempt to study it fully. Moreover, I realize that most people may have heard of it but don't have a working knowledge of what the expression *Trinity of God* means. Therefore, as we approach the seven reasons for marriage, I believe a background explanation is in order. We need to understand who the Trinity is, why God created the first two human beings, and why He joined them in something called marriage. So, let's get started.

Who Is the Trinity?

"Then God said, 'Let Us make man
in Our image, according to Our likeness.'"
—GENESIS 1:26

Have you ever asked yourself whom God was speaking to when He said, "Let Us make man in Our image"? Was He speaking to Himself? No, God is not schizophrenic. He is referring to the other Members of the Godhead, which together make up the holy Trinity. You see, God is a Trinity, a tri-unity. He is the blessed three-in-one sovereign God, not 1+1+1, but 1x1x1, which equals one.

Thus, the Trinity is made up of three Persons called the Godhead. What is so incredibly special about this, and the primary reason that it is difficult for humans to comprehend, is the nature of a relationship where the members participate in a co-equal existence and interact in voluntary submission to one another. Even so, we do have some understanding of what the word *relationship* means because quite often we grapple with various relationships over the course of our lifetime. But within the context of our finite minds and a limited capacity for imagination we do not readily grasp what the divine relationship of the Trinity looks like.

Nevertheless, this is God's desire for us—to conform to the image in which He created us and to imitate the pattern of the Trinity in our earthly relationships. And, if our desire is to please God, our Creator who has made every provision available to us, it is our task to not only embrace His plan but to also emulate it. God declared it to be so when He said, *"Let Us make man in Our image."* It's like this: When a man and woman have children, naturally, they want their offspring to look like them. Moreover, people want their children to grow up and reflect the values they have instilled in them. It is no different with our heavenly Father. He desires for us, His children, to look like Him. He takes pleasure in us when we behave in the way that He expects us to; that is, in conformity with the teachings in His Word. For this reason, we must rely on our faith in Him that He will make the truth of His Word a reality for us.

Now, at first glance, we may find it difficult to see ourselves in the image of God; we don't see it reflected in our marital relationships either because we don't easily get this idea of equality and submission that the Trinity is made of. Somehow these two words don't even seem to fit in the same sentence. But, they do fit together and God wants us to learn how we can connect them in our lives by studying His own design. Because it came from the very mind of God, this is a spiritual concept that will produce a spiritual reality in our lives. As such, it is attainable for us through the grace and power of God.

When you look at society today, it is becoming increasingly difficult to see the distinctions God wove into the fabric of the male and female DNA and what that means in the marriage relationship. But, that is the very reason we don't look at society for our cues. Instead, we look to the Bible, the Word of God. It should remain our source for direction in life. So, don't get caught up in the tide of current events going on in this world. You and your mate, as believers in Christ Jesus, are joined in holy matrimony. You took a vow before God that He expects you to honor and uphold. And by the power of God, you can make your marriage reflect the love and beautiful relationship that the Trinity shares. After all, this is God's desire for you and He is your assurance that it will become real and tangible for you. Jesus said it in two simple words, *"Only believe."*

The Trinity is the sum of the complete essence of God. In every way, each Person of the Trinity is equally submissive to the others. The Father glorifies the Son (John 17:1–5), the Son glorifies the Father (John 15:8), and the Holy Spirit glorifies the Son (John 16:13–14). They are always putting one another first and none of Them take glory for Themselves alone.

Furthermore, the Bible teaches the eternal procession of the Son from the Father. This is shown in Scripture where it discloses, *"No one has seen God at any time. The only begotten Son, who is in the bosom of the Father, He has declared Him"* (John 1:18 NKJV). So, the Son proceeds from the Father and they share the same essence. Jesus also introduced the Holy Spirit as proceeding from the Father and the Son. Later on He informed His disciples of a coming event, *"When the Helper comes, whom I will send to you from the Father, that is the Spirit of truth who proceeds from the Father, He will testify about Me"* (John 15:26; John 14:26). So then, the Holy Spirit proceeds from the Father and Son in eternal procession. In other words, this means that They all partake of the same essence and together make up the holy Trinity.

When God the Father, God the Son, and God the Holy Spirit had a meeting in eternity, They decided to create man in the image of God; that is, after the divine pattern of the Trinity. Thankfully, this was a meeting of the Trinity and not a mere committee of human design. Had the decision involved humanity it may have ended up a three-way tie instead of the unanimous agreement that it was: a complete reflection of the supreme wisdom and sovereignty of God.

So then, what does it mean for us to be made in the image of God? Fundamentally, it means that, as God's highest created being, we are also a trinity. We were made with three dimensions: spirit, soul, and body. The spirit of man gives us a God-consciousness, the soul gives us a self-consciousness, and the body gives us a world-consciousness. It is the spirit of man that allows us to commune with our Maker, who is also Spirit. The soul is the aspect of man that is comprised of conscience, imagination, emotion, intellect, and will. The body is the material aspect of man that helps us to relate to the physical world. In essence, God gave man both natural and spiritual characteristics so that he could exist in an earthly world, interacting with the other creatures of nature with his body and soul. Yet, with man's spirit, he can also relate to the Creator, who is Spirit.

Who Is Man?

Ultimately, everything that pertains to God is wrapped up in one word—*relationship*. God used the pattern of the Trinity to create a being that He called "man" because God is a God who is in a relationship with Himself. He wanted a creature with whom He could relate, one who would reflect His divine presence in the earthly world. So He created man in His image, after the pattern of Himself. Since God made Adam according to His own likeness, Adam was made to be an earthly being with a reflection of God's Trinity in heaven. This is how it happened:

> *"Then the Lord God formed man of dust from the ground,*
> *and breathed into his nostrils the breath of life;*
> *and man became a living being."*
> —GENESIS 2:7

Can you feel the loving touch that is spoken of here? You should be able to because the Word of God is talking about you. God "formed" man and "breathed" life into him. Until this point, He had spoken into existence all of the creative elements that He had produced. For example, when He spoke light into existence in Genesis 1:3, He said, *"Let there be light,"* and the light appeared.

But for man, the highest form of earthly creation, God took the time to get intimately involved in the process. He reached down and used the dust, or clay, of the earth and shaped the man's body. To add the final touch, God then breathed His own breath into the man to give him a part of Himself that no other creature on earth would possess.

But God was not finished yet because He didn't want Adam to be alone. To accomplish all the things that God expected him to do, Adam would need a special relationship. So in Genesis 2:18, God gave Adam a wife, a partner, whom he named Eve. For the sake of companionship and interaction with Adam, Eve was created.

We truly have a loving God who didn't have to create us, but He did. And we don't even come close to showing our appreciation for the goodness and mercy that He shows to us each and every day. The psalmist David seemed to have a glimpse of this understanding. Think about what he said to the Lord,

> *"What is man that You take thought of him,*
> *And the son of man that You care for him?"*
> —PSALM 8:4

Can you imagine a greater blessing than to exist in the mind of God? Because of His great love for us, we were chosen by God to be a reflection of Him. God carefully placed within the first man, Adam, His own divine attributes. Through Adam, God ordained a specific role and expectation for humanity to play. Adam was given the responsibility to represent God in this earthly realm. His job meant that he would rule and reign over all the other creatures that God had created. The Bible speaks of this truth in Romans 1:20 (NKJV) when Paul attests,

> *"Since the creation of the world His invisible attributes are*
> *clearly seen, being understood by the things that are made,*
> *even His eternal power and Godhead."*

Scripture clearly draws the connection between God's earthly attributes that we can visibly see and the Godhead in heaven that we cannot see. Here the Bible assures us that it took the power of God to make the earthly creation reflect the divine attributes of the Godhead. As fellow human beings, we only need to observe one another and the things of nature to know that God's presence is very real and there is no greater power.

At this point you may be wondering why a book about marriage is beginning to sound like a book on theology. Trust me, it's not to add pages to this book. Just hold on because I am going to turn the theology I have spoken of into *doology*. There is a meaning to my method. I am going to take you from revelation to application. I will present doctrine to you that will articulate your inherent duty as a Christian believer. Moreover, as a model for how God expects you to operate in your marriage, I will show you that God set forth His pattern to be a demonstration of what a marriage should be.

God's intentions for marriage are deliberate and the way that you view your marriage should be as well. But we don't fully understand His purpose for marriage, and that lack of understanding is the number one reason why most marriages don't work.

Why God Instituted Marriage

"It is not good for the man to be alone;
I will make him a helper suitable for him."
—Genesis 2:18

When God created woman He was taking His purpose for creating man one step further. Not only does He want man to reflect His own image on earth, now He wants man to have a counterpart, someone to be in relationship with him.

Marriage was designed to be a demonstration of the Trinity. The biblical account of marriage was set forth in Genesis chapter 2 when God declared,

So the Lord God caused a deep sleep to fall upon the man,
and he slept; then He took one of his ribs
and closed up the flesh at that place.

The Lord God fashioned into a woman the rib which
He had taken from the man, and brought her to the man.

The man said, "This is now bone of my bones,
And flesh of my flesh; She shall be called Woman,
Because she was taken out of Man."

For this reason a man shall leave his father and his mother,
and be joined to his wife; and they shall become one flesh.
—Genesis 2:21–24

This is the way God set it up from the beginning. God Himself officiated the first wedding ceremony when He joined Adam and Eve as man and wife. At that moment, marriage became the strongest bond in all of human relationships.

Many years down the road, the apostle Paul picked up on what God had done. He wrote of the great mystery that surrounds the likeness that God drew between the joining together of a man and woman in matrimony and the direct reference it has to Christ and His church. The Spirit of God used Paul to teach the church what this marriage thing is all about. In the book of Ephesians, Paul addresses how we are to live out the marriage commitment. He spells out the comparison between a husband and wife relationship and the connection it has to Christ and His bride—the church. This is the pattern of the Trinity as it relates to the union of marriage:

> For the husband is the head of the wife, as Christ also is
> the head of the church, He Himself being the Savior of the body.
>
> But as the church is subject to Christ, so also the wives
> ought to be to their husbands in everything.
>
> Husbands, love your wives, just as Christ also
> loved the church and gave Himself up for her. . . .
>
> So husbands ought also to love their own wives as
> their own bodies. He who loves his own wife loves himself;
> for no one ever hated his own flesh, but nourishes
> and cherishes it, just as Christ also does the church,
> because we are members of His body.
>
> For this reason a man shall leave his father and mother and shall
> be joined to his wife, and the two shall become one flesh.
>
> This mystery is great; but I am speaking with
> reference to Christ and the church.
>
> —EPHESIANS 5:23–25, 28–32

By showing us the love that Christ has for His church, it is evident that God wants us to imitate that same kind of love toward each other. God defined the husband's role to show care and concern about the things of the wife. And conversely, the wife's role was to be caring about the things of the husband. The two are now one. And as such, they are intended to share in a mutual exchange of love and honor—just as the Members of the Trinity love and honor one another. God was saying to His creation: *You have been made in Our image. I want to teach you how to conduct your marriage by giving you the Trinity as the pattern.* As descendants of the first couple, God is speaking to us in the same way because we mirror the same roles in marriage as the first couple.

Now, I realize that understanding the connection between marriage and the likeness of the Trinity may be somewhat difficult to comprehend since the traditional roles of a man and wife are constantly challenged in today's society. Our God-given functions have become increasingly blurred to the point that even Christians are often confused by what they see happening in our culture. But know that God does not change. He is the same today, yesterday, and forever (Hebrews 13:8). And His intentions remain steadfastly focused. At the end of the day, we still have to answer to Him for how we treated His most sacred union.

That is why God laid it on my heart to share His reasons for marriage with you. We can get this only if we apply ourselves to doing everything that we can to understand God's intentions. Our marriage vows are on the line. We must be deliberate in pursuing God's reasons for marriage and turning to His Word to see what He has to say about it. That is where the answers to our questions lie. Ultimately, we must do our very best to rise above the worldly influences that would cause us to stray from God's plans for this thing called marriage.

The Word of God is the Manual that outlines the instructions He has given us on how to put our marriages together so that they function properly. Just as each individual part of the bicycle works together to make it function, each of God's reasons for marriage is a vital component to the making of a godly marriage. My goal is to lay out those reasons for you so that you can incorporate any piece that is missing from your relationship and let God work on you and in you so that you will experience all the fulfillment and success God has intended for your marriage to enjoy.

I trust that your marriage will be richly blessed as you read *Seven Reasons Why God Created Marriage.*

Reason #1

The Pattern
of the Trinity
Reveals a
Spiritual Reality

Almost two years ago, in a quiet moment, my wife looked at me through her pain and tear-filled eyes and said, "I know you are tired of having to do everything without my aid and assistance. I know you are tired of not being able to enjoy the things that most husbands enjoy, like coming home to a cooked meal and a clean house instead of having to come home and cook the meal and clean the house yourself. You have been taking care of me for sixteen years without much help and without much of a break. Besides that, you have also been taking care of my mother with her Alzheimer's disease.

"Sometimes I really feel bad that I cannot help you more. I long for the days when I was whole and able to take care of my man and my home. I am tired of me being sick and I know you are tired of me being sick too. I know you are ready to leave me and give up on our marriage. At least I feel like that is what you probably want to do."

At that moment, she was making a reference to her sixteen years of debilitating illness that includes four nervous breakdowns, three major surgeries, five minor surgeries, complications from Type 2 diabetes, high blood pressure, chronic back pain, and severe migraine headaches, which have generally ended up with us at the hospital so that she could get a shot for relief from the insufferable pain. These excruciating setbacks have rendered her virtually unable to perform even the most simple of tasks.

By God's grace, for the past eighteen years now I have had to do all of the shopping, all of the washing, most of the cleaning of the house, and the cooking, among other things. As I reflected upon the faithfulness of the Lord Jesus Christ, He showed me that my greatest problem in my marriage was not with my wife but with me. I thought about how He has taught me that in order for my marriage to be successful, like Him, I have to die to self.

With those thoughts in mind, I gingerly took her hand in mine and stroked it as I lovingly gazed into her pretty brown eyes and said, "I love you and I have loved you from the first day I met you. Do you remember that I told you on that first day that I would marry you even though you were only eight years old and couldn't spell the word *marriage*? The Lord has matured me to the point in our marriage that even though I may get tired *in* serving you, I don't get tired *of* serving you because I can do all things through Christ who strengthens me. So, even if you never get better I have already decided to take care of you for the rest of my days. I am not saying that I haven't had struggles. I am saying that sometimes I too wish that you were fully restored and things were like they were prior to your getting sick. But long ago the Lord taught me that marriage was not about finding the right person but about being the right person.

"He has enabled me to love you as much in your sickness as I have loved you in your good health. All glory goes to Him! And besides I always tell you that I am so committed to you that if you ever leave me, I am going with you. I know that a successful marriage is one that is able to weather the fiercest storms of life."

Tears now were freely flowing from both of our eyes as I drew her close to me in a warm embrace and softly kissed her lips and reaffirmed my love for her. She fell asleep in my arms and I thanked the Lord Jesus for His sustaining strength and for teaching me how to utilize the first principle of marriage—the pattern of the Trinity.

A Spiritual Foundation for Marriage

The Trinity of God is a spiritual family based on a divine relationship. Since it is God's intention that the marriage relationship reflects His relationship with Himself, it is crucial to our success that we line up with God and keep Him at the center of our marital relationships. There is only one way that we can achieve this goal. A godly marriage that is grounded in the Lord must have a spiritual foundation.

As I tried to console my wife and ease her concerns, I asked her, "How often have you heard me preach from the pulpit that, in the spiritual sense, *I* am a wife because I am part of the church, the bride of Christ? But, in the natural realm, I am a husband married to you, Leslie Ford, my loving wife. But if I am to love you in the way in which God desires for me to love you, I must first submit in the spiritual to my Husband, the Lord Jesus Christ. He cares for me as I submit myself to Him. Then I step off into the natural, and what my Husband in the spiritual does for me as His wife, I do the same for you. If I'm going to be a successful husband in the natural I must first submit to my Husband in the spiritual, the Lord Jesus Christ. Everything that He does for me in the spiritual, I step off in the natural and, by His power, do that for you. So, if I were to fail as a husband in the natural it would be because I first was a failure as a wife to the Lord Jesus Christ in the spiritual. This is how I am able to care for you in the way that God intends for me to do."

I have no doubt that God intends marriage to follow the pattern of the Trinity because my own marriage has proven to be a reflection of the essence of biblical truth: *"Husbands, love your wives, just as Christ also loved the church and gave Himself up for her"* (Ephesians 5:25). Brothers, know that this is very real. The God of the universe is saying to you: when you become a husband, loving your wife unconditionally is not simply an option—it's a necessity.

Once vows are exchanged, it is the same for every married couple. In a traditional marriage ceremony, we present a ring to our betrothed. When a man puts a ring on his wife-to-be, he is saying that it is a symbol of his love and commitment to her. It is a symbol of protection that is supposed to make her feel secure as she is encircled with the love and protection of her mate. The ring is made of a precious metal that is to give a foretaste of what the man's provision will be. He wants her to know that he will take good care of her. When he places the ring on her finger, she wears it in open display. The man is saying to her that he will always display her as his glory in that same way.

Another good example is found in a traditional Jewish wedding ceremony. The husband makes a solemn commitment to his wife by removing his outer tunic and putting it around her. He is saying to her, from that point on, she will never be naked or cold. She then accepts this gesture by wearing the coat throughout the rest of the ceremony.

What better way to begin a marriage than with a covenant agreement that expresses the depth of your love and a desire to care for each other. However, it's after the ceremony when it's "put up or shut up" time that your covenant agreement has to be backed up with some serious action from both partners. What I'm saying is, you can't just go through the motions; you have to live it out through the good times and the bad times. As I have shared from my personal experience, I am not telling you something I do not know firsthand.

Allow me to reiterate that if a man is not a good husband in the natural, it is because he is not a good wife in the spiritual. It's all about your relationship with Christ that positions you to receive the goodness of God and then transfer that goodness to your marital relationship. Brothers, this one is exclusively for you. Remember what Scripture says: *"He who loves his own wife loves himself."* If you want to get better as a husband in the natural, then hook up with Jesus in the spiritual and He will help you put your marriage in order.

There are some practical things that you can do. For your marriage to work, you must follow the Guidebook, that is, the Word of God. If you are not already doing so, I strongly recommend that you join a consistent Bible study group particularly designed for married couples. Christian marriage counseling can also be an effective means in helping to sort through the typical day-to-day issues that arise in married life as well as offering assistance in working through major problems. You must also develop a consistent prayer life because sincere prayer can only serve to improve your situation. As a married couple, these are the tools that will help you line up with God's Word. The essence of Christ will start to fill your spirit, soul, and body, and you will begin to see His influence in each other. When you are able to see Christ in your mate, it will help you to realize that submitting to each other in love is possible just as you are learning how to submit to Christ.

Prayer Holds the Key

It is not too difficult to understand why we don't get this. But it is truly a shame that many Christian couples do not even pray together on a regular basis. Spending time together communicating with God is necessary to keep your marriage healthy and stable. If asked the question whether you and your mate have a daily prayer time, would you be embarrassed to answer? Part of the problem is, too many couples don't even have meaningful conversations with each other. So, let me suggest that you turn off the TV so that the two of you can begin a routine practice of talking to God together. It would even make it easier for you to talk to each other. Try it, you might like it. And know that God will be there to join in with you whenever you're ready.

You see, when you invite God in as a partner in your marriage, you do so through prayer and obedience. Prayer is what holds us together. In fact, it can be the difference between staying together and improving your marriage or getting a divorce. A poll on "Couples Who Pray" taken by Baylor University and George Gallup compared those who "pray a lot" with their spouse versus those who pray "sometimes." The results were as follows: 78 percent vs. 60 percent say their marriage is happy; 91 percent vs. 74 percent say their spouse is their best friend; 75 percent vs. 64 percent agree on how to raise their kids; 60 percent vs. 58 percent agree on finances; and 72 percent vs. 52 percent say the quantity and quality of their love is good.[1]

Sincere and consistent prayer can be an effective prevention method to steer a failing marriage toward reconciliation. Why? Because God honors the earnest prayers of His people. James, the apostle, understood this principle. He encouraged the believers to pray because *"The effective prayer of a righteous man [or woman] can accomplish much"* (James 5:16).

Now, I realize that a commitment to pray faithfully as a couple united in love can't be a "one size fits all" approach. You and your spouse have to agree on the proper time and manner in which to come together in prayer. However it works for you is best. But with the divorce rate today being one in every two, the point is that it is important to be determined to make your marital relationship the strongest it can be. And simple but heartfelt prayer can go a long way.

My wife and I make it a practice to pray together on a regular basis. I can readily attest to the fact that it's very difficult to pray together and still be angry with each other. At the same time, we try to obey Ephesians 4:26–27: *"Be angry, and yet do not sin; do not let the sun go down on your anger, and do not give the devil an opportunity."* To keep from giving the enemy a chance to destroy what we have built together, we attempt to find resolution to our problems before going to bed. Generally, we're able by God's grace to resolve an issue in this way even though sometimes we've had to stay up for five days in order to obey the Scriptures. Seriously, though, my wife and I pray together almost every day and have a devotional time together two to three times each week. As we have tried to follow His lead, God has used our efforts to strengthen our marriage relationship tremendously.

Food for Thought:

- To combat the challenges and obstacles that face married couples today, you will have to take some other deliberate steps toward keeping your marriage alive and well. Spending quality time together is the best way to create a deep sense of belonging and intimacy. When is the last time you and your mate went to bed at the same time? Many couples are missing out on chances for building intimacy by not going to bed at the same time (and I'm not talking about solely for the purpose of having sex, although that's also good).

- Do you and your spouse have a regular date day? This is a time you set aside to be together—with no children and no in-laws—nobody but you and your spouse. To counteract the pressures and strains of day-to-day life, do something that you both enjoy, and do it often. Lord knows there are enough difficulties that you must face as the two of you overcome the issues of life. You need to create a sense of balance that comes from a steady effort to reinforce the fact that she knows that you are hers and you know that she is yours.

Leslie and I have a regular date day and one of the activities that we share has facilitated our love in a big way. We call it our "Spiritual Leadership Schedule." It is our effort to be proactive rather than reactive in our marriage. During our quality time, we discuss each of the items on the following list.

SPIRITUAL LEADERSHIP SCHEDULE
1. Discuss upcoming date
2. Share Bible memory verses
3. Discuss budget
4. Pray together
5. Evaluate personal quiet time
6. Plan weekly schedules together
7. Schedule/plan family devotions
8. Discuss wife's outside activities
9. Conduct exercise program
10. Set projects (spiritual and home)
11. Discuss spiritual successes and failures
12. Set personal goals
13. Minister to each other over meals
14. Schedule next spiritual leadership time

Feel free to adapt this list to your personal needs. The point is to set aside quality time to spend with each other and use it to establish definite goals that will benefit you and your relationship. And remember to be proactive and not reactive!

A Perfect Relationship

"That they may all be one; even as You, Father, are in Me and I in You, that they also may be in Us . . . The glory which You have

given Me I have given to them, that they may be one, just as We are
one; I in them and You in Me, that they may be perfected in unity."

—JOHN 17:21–23

Speaking to the Father on our behalf, Jesus prays for those who believe in Him. It is clear from His words that Jesus wants us to be included in the picture of the Trinity. Here He describes the perfect relationship that is indicative of the Trinity. We should be thankful that, through God's infinite love, He desires to unify us and make us perfect by our close association with Him. Since the concept of family existed in the Trinity first, when God designed man—both male and female—He did it so that the relationship would look like the Trinity. When you look back at the beginning of human existence, notice that it all started with a family—a man, a woman, and their children—which becomes a mirror of the Trinity.

This is a glorious thing. Not only are we in relationship with each other, but most importantly, God, our Creator, is at the center of that relationship. That's the connection needed to make our marriages work; it's the complete picture—a picture of perfection.

Then what does a godly relationship look like when it reflects the Trinity? The Members of the Godhead unequivocally honor and reverence one another. They don't look to see who is number one on the marquee. The Father is always pointing to the Son and the Son is always pointing to the Father and the Spirit is always pointing to the Son. There is never a vote among the three on who will be promoted in the relationship. No one is complaining about the rotation. You won't find the Trinity having arguments about one of the three always getting more attention than the other.

When you think about the Trinity, envision a picture of a relationship where there is no selfishness, only true harmony and perfection. The Father is not concerned about the Father; He is concerned about the Son. The Son is not concerned about the Son; He is devoted to the Father. The Spirit is not concerned about the Spirit; rather, His attention is focused on the Son.

Does this sound like the relationship between you and your mate? If so, let me be the first to commend you. If not, then you are like so many others. If you recognize that your marriage is in need of improvement and you want a better relationship, then why not pray and get into agreement with God so that you and your spouse can get ready to make some real and positive change happen. It took some time before I reached the place in our marriage that I could accept what I could not change in my life. But, after much prayer, I recognized that a change needed to take place in me. The Holy Spirit then brought this Scripture to my attention: *"Let this mind be in you which was also in Christ Jesus,"* (Philippians 2:5a NKJV). Over and over I have prayed these words in my marriage, so that I would exercise the servanthood and humility of our Lord and that He would empower me to fulfill the vow that I made thirty-seven years ago—to have and to hold, in sickness and in health.

Someone has to take the first step in recognizing the need for change. Take a minute and reflect on your situation. Could it be that one or both of you may not think you're ready? Often human nature is such that it just seems easier to do nothing and to deal with the status quo. If the climate in your marriage is less than desirable but you find it difficult to try and do anything about it, ask yourself, "So, what is it that's holding me back?" Well, read on and allow me to show you some things. You might even recognize yourself and decide that you're ready to do your part so that your marriage is more in alignment with God.

Selflessness versus Selfishness— How Do You Measure Up?

God wants us to grow continually in our marital relationships until we begin to imitate the Trinity. The nature of the Godhead, the pattern of the Trinity, is a selfless union. Therefore, I want to point out that this is a key ingredient that is lacking in many of our marriages—it is an attribute called *selflessness.* You need to understand that God would not have designed marriage to be like the Trinity if He had not made it possible for it to be so. But, as human beings, we have a problem that holds us back from assuming our rightful place in God. The issue is that all too often we operate in a mode of *selfishness* instead of selflessness.

Selfishness is the number one problem in marriage. It could be at the root of your problems too, and it's very easy to test yourself and determine where you stand. Three simple words can reveal whether you are operating in your marriage with a selfish attitude. They are: *I'm not happy.* It's not uncommon for us to be concerned about three persons: me, myself, and I. It says that your focus is not on pleasing God and having a desire to please your mate. Instead, your attitude shows that it's all about you.

Here's an "aha!" epiphany moment that is worthy of your consideration: God attuned marriage to the pattern of the Trinity so that you could understand that it's not about you. Rather, marriage is about you and your mate lining up with His Word. Sadly, it is an attitude of selfishness that causes us to break the model God has set with the Trinity. We spend a lot of time trying to figure out who is investing the most in the relationship. We waste time and energy trying to make sure the relationship is a fifty-fifty proposition. We are concerned about being taken advantage of and are overly cautious to avoid being "used." (Let me be clear, I am not talking about abusive situations here. This discussion is about plain old human nature and its tendency toward selfishness.) Too often getting our own needs met is more important than meeting our spouse's needs.

Instead of following the pattern of a perfect relationship set by God—a pattern of showing unconditional love, honor, and reverence for each other—many times we become record keepers in our marriages. We keep mental notes of what we do for him or her and whether or not our benevolence is being properly reciprocated. We are trying to make sure the other person isn't getting more out of the relationship than we are. That is not how the Trinity operates and it's not how God would have our marriages work either. The Word of God speaks succinctly to us through Philippians 2:3:

> *"Do nothing from selfishness or empty conceit, but with humility of mind regard one another as more important than yourselves."*

Now, think about this. Close your eyes for a moment and imagine what life would be like for you and your spouse if both of you treated each other the way that you personally want to be treated. Giving the highest amount of respect and adoration to each other would be a good thing, wouldn't it? There's nothing wrong with the two of you working together to make this a reality; in fact, it's about all that is righteous and good. And Jesus is with you on this, backing you up with a simple command to show you where He stands:

"Treat others the same way you want them to treat you."

—LUKE 6:31

The principle is very simple, yet we have such difficulty putting it into practice. How could you possibly go wrong with putting your mate first when at the same time he or she is putting your wants, needs, and desires before his or her own? When you get this, I guarantee that your life will be better; you'll enjoy a far greater amount of success in your relationship. You'll discover that life is much sweeter when you live it God's way.

But somehow, we've got it all backwards. The pursuit to get married should not be an exercise in finding someone to do something for you: someone to take care of you, someone to keep you company, someone to protect you, someone to comfort you, or even someone to support you. That is not to say that these things should not happen in marriage—it's just that they should not be the reason why we go into the marriage. Rather, we should be thinking the reverse and want to share our lives with someone whom we can love and support. There should be a strong desire to demonstrate godly care for one another, which is the result of each one placing the other first. That is how you get the most out of your marriage because that is how God designed it to be.

The truth is, if we would spend as much time worrying about our spouse's needs as we do about our own, many problems in our marriages would be eliminated. Marriage is not about finding the right person; it is about *being* the right person. As a pastor, this is one of the reasons I am a strong proponent of premarital counseling. It is my opportunity to teach a couple why God created marriage and equip them with an understanding of the right reasons for getting married. They will then be better prepared to form a godly union that resembles the Trinity.

In fact, because God wants us to operate in a mode of selflessness, the Bible has a lot to say about what we are to do for each other. These declarations are commonly referred to as the "one anothers." The "one anothers" are not just to govern our relationships with others in the body of Christ; they should also be applied in marriage. To find out how you and your spouse measure up, check out the following chart. It lays out some food for serious thought on how, as believers in Christ, you are to treat each other (and everyone else that you encounter in life).

Mark 9:50	be at peace with one another
John 13:34–35	love one another
John 15:12, 17	love one another
Romans 12:10	be devoted to one another in brotherly love; give preference to one another in honor
Romans 12:16	be of same mind toward one another
Romans 13:8	owe nothing except love to one another
Romans 14:13	don't judge one another
Romans 14:19	build up one another
Romans 15:5	be of same mind with one another
Romans 15:7	accept one another
Romans 15:14	admonish one another
Romans 16:16	greet one another
1 Corinthians 7:5	stop depriving one another

The Word of God is the first source to tap into to help you avoid the pitfalls of selfish behavior. These verses tell you what God expects of us in our daily interactions. Let me suggest that you make a commitment to spend some quality time with this as a joint exercise. Studying these Scriptures together will give you and your mate a greater advantage. In other words, marriage is strengthened when a couple focuses on ministry to each other and is not focused on a selfish display of protecting "my rights."

Well-known Christian author and Bible teacher Dr. Charles Swindoll makes a profound statement to married couples as he explains, "Being committed to one's mate is not a matter of demanding rights, but releasing rights .... God has a better way: Surrender your rights. Lay down your arms. Release your grip on the things you've been fighting for. Commit the risk to God. Trust Him to defend you and keep you from being ripped off. I say that to husbands just as much as I do wives. Releasing rights, ideally, is a mutual thing—a duet, not a solo."[2]

This is great advice for anyone who is interested in strengthening their relationship. Just think of the benefit your marriage would receive if you applied these words of wisdom in your situation.

The Art of Dying to Self

One rich man told his wife, "I think you only love me for my money. If I lost all my money, would you still love me?" She responded, "Of course, I would still love you! I would miss you, but I would still love you."

Here's the problem. Before there is one marriage, there needs to be two funerals. For the sake of your marriage, you must first die to yourself. If you don't, you will end up with one wedding and two funerals. I'm talking about the need to die to your old self, that aspect of you which is wrapped up in selfish ways and tendencies so that your marriage can thrive.

If this sounds at all familiar and you know that your marriage is in trouble because of your selfish attitude, I strongly urge you to surrender to God—it's the only way to get your marriage on the path to success God's way. If you're worried that you'll be giving up your own rights, keep this in mind: When you both come into agreement to turn your marriage around, you won't be losing anything by sacrificing your personal needs. In fact, just the opposite will be true. You have everything to gain.

Let's face it, to fulfill God's reasons for marriage you must have an unselfish mind-set. It's absolutely the only way that you will be able to put away your own self-seeking desires and love your spouse with the love God expects from you. Far too often people get caught up in planning the wedding day and give little regard to the many days that will come after the ceremony is over and all of the wonderful festivities that go along with it. This is a trap that has led countless people from the altar to the courtroom in quick fashion. When asked why a couple ended up in divorce, someone once said that they never had a marriage, they only had a wedding. This is a sad but true commentary in so many cases.

It is a well-kept secret, but overlooking the example of the Trinity as it applies to marriage illustrates the number one reason why marriages are deteriorating at such an alarming rate. Following the pattern of the Trinity is the right prescription for marriage; it's the missing ingredient. God Himself has set the pattern for behavior by modeling what the relationship should look like. But instead of honoring each other as a married couple with the kind of reverence that the Members of the Trinity honor one another with, you have a problem with submitting to your mate. God is calling you to put away your old motives and die to your old self. When you don't give preference to your spouse's needs over your own, it won't work as God intended.

Let me give you some background to help you understand why it is absolutely necessary to answer God's call and align yourself with His desire for you to pattern your marriage after the Trinity. In Genesis chapter 1, God's focus is on the essence of the man and woman. They have co-dominion of the earth based on the equality that comes from the fact that both were made in the image of God.

Let me reiterate this important truth! Having dominion rights is based on the fact that man and woman possess the same essence because they were both made in the image of God. Clearly, then, God establishes the indisputable fact that man is not superior to the woman and the woman is not inferior to the man. It is an undeniable truth that they are equal because God patterned them both after the Trinity. Although they were not created at the same time, the account in Genesis chapter 1 is a summary of the creative process that combines the creation of two separate beings into one storyline. It is presented in this way so that no one would be confused when He delineates the functional order of the two beings in Genesis chapter 2.

Then, in the second chapter of Genesis, God gives the chronology of Adam and Eve's creation. It is understood that they were not created at the same time even though God made them equal in essence. They were designed to have different functions, and, like the Trinity, will align themselves in a functional order to accomplish God's purpose for them.

To further illustrate how the pattern of human creation and the pattern of the Trinity demonstrate equality as well as function, 1 Peter 1:1–2 delineates the function of each person of the Trinity as it relates to man's salvation:

> *"To those . . . who are chosen according to the foreknowledge*
> *of God the Father, by the sanctifying work of the Spirit,*
> *to obey Jesus Christ and be sprinkled with His blood:*
> *May grace and peace be yours in the fullest measure."*

So then, the apostle Peter lays it out like this: God the Father appointed us to our salvation; God the Son atoned for us in salvation; and God the Holy Spirit applied our salvation to us. Even though the Members of the Godhead are equal in stature, they voluntarily aligned themselves in a function order for the purpose of providing salvation for us.

Paul takes this very practical analogy of the truth and applies it in 1 Corinthians 11:3 when he states, *"But I want you to understand that Christ is the head of every man, and the man is the head of a woman, and God is the head of Christ."*

Here's the parallel. When you became a believer, you entered into a marriage relationship with Christ, who is the Head of the church just as a husband is the head of his wife. This symbolic act is a bedrock tenet of our faith in God. Once you are a new creation in Christ, your old self has been put away and God has given you a new nature (2 Corinthians 5:17). But for the "new" you to come forth, you have to work with God. Listen to the words of the apostle Paul:

> *"For if you are living according to the flesh, you must die;*
> *but if by the Spirit you are putting to death*
> *the deeds of the body, you will live."*
>
> —ROMANS 8:13

He is saying that you have to overcome your old ways and thoughts and give the Spirit of God room to help you live a new kind of life. The life that God wants you to have is one that is not selfish and self-centered but rather it is focused on serving Him and putting others first. Paul paints a picture of how this plays out in our relationship with Christ:

> *"Therefore I urge you, brethren, by the mercies of God,*
> *to present your bodies a living and holy sacrifice, acceptable to God,*
> *which is your spiritual service of worship. And do not be conformed*
> *to this world, but be transformed by the renewing of*
> *your mind, so that you may prove what the will of God is,*
> *that which is good and acceptable and perfect."*
>
> —ROMANS 12:1–2

We belong to Christ, we are members of His spiritual body—the church. When you make a commitment to God to live a new life in Christ, your decision requires you to give up your own fleshly desires to be more like your heavenly Creator God. However, you cannot do this without constantly feeding your mind and your spirit with the Word of God. It is the power that allows you to live according to the Spirit of God and to maintain vital fellowship with God.

Here's the solution. A marriage union can and should be a reflection of the Trinity. After all, this is God's first reason for marriage. Marriage is sacred to God, and He expects us to treat it that way. Paul was talking about this when he said we are to present God with a living sacrifice. It means dedicating your life and your marriage to Him. So, we should approach the state of matrimony by recognizing the pattern God designed for it. I know that you want to honor God with your marriage because it's a part of your responsibility to please Him in everything that you do. But you should know that you cannot accomplish this without giving to God what He asks of you—that which is a good and acceptable and perfect self-sacrifice.

As followers of Christ, it should be our desire to be like Him in every way possible. But we have to begin with exchanging our natural mind-set of selfishness with a spiritual mind-set of selflessness. This will only come by studying the Word of God and putting it into practice. When you and your spouse cooperate with God, He will bring abundant blessings to you that will make your marital union a spiritual reality—a reflection of God's Trinity.

God has blessed us with so many blessings that we can't even begin to count them all. All He asks of us in return is to obey Him. It should be a direct response to His love and the mercy and grace that He showers on us. But obedience requires you to connect with the Holy Spirit and allow Him to change your heart and your mind so that you view your life and your marriage with a heavenly minded perspective. He is just waiting for you to get in line with Him so that He can fulfill His work in and through you.

The Bible calls us as believers to follow Jesus' example and emulate His selfless behavior. So, perfecting the art of dying to self needs to be a constant goal. Our good friend Paul, the apostle, spoke of the seriousness of putting this idea into practice. He brilliantly captured what we have to do in our walk with Christ when he said,

"I have been crucified with Christ; and it is no longer I who live,
but Christ lives in me; and the life which I now live in the flesh
I live by faith in the Son of God,
who loved me and gave Himself up for me."
—GALATIANS 2:20

In the same way that Paul recognized the change that took place in him when he became a believer, you have to realize the contrast between how you once lived and how you must allow the power of God's Word to put that old life to death in you. If you want your marriage to be pleasing in God's eyes, I can't stress enough that the old life in the flesh and its negative behavior that resisted the idea of submission has to die.

Giving up your personal desires for the sake of your marriage means that you have to renew your mind and build up your faith. As Paul acknowledged, you must get to the point that you are able to "die daily" (1 Corinthians 15:31). There are no shortcuts. You have to cooperate with the Spirit of God. As you yield to Him and allow God's Spirit to live large within you, your flesh won't win. It can't win over the power of God. You will get the victory and that's a promise from God. I know for certain that I could not have made it through some difficult times without relying on God's power and grace. I love my wife and throughout our marriage Jesus has taught me how to overcome our difficulties by serving her with the mind of Christ and not my own. I cannot take any credit; I can only look at us through the mirror of our struggles and see how the selflessness of the Trinity is at work.

So, find out where you are concerning your marriage. Do so by using the Word as a mirror and asking God to show you your true self. A good place to begin transforming your mind is to meditate on Philippians 2:2–5. These verses beautifully describe the real deal that must be at the foundation of every marriage:

"Make my joy complete by being of the same mind, maintaining the
same love, united in spirit, intent on one purpose. Do nothing from
selfishness or empty conceit, but with humility of mind regard one
another as more important than yourselves; do not merely look out

for your own personal interests, but also for the interests of others.
Have this attitude in yourselves which was also in Christ Jesus."

Whether you are already married or planning to get married, the road to victory is the same. It starts with your commitment to a godly relationship. Having a relationship with God at the center will make your marriage connect with the pattern of the Trinity. All I ask is that you be honest with yourself. If you are willing to take a long, hard, prayerful look at yourself, you may find that you must put aside some old ways that aren't working to benefit you and your mate. I strongly encourage you to examine your current motives and behavior since they may be serving to hinder the success of your relationship and keeping you from pleasing God. It's never too late to change; you just have to begin the process of hooking up your marriage with God.

So, prepare yourself: your awakening will come through constant and fervent prayer and placing your trust and confidence in God with a sincere heart.

A Spiritual Reality—Getting Connected

Often as we read the Bible we envision the people in biblical history as pristine characters. In other words, we don't see the people in the Bible as *real people* who had flesh and blood and emotions like us. Pick a soap opera, any soap opera. It won't be any more entertaining than many of the stories you find in the Word of God. That is, if you read it with the right eyes.

The Story of Joseph and Mary

When I read the Bible, sometimes I find myself saying, "Lord, I don't need television!" There are some stories in the Bible that would make hit television shows. Like Joseph and Mary's story, for example. When Mary discovered that she was pregnant, they were legally married. They had commenced their marriage but had not consummated it, meaning they hadn't had sex yet. In fact, custom dictated that they had to wait for one year. So, put on your sanctified imagination and picture this scenario.

Joseph goes over to Mary's house and this is what happened. "Hey, Mary! Girl, you've gained weight! What have you been eating! You haven't been eating pork, have you?" Mary responds, "Joseph, I have something to tell you. It may sound a little strange, even unbelievable, but I need you to trust me and to remain calm. Joseph, I am pregnant." Joseph reacts with shock, "What! What did you say? Wait a minute! Did you just tell me that you are pregnant? I know for a fact that we haven't consummated our marriage."

Mary pleads, "Please calm down and let me explain." Joseph says with indignation, "What is there to explain? You're pregnant and it's not mine. Exactly what is it that you want to explain?" Mary continues, "I am trying to tell you how it happened." Joseph retorts, "Oh, I think we both know how it happened. I'm more interested in why." Mary responds, "Please, Joseph. You really don't understand." Joseph questions, "What don't I understand, Mary? You are my wife. We have not had sex. You are pregnant. It is not mine! What am I confused about? What is it that you need to explain?"

"Joseph, please listen to me. I'm pregnant by the Holy Spirit," Mary explains. "You're what! Whose is it? The Holy Spirit! From the looks of things, I think you've had time to come up with something better than this. I know that's not the best you can do for an explanation. I'll give you a few minutes to try again." Joseph is furious.

"I am telling you the truth. I am pregnant by the Holy Spirit," Mary says. "Since when does the Holy Spirit go around impregnating other men's wives? If I were to believe that, then tell me how holy can He be if He gets my wife pregnant!" Joseph shoots back. "No, Joseph, you don't understand," Mary goes on. "An angel appeared to me and said I would become pregnant by the Holy Spirit."

"Mary, I need to get away from you for a little bit. I don't understand why you wish to insult my intelligence in this way, but I think it is best that I remove myself from your presence right now."

Now, what could be a bigger problem than that? This is a huge problem! He could have had her stoned to death, but Joseph was a good man and made up his mind that he would just put Mary away privately. If he had done so, Mary would have had no choice but to accept his decision. She would then need to find her own way in life as an unwed mother. That could not have been an easy road to take for either of them—particularly since they would have been outside of God's will. But, thanks be to God, we know that is not how their story ended.

Allow me to serve you notice: the problem with your marriage—however you might see it—is not the problem. It's the way that you and your spouse handle your problem that is the problem. Joseph and Mary were confronted with a major predicament that could have split them up and changed their lives drastically. According to the law of the land, he should have had her stoned or at least divorced her. That was the law, it was his legal right.

Why didn't that happen? The first thing they did was receive God's Word about their situation. Luke reported that the angel visited Mary with the news of her pregnancy (Luke 1:26–38). Mary accepted it and submitted her will to God. The book of Matthew records that the angel came to Joseph and told him not to worry about it because Mary was telling the truth (Matthew 1:18–25). When the angel confirmed the truth to Joseph that she was pregnant by the Holy Spirit, he acknowledged that word and acted in obedience to God's will.

There is a powerful thing about how Joseph and Mary handled their dilemma; not only did they *hear* the same message, they heeded the same message. They trusted God. We can learn a critical lesson from their story because this is where we often miss it. Joseph and Mary were on the same spiritual wavelength. That is what enabled them to hear the same message and respond positively to God's direction. They may have had to face some difficulty because they chose to obey God, but they made the right choice anyway. As a result, they found themselves in alignment with God's will. Lining up in obedience to God and what He tells you to do may not always seem like the easiest route to take, but it will make all the difference in the world for you—just as it did for Joseph and Mary.

Don't miss this point. They could not have succeeded in making the right choice if they were not connecting on the same wavelength, getting the same message, and responding to it in the same way—in obedience to God. Moreover, Joseph and Mary didn't hear the same thing and come up with separate responses. If they had taken another approach and ignored God's message, solving their dilemma would not have been possible. They would have been forced to face the consequences of their actions. Instead, they both surrendered in obedience to God and followed His path for their lives.

That's what is wrong with many marriages today. Husbands and wives are not on the same spiritual wavelength. They are not connecting with God. And when conflict arises, one partner is on an AM frequency, the other partner is on an FM wavelength, and God is beaming through on satellite. They haven't tuned in to God and what God is saying. They are not connecting to the Source from which all blessings flow so they can hear clearly what God is saying to them. You have to first connect with Him and then trust Him enough to line up with His will.

When conflict arises and you and your spouse are having trouble handling it properly, you are probably on two different wavelengths. After making a decision to try to fix a problem, do you ever regret the outcome? Think back on some of your difficulties—does this sound familiar? If so, you probably weren't connected with God's purpose in the way that Joseph and Mary succeeded in doing. When you are in tune with God, you will know when your struggle has been resolved with God's help.

God will intervene in your situation and send word about how to solve your marital conflict. But it's how you receive the message and then respond to it that matters. It all comes down to hearing and obeying God's Word; but first you have to be on the same frequency with Him to even hear the same thing. That is what determines whether you and your spouse will experience victory in God.

Joseph and Mary allowed themselves to be on the same spiritual wavelength and that made them a spiritual couple. As a result, God was able to minister to them. Theirs was a true picture of the pattern of how the Trinity works together for our good. Joseph was willing to do what he knew was best for Mary at the expense of his own reputation. He gave up his right to vindicate himself and have her punished. And Mary humbly allowed God to have His way in her life. Both of them were rewarded for their faithfulness. This kind of love comes directly from obeying God and creates a strong foundation for marriage. It is the giving up of one's rights for the benefit of the other. And that is something that we need to see more of in our marriages today.

When you and your spouse make the connection with God's Trinity, the Word of the Lord will become true in your marriage, *"With God nothing will be impossible"* (Luke 1:37 NKJV).

Making It Happen

1. With an open and receptive heart, ask God to help you understand how to apply His reason for creating marriage (as a pattern of the Trinity). He will hear your sincere prayers and help you to transform your marriage into a reflection of His image.

2. Keep in mind that strong communication between you and your spouse is of utmost importance to the success of your marriage. If you haven't already done so, start a regular prayer and spiritual leadership time with your spouse where you talk about your concerns and your victories.

3. Both of you should then set aside some regular personal devotion time to spend with the Lord. When you go before the Lord, ask Him to help you understand His seven reasons and how they relate to your marriage. Ask the Lord to show you how you can begin to implement them in your relationship. Ask the Lord to give you the grace daily to help you focus on the adjustments you need to make.

4. Begin a personal journal by writing a brief statement that expresses your and your spouse's reasons for getting married. Talk about your dreams and aspirations. What do you plan to accomplish through your marriage? Share with each other how you will work toward achieving your personal plans and how they work together with the overall reason for why you got married. Record your individual thoughts and feelings on these subjects.

5. Break down the results of your discussion so that you can set some practical goals. Write out your goals and how you plan to reach them. Review them regularly during your spiritual leadership time. Begin by answering the following questions and add others that are appropriate for you and your spouse: What are your spiritual goals? What are your financial goals? What are your health and fitness goals? And so on.

6. Describe in as much detail as you can how you will reach your goals. Define what the results will look like in your life and marriage.

7. List the areas in your life that you need to yield to the Lord so that He can help you be a better spouse.

8. Search the Scriptures and write out some key verses that will reinforce your ability to implement the new actions you will take in your life and marriage. Commit the verses to memory.

Reason #2

A Partnership
in God
Recognizes a
Spiritual Role

The story is told of a wealthy man and his wife who were traveling home from a long distance trip. After taking a wrong turn, they happened to end up in the seedy part of a town. Running low on fuel and in desperate need of directions, the man pulled into a small, rundown gas station with just one pump. He went inside to ask for directions on how to get back to the freeway. With a renewed sense of confidence, he left the tiny office where another worker had given him some advice.

As he approached his car, he saw his wife talking to the gas station attendant. The attendant was shabbily dressed in a striped shirt with checkered pants that rose up to show his polka dot socks running over his worn-out brogan boots. His curiosity grew as he noticed that the conversation they were having was quite animated.

After the couple was back on the road again, the man asked his wife if she knew the attendant. She told him that the man had been a boyfriend of hers many years ago. It was, in fact, when she was in junior high school. Her husband responded by telling her how fortunate she was that she had married him instead. If she hadn't, she could have been the wife of a mere gas station employee. Feeling as though he was

overlooking her part in his success, she quickly took issue with his statement. She pointed out to her husband that he was making a broad assumption by judging that he would have been successful whether he had
married her or not.

As it turns out, what the woman told her husband was correct. No matter the outcome, the fact remains that marriage is a partnership and both
spouses have a responsibility to significantly contribute to each other's lives.

A man named Nathaniel once discovered the reality of this truth. When
he had been fired from his job, he reluctantly went home to inform his wife,
Sophia. Surprisingly, she told him that was a good thing because now he
could devote his time to his passion for writing. He asked her how that
would be possible in light of the fact that he would no longer be able to produce an income. She then told him that she had been saving a little money
from her household expense allowance. The sum she had accumulated was
enough to sustain them for at least a year.

As a result of their circumstances, our world was enriched because of
this couple's partnership. The book that he wrote is entitled *The Scarlet Let-
ter*. Nathaniel Hawthorne went on to become a literary genius. But it possibly would have never happened had he not been married to Sophia
Peabody Hawthorne.

Dr. Patricia Valenti made the following observation in her book on the
life of Sophia Hawthorne: "She changed the way he thought. It was not acknowledged but people now recognize the marital relationship and the influence of a wife on her husband."[1]

> *"It is not good that man should be alone."*
>
> —GENESIS 2:18

With one supernatural declaration after another from the Creator God
about the good work of His hands, there was an extraordinary moment
when God looked at Adam—the only human creature on earth—and God
said that it was not good.

I ask the question, why did God say that it is not good for man to be
alone? After all, God was there; He was with Adam. And with that being so,

how could man have been by himself? There had to be some other way in which man was alone in God's mind.

This question took me on a spiritual journey, and I started to think about what God said about the Trinity. He revealed in His Word that *"God is spirit, and those who worship Him must worship in spirit and truth"* (John 4:24). I also thought about the presence of fellowship that exists in the Trinity: *"For there are three that bear record in heaven, the Father, the Word, and the Holy Ghost: and these three are one"* (1 John 5:7 KJV).

Furthermore, I reasoned that man is a spiritual being—but his essence is not deity, it is humanity. For man's design to pattern after the image of the Trinity as God stated in chapter 1 of Genesis, Adam needed someone made of his own essence to fellowship with. Yes, God and Adam shared fellowship with one another, so he was definitely not lonely. But God as Deity did not correspond with Adam as human. They could relate Spirit to spirit, because God gave man a spirit, but they could not relate on a deity-to-humanity level. Consequently, one can take from God's declaration that there is a fellowship God wanted man to have, which God Himself would not supply.

God is the ultimate Provider. He had already surrounded Adam with all kinds of creatures for him to interact with and reign over. But when He said these words, *"I will make him a helper **comparable** to him"* (Genesis 2:18 NKJV, emphasis added), God acknowledged that Adam would be living in solitude without the companionship of someone who could communicate with him on his level, for no other being created thus far reflected God's image in the same way as Adam did. This is the reason God said that Adam was alone. It is what compelled God to create a counterpart for Adam, thereby fulfilling a need that not even God was going to satisfy for him. Thus, the idea of a partnership was born when God gave Adam a companion with whom he could fellowship.

As his mate, Eve fit that role precisely. She was the companionship that was right for Adam. Eve was that special someone to share life with him. It's what partnership is all about. In so many words, God was saying to Adam, "I'm giving you somebody who resembles you; she will be your counterpart. I am giving you a partner who has your same essence but who will have a different function. She will be your helper." However, it is important to note that her role as his helper did not make her inferior to Adam. It simply takes two to make a partnership. Eve was created to share dominion of the earth with Adam. She was intricately designed by God to function as Adam's partner and be the "one who helps."

This is how the marriage of Nathaniel and Sophia worked as a beautiful partnership. As he set out to work and provide for his family each day, little did he know that his wife was wisely creating a nest egg that would eventually become so important to their welfare. After one means of support went away, Nathaniel needed time to sit down and write a significant piece of literature. Understanding that she was his support system, Sophia stepped in and provided that means of support which would allow him to do just that. Just as God had designed the marriage relationship to work, he was the provider and she was the one who helped him. As they both mirrored their God-given functions, they were in sync and their future together was made more secure.

The Heart of Equality

"God created man in His own image, in the image of God He created him; male and female He created them."
—GENESIS 1:27

When God set about making Adam and Eve, His main focus was on creating the dimension of man that makes us look like the image of God. It is this aspect of humanity that contains our spiritual essence and our eternal nature. He then took this idea and produced two physical genders—male and female—and applied one collective term that describes them both. This phenomenon is at the heart of what made them equal partners.

So, when God used the word *man* in Genesis 1:27, He was using it in a generic sense. Just as there is no distinction in equality between the Members of the Trinity, He was showing no distinction in the equality of the two human beings. As a result, when God spoke of man, He was referring to both the male and the female genders. Thus, it was the spiritual essence of Adam and Eve that caused them to resemble the partnership reflected in God's Trinity. Moreover, the image of the Trinity is a perfect expression of divine equality. Just as the very first couple was designed to imitate this pattern, it stands to reason that God established gender equality as the center of a marriage partnership.

From the moment Adam and Eve were united, they were two individuals sharing equally in an earthly existence as husband and wife. Now, the picture of the Trinity was fully represented in God's creation story. With God in their midst, Adam and Eve were of equal stature and had everything they needed, including each other, to carry out their functions as man and woman on earth.

However, God didn't stop there; He made the situation even more intriguing. Beginning with the first couple, God gave the two genders separate identities by assigning them unique traits and characteristics. He did so because He intended the partners to have specific functions in the marriage relationship. Yes, we are equal in essence, but we cannot overlook the fact that a husband and wife differ in a functional sense. On the other hand, our roles are different but that does not diminish our equality in God's eyes. We will talk in-depth later on about the differences in the functions of marriage partners.

But here's where human partnerships get somewhat complicated. There is a little something called *submission*. Please be aware, submission has a stigma attached to it because of the bad rap it has taken over the years. Know that we have to break through such barriers. It is the only way to accomplish God's desire for us to experience true partnership in marriage. Husbands and wives have to do their respective parts by submitting to each other out of love. Clearly, Nathaniel and Sophia Hawthorne understood their functions, which greatly contributed to their successful marriage partnership. His love for her made him go to work and his desire to provide for her also made him distraught when he lost his job. Her love for him caused her to sacrifice the ability to buy more "things" and put that money away instead as she quietly saved for a rainy day. This is the kind of attitude that God wants to see in His children—a demonstration of love and commitment to each other. True love and submission go hand in hand. And together they make up a recipe for a successful marriage that looks like the Trinity.

The Principle of Equal Submission

Yes, this thing called marriage goes far beyond choosing a beautiful wedding dress and just the right banquet hall. There is a thing called "equal submission" that is identified in the following verse. This principle must be taken into account if a couple wants their marriage to last.

> *"Giving thanks always for all things unto God and the Father*
> *in the name of our Lord Jesus Christ; **submitting** yourselves*
> *one to another in the fear of God."*
>
> —EPHESIANS 5:20–21 KJV, emphasis added

The term *submitting* that is used in Ephesians 5:21 does not refer to one person having complete power over another person; rather, it means that one willingly puts oneself under the authority of someone else. This is how the Trinity works. On many occasions Jesus taught His disciples about the relationship that He shared with His Father in heaven. To better understand how submission works in the Trinity, listen to the apostle John speaking of Jesus:

> *"For this reason therefore the Jews were seeking all the more to kill*
> *Him, because He not only was breaking the Sabbath, but also was*
> *calling God His own Father, making Himself equal with God.*
> *Therefore Jesus answered and was saying to them, 'Truly, truly, I*
> *say to you, the Son can do nothing of Himself, unless it is something*
> *He sees the Father doing; for whatever the Father does, these things*
> *the Son also does in like manner. For the Father loves the Son, and*
> *shows Him all things that He Himself is doing; and the Father will*
> *show Him greater works than these.'"*
>
> —JOHN 5:18–20

Now hear what Jesus said of Himself:

> *"Do you not believe that I am in the Father, and the Father*
> *is in Me? The words that I say to you I do not speak on My*

own initiative, but the Father abiding in Me does His works.
Believe Me that I am in the Father and the Father is in Me."

—JOHN 14:10–11

Jesus is talking about the deepest kind of love that exists: God's love. He is saying that the relationship between the Son and the Father is so intimately intertwined that they wholly and willfully defer to one another in love. Although He is the Son of God, Jesus did not speak on His own authority, He spoke for His Father. The Father loves the Son and did not withhold anything from Him. To complete the picture of the Trinity, Jesus went on to include the Holy Spirit by saying that He would pray to the Father to send the Spirit of God to help us through life (John 14:16–17). Do you see the beauty of a relationship that is based on love and submission where no one person is greater than another?

The principle of equal submission comes from the very heart and mind of God. Therefore, it is based on God's unconditional love. And you can rest assured; God does not leave us alone to figure out whether we are able to lovingly submit. Scripture tells us that we are capable of loving as God loves by reminding us that *"the love of God has been poured out within our hearts through the Holy Spirit who was given to us"* (Romans 5:5). We have to acknowledge this because we can do nothing without the power of the Holy Spirit backing us up. He is the One who gives us the power to make our marriages a picture of God's love by submitting to each other in a mutual love. We simply have to learn to rely on Him.

When many people get married, they don't have a clue about understanding what a loving and submissive relationship is all about. And the marriage experiences trouble from the very beginning. They don't see that the foundation of marriage is based on submitting to each other out of a loving heart. I'm not talking about the kind of love that is here today and gone tomorrow—when things don't go as planned. In other words, these marriages are in trouble because they don't get the connection to the Trinity. They have not made expressing love and submission to each other a priority.

Nevertheless, if this description applies to you, it will be evident in your relationship. Know that you and your mate are first and foremost accountable to God. It is up to you to find out from God's Word what He expects from you regarding your marriage. The best way to equip yourself is to first get the knowledge that you need. As part of your Christian duty, the apostle Paul says, *"Be ye not unwise, but [understand] what the will of the Lord is"* (Ephesians 5:17 KJV).

You have to realize that you have the power to make your marriage be what God intended. God is telling you that it is possible for you to submit to your mate if you allow Him to influence your thoughts and behavior. God has made a provision of power to enable us to accomplish what we ourselves find difficult or impossible to do. It is the filling of the Holy Spirit that Paul refers to in verse 18. The Holy Spirit will produce in us the fruit of the Sprit when He fills us. He is resident in every believer but He must also be president of a believer to release His power for living. That is, we must give Him control of our lives.

How filled with the Spirit should a believer be, you ask? We should be so filled with the Holy Spirit that if a mosquito bit one of us he would fly away singing "There's power in the blood!"

But seriously, my wife and I utilize a simple formula that I call the C-Method for being filled with the Holy Spirit. Let me suggest that you do the same. It goes like this.

Start by spending time alone with God with a regular devotional time. Get up a half hour earlier than usual to meet with the Lord. This time should consist of prayer and Bible reading. Ask the Lord to fill you with His Spirit so you can be empowered to fulfill His purpose. Read and meditate on these Scriptures to do the following:

- Confess your sins to the Lord (1 John 1:9)
- Commit your body to the Lord (Romans 12:1)
- Conform your mind to His Word, His will, and His ways (Romans 12:2)
- Claim by faith the filling of the Holy Spirit (Galatians 3:1–4)

As you follow this basic plan, you will begin to see the following changes taking place in you:

- Your Character will change (Galatians 5:22–23)
- Your Conduct will change (Ephesians 4:25–29)

- Your Conversation will change (Ephesians 4:31)
- Your Concern for souls will change (Romans 1:13–16)

The first 4 C's will produce the fruit of the Spirit in your character and the last 4 C's are the evidence of being filled. Remember that you are a work in progress, but when you are filled with the Spirit you will begin to edify your spouse and others as well. This will be a source of great encouragement for you to continue on this path.

So, knowing God's will and being filled with His Spirit will prepare you to pattern your marriage after God's Trinity. This exercise will facilitate you and your spouse doing your part in submitting to one another. If more couples would practice the principle of submission, we would have stronger marriages and far less divorce. Unfortunately, a lack of knowledge is at fault because we haven't been taught the entire lesson on God's vision for marriage. Let me start by introducing you to a critical omission that is at the core of this problem.

The Whole Truth and Nothing but the Truth

The Word of God provides clear instructions for a husband and wife to carry out the mandate to place themselves in equal submission to each other. But to get a right understanding of this truth you must follow the instructions given by the Manufacturer. Believe me, no one else but the omniscient God can make this a reality for you. Read the following verses to see the blueprint that God set for a husband and wife to achieve a successful marriage—His way.

- *"Submitting yourselves one to another in the fear of God."* (Ephesians 5:21 KJV)
- *"Wives, submit yourselves unto your own husbands, as unto the Lord."* (Ephesians 5:22 KJV)
- *"Husbands, love your wives, even as Christ also loved the church and gave himself for it."* (Ephesians 5:25 KJV)

Here's how equality and submission come together in your marriage. God has set this up so that husbands and wives submit to each other in different ways. Moreover, the individual functions we were given by God drive this process. What these verses refer to is the action expected of both partners that together display mutual submission as they rely on God's love to lead them.

If you are a wife, submission to your husband is something that you do voluntarily as a result of your love for God. What does that mean? Think about your relationship with God and how you submit your life to Him. It's not just about how you do your very best to obey God and please Him—but also how you share all of your joys, victories, worries, doubts, fears, and concerns with God. Well, God wants you to submit yourself to your husband in that very same way. It becomes a matter of faith because you have to trust God that He is orchestrating your marriage in a way that your husband is also doing his part. It takes two. On the other hand, your husband is to return the love and obedience you show him with his own sacrificial loving submission to Christ. In other words, the husband must fulfill his duty to his wife by imitating Christ and the way that our Lord loves His church.

But here's the missing ingredient that must be done first; that is, the act of *submitting to each other*. In addition to the tasks outlined above that a husband and wife are to carry out, just as importantly, verse 21 shows a joint responsibility to *mutually* submit. It is not just about the wife submitting to the husband and the husband submitting to Christ—they must also submit to each other. This is the proverbial "glue" that keeps the whole act of submission intact. However, this vital consideration often gets omitted when Ephesians chapter 5 is used to teach the principle of submission in the context of marriage. It happens when we use verse 22 as the focal point; you know, the point about wives submitting to husbands. The problem is, we should actually start at verse 21 so that couples learn that they are to submit to each in the fear of God. Because this verse immediately precedes verse 22, it brings the entire relationship into focus. But when it is omitted, an important part of the complete context of God's message on submission is overlooked.

Granted, submitting ourselves "one to another" is a general Christian duty to be practiced by all believers. But for the express intention of this discussion, we're talking about a mutual exchange of respect and esteem between two spouses. There is no doubt that this command has a special meaning for marriage partners who must practice submission as their respective duties are outlined in verses 22 and 25. This is the Trinity at work within the marriage framework. We also have to take into account the special emphasis placed on the key phrase, *in the fear [or reverence] of God.* This direct reference to why we obey God's command to submit draws attention to the complete admiration of the Lord that we cherish. In other words, we should want to obey God and submit to each other because our love for Him makes us want to do His will. So, it comes down to, if you love and respect God, you will want to follow His commandments in the order He has established.

God wants us to understand that there is equality in marriage and the act of submission takes two willing partners. One spouse is never expected to dominate the other, and God has not given any right to do so. It is an equal partnership. The husband is to submit to the wife and the wife is to submit to the husband. Both partners share the same duty toward each other. When you take submission to heart, you are demonstrating to God that you not only hear Him but that you also love Him enough to fear Him. In fact, this is what unites two people with the same intent—loving God first and then each other. And when you and your mate function in your roles, the three of you make a complete picture of the Trinity.

In case you are still not convinced, I want to point out a significant connection between the image of the Trinity and what it looks like in a marriage partnership that is based on true equality. This idea is inspired by some companion Scriptures that draw comparisons to the pattern of the Trinity. It may be helpful to look at the following chart to see how it explains the similarities between the equality and function in the marriage partners.

Verse	Equivalent Verse	Meaning
Ephesians 5:21 NKJV: *"Submitting to one another in the fear of God."*	Genesis 1:27 NKJV: *"God created man in His own image; in the image of God He created him; male and female He created them."*	Points to the God-ordained equality between the man and woman.
Ephesians 5:22 NKJV: *"Wives, submit to your husbands, as to the Lord."*	Genesis 2:18 NKJV: *"And the Lord God said, 'It is not good that man should be alone, I will make him a helper comparable to him."*	Applies to the function of the woman as she and her husband submit to each other.

Notice the counterpart to Ephesians 5:21, which further emphasizes the equality between two spouses. It is found in Genesis 1:27 and together these two verses explain why the husband and wife are to be in submission to each other.

The same is true of two other Scriptures: Ephesians 5:22 and Genesis 2:18. They both highlight the distinction in function between the man and woman. The woman was created to carry out her part in helping the man fulfill the role of leadership God gave him.

Collectively, these Scriptures lay out the principle of equal submission and how it is related to the equality and submission that each member of the Trinity demonstrates in their respective roles. Please take as much time as necessary to allow this information to sink in. We have to understand this because it is so much a part of the big picture God designed for marriage. It is so important that we should not move from Ephesians 5:21 until we grasp its meaning. This is the principle of equal submission at work. Notice the verb *submitting* used in verse 21 represents a present participle; it denotes continuous action. A man and wife are never to stop submitting to each other.

Marriage is not a game or a simple undertaking. It takes real work to make it strong and enduring. We have reached the point in a serious effort to understand why marriage is to be a successful partnership. Some very thoughtful prayer and an earnest approach to studying the Word now become extremely necessary. You have to look at God's plan for your life in its entirety; only then can you find out why God says it is necessary for you to submit to your mate.

This is the way a marriage partnership can work like the Trinity. Both partners must connect with the fact that God wants them to submit to each other. Then they can move on as the wife submits to her husband out of her love for him. She submits to him effectively by mimicking how she submits to the Lord. It is her love for God first that puts her in a place of voluntary submission to His authority. Under her voluntary submission to the Lord, she is then able to carry out her role of submitting to her husband's authority.

For her to do this, the husband has to obey God's commandment to love his wife in the same way that Christ loves the church. Christ loves the church and sacrificed Himself for her. When a husband loves his wife with a sacrificial attitude, she will have no problem loving and submitting to him. They are both acting out of their respective duties to submit according to God's direction. A wife can trust her husband to lead her and love her and not abuse his authority over her.

Furthermore, because God holds the man accountable for the marriage overall, he was given responsibility to imitate Christ and demonstrate the kind of godly love that a husband is to have for his wife. But, here's the deal. Along with authority comes accountability. If he obeys the Scripture, he is obeying God's command to submit himself to Christ. As a result, he is not abusing his role and lording it over her. That is not why God gave him authority. On the contrary, he is to love his wife with a godly display of love. In fact, a husband has the job of tending to every aspect of his wife's needs. He is to anticipate everything that pertains to her and use his God-given position of authority in the marriage to make sure she has every opportunity to be successful in life.

The keyword for submission is *reverence*. When you get this right it means that your partnership is working; you are connecting your marriage with God's Trinity. If you follow God's pattern and learn to reverence each other, you will have developed what I call a "face-to-face" relationship. That is the position of fellowship—just as it is in the Godhead. The two of you will be performing your spiritual roles by lining up your marriage in reverence to God. It is the true pattern of the Trinity.

Show Me a Picture

So, you might ask what this pattern of the Trinity is supposed to look like in your marriage. If you are wondering, *How is it that I am not supposed to put myself first but rather I am to submit to my spouse?* well, I'm glad that you asked. I have often illustrated the principle of equal submission using a married couple in a live demonstration.

Scripture offers married individuals a biblical picture of how they are to submit to each other. There is a two-part illustration here.

Biblical picture number one is of the wife as she mirrors her role in the Trinity. It begins with this admonition to the wife:

"Nevertheless let every one of you in particular so love his wife even
*as himself; and **the wife see that she reverence her husband.***"
—EPHESIANS 5:33 KJV, emphasis added

The word *reverence* used here means "to fear." It is taken from the word
phobia, which means a fear of something or someone. The word *phobia* is
derived from a word that means "to bow down; to pay homage to."

In my attempt to illustrate what this looks like, I ask the wife to bend
forward and face her husband. She is then in a bowing position to her husband. Now, I know that this is a picture most women envision when they
hear the topic of submission preached. It is what causes them to react like the
word *submit* is a dirty six-letter word. I can only imagine what goes through
their minds. A woman could possibly say such things as "I mean, who does
he think he is? I'm just as good as he is. I have a better education and a better job." But ladies, please don't stop reading. The situation gets much better.

This picture is incomplete without its counterpart. So, here is the rest
of the story:

"Likewise, ye husbands, dwell with them according to knowledge,
*giving **honour** unto the wife, as unto the weaker vessel, and as being*
heirs together of the grace of life; that your prayers be not hindered."
—1 PETER 3:7 KJV, emphasis added

This verse speaks to the husband and commands him to give honor to
his wife. God has given the husband a unique responsibility toward his wife.
And He will hold the man accountable for honoring her. In fact, a man's
obedience to the commandment God gave him directly affects his relationship with God.

So, here's what biblical picture number 2 looks like for the husband.
The word *honor* comes from the word *timen*, which at its root means "to put
on a pedestal." If a man loves his wife as he is directed in Ephesians 5:25, it
becomes the equivalent of putting her on a pedestal. That means he will
show his love for her in the way that the Bible describes—in the same way
that Christ shows His love for the church. The result will be that a man
treats his wife with the utmost respect and consideration.

Therefore, the picture is complete. A husband puts his wife on a pedestal by showing her honor, which then translates into a face-to-face encounter where she is bowing to him in reverence.

Do you see it? The husband puts his wife up on a pedestal and she looks down at him so that they can see eye-to-eye. If this is done with consistency and intensity, their actions will place them in direct fellowship with each other. What a powerful image that is conjured up by the posture described here when these two verses are united: Ephesians 5:33 admonishes the wife to reverence and respect her husband, and 1 Peter 3:7 admonishes the husband to honor and respect his wife.

You probably have some preconceived notions about why you and your wife don't always see eye-to-eye and why things may seem to be out of sync in your marriage. But when you can envision this, you will see the biblical picture of what a godly marriage should be. I really hope that you get this image in your spirit so that you'll begin to submit to each other in the way God set it up for marriages to work.

The Bible says that *"an excellent wife is the crown of her husband"* (Proverbs 12:4). Now, a brother with a crown on his head is a king. If he is a king, then what does that make his woman? That is right—a queen. If we treat each other as kings and queens, doesn't that look like the picture of a marriage pleasing to God? Would a woman reject a man who honors her and puts her on a pedestal? And would a man reject a woman who shows him the proper respect and reverence that he deserves? I don't think so.

Together, But Different

To briefly summarize God's view of a marriage partnership, when God put the first couple together, He made them equal partners—but they were also different. God perfectly paired them with each other and they fully recognized their individual roles. Within the dynamic of their relationship, the husband was the protector and provider and the wife was his supporter.

The news is that Eve had no desire for Adam to be like her and Adam didn't want Eve to be like him. Keep in mind that this was the first couple and it was marriage in its purest form. God surely didn't make the woman to be like the man or the man like the woman. Furthermore, it appears as though they were satisfied with being together as God intended them to be—similar to how the Members of the Trinity relate to each other. Although the Bible doesn't supply a wealth of information about their relationship, it doesn't seem like they had trouble living with the way in which they were created. We know that there was bliss in the garden and all was content—at least for a while.

Okay, so we know that marriage partners are equal partners in God's sight. However, it's not an easy task to maintain partnership, and that's where our story begins. When life gets in the way and stuff starts to happen, difficult times arise. Let me ask you this: "At the end of any given day, what do husbands and wives argue about?" Whatever answer you supply, it can most likely be traced back to the differences between their roles as husband and wife.

For example, let's look at a fairly common situation. In today's economic situation it usually takes two incomes to support a family. Many times a wife has to step out of the basic role of helper and get a job to pay the bills. When that woman makes more money than her husband, which is often the case, it reverses her husband's function as financial provider. In that capacity his role becomes that of helper. Perhaps he even stays home and takes care of the household. When their roles are switched it can breed disagreement and disorder over who controls the money. Now, I am not saying that this is always the case, but marital relationships can become susceptible and vulnerable to challenges like these. Do you see how situations such as this can cause disagreements in the fundamental way that the family structure is supposed to operate?

God has set the order of marriage and the distinctive roles that grow out of that institution. The reason disagreement over the roles in a marriage partnership can be a major problem for married people is because God designed marriage to pattern after the Trinity. But guess what? The Members of the Trinity don't argue over differences. God the Holy Spirit isn't troubled by the fact that it was God the Son who offered Himself for our salvation. The Holy Spirit isn't upset by that; He has His own role to play in helping us to work out our salvation.

This is where we miss it. For some misguided reason, we want our partners to be like us, to behave the way that we do. Perhaps it is because we are under the assumption that life would be easier if both partners think and react exactly the same in a given situation. But the truth is, men and women don't think alike. Not only did God give us separate roles, He gave us different characteristics. Female and male traits are distinctly different in many ways. It is part of God's intricate design and it informs us how we behave in our respective roles.

Do you know that men think in mono and women think in stereo? At least, that is the conclusion I have drawn. However, it is also based on the fact that a recent scientific study has shown that men predominately use only one side of their brain and women use both.[2] As a result, women have a tendency to be more creative and men are prone to be more focused. For instance, if I am washing the car, I have to wash the car, period. That is my focus. On the other hand, my wife has the ability to take care of the baby, cook a meal, talk on the telephone, watch television, and help the kids with their homework—all at the same time. That takes a great deal of creativity.

Furthermore, this is also one of the reasons I believe that a man will never win a verbal battle with a woman. It is my observation that during a conversation, men tend to stay on one subject while many women have the ability to talk about five different things at the same time. The amazing thing is that they don't skip continuity in any part of the conversation! Men are just not geared that way. We are mainly action-oriented and easily become overwhelmed by a woman's ability to produce a simultaneous stream of words directed toward a number of subjects. Tragically, some men start thinking about using their hands when they become frustrated and realize they just cannot win the battle with mere words. God help us.

Allow me to let you in on a little secret. What we actually disagree over is the fact that we are different. This is a losing battle all the way around because men are not going to ever change women and women are never going to change men. And that is a reality. God made us with some fundamental differences and no matter how hard we try, we cannot alter that fact. Instead, what we have to do is learn to respect the differences. Yes, we are made different, but praise God for the differences! If the truth were told, men and women wouldn't like each other if we were just alike.

I am so glad that my wife is not exactly like me. I haven't always been glad about that, but I am now. I've learned some things through experience about the differences between men and women that have made me appreciate the differences between us. I believe it is because we have learned about the power that we've found in agreeing with each other.

Scripture asks a very important question: *"Do two walk together unless they have agreed to do so?"* (Amos 3:3 NIV). If you think about your marriage with this Scripture in mind, you will begin to see something different. You will begin to experience the benefit that is found in agreement. Let me put it like this. As you travel along in the car of life and things aren't going the way either one of you want them to go, guess what you need? In the automobile industry it's called dual climate control. This feature was designed to allow passengers to respect their differences as they travel together.

When my wife and I are in the car, sometimes she's cold and I'm warm. Fortunately for us, my car has this great feature so she is able to heat up her side without overheating me. Now, think about it, we are in the same car, going in the same direction, yet we are traveling comfortably in two climates. We are able to stay the course because we are operating in an environment that keeps us both satisfied, even if the ride gets a little rough. We are still able to respect our differences. We're together, but different at the same time.

Married couples really have to get a handle on this so we can function like the partners that God made us to be. This is another comparison to the man's role as the thermostat in the marriage and the woman as the thermometer. God is our facilitator; He helps the husband set the climate that enables peace and contentment to preside over the marriage. Then, when things go wrong and the two don't see eye-to-eye, husbands and wives don't break out and run from each other or break down and quit.

Rather, they rely on divine direction to keep moving along the right course in life in a unified way. That makes it a necessity to look to God to give us the guidance we need and stay in alignment with Him. In other words, we have to follow the Leader if we want the journey to take us to the destination in life that defines His will for our lives.

You see, we need to understand that different is not wrong—it is just different. Different is not better—it is just different. Different is not superior—it is just different. We take different approaches to life because that is how we were engineered. Men gather around events and recreation and we build relationships in that way. Women gather around relationship and, subsequently, have a tendency to gravitate toward things based on their strength in managing relationships. I like to put it this way: men are like microwaves; they heat up quickly. Women are like crock pots; they heat up slowly. In other words, men want to deal strictly with the facts and get right to the point of a matter. Women have a tendency to relate their ideas through a set of various circumstances and build on the details, presenting one idea at a time and culminating with a crescendo of ideas that collectively make perfect sense.

Nevertheless, in spite of our obvious differences, married couples are partners and companions. We balance each other. We complete each other. But what some need to understand is that we were not designed to compete with each other. Too often we get caught up in disagreements because there is a breakdown in communication and in times like these it would serve us well to remember that we are to correspond to each other. Our roles are not in opposition; rather, they are meant to complement each other. Say, for example, in the way that a lock and key work together. For either one of them to have true meaning, they need each other.

The Key to Partnership

Let me illustrate this idea for you. Imagine that you are holding a lock in one hand and a key in the other. Now consider this—which one is more important? If your answer is the lock, you are wrong. If your answer is the key, you are wrong. Inherent in the two items is their function; that is, they go together and neither is any good without the other. They need each other. Not only that—they must match. You can't combine any key with just any lock and expect them to work together. Every key is made to fit into a specific lock. Every lock is meant to be opened by a specific key. So, they cannot function without each other.

That's a partnership. You could also compare a lock and a key to a marriage relationship. The man is the key and the woman is the lock. Which of the two is more important? Both are equally important. What is a lock without a key? How useful is a key without a lock? They are exclusive to each other just as a man and a woman who are joined in matrimony. This is a reflection of the partnership that God established for a husband and wife. He made one to function as a lock and the other as a key. If you throw away the lock, the key is no good. If you dispose of the key, the lock does not function by itself. Actually, this is the case when a marriage is broken.

A problem occurs when a man struggles to make his woman a key when she is not a key and never will be. She does not behave in terms of how a key operates. And he should respect her as a lock and seek to appreciate what a lock is designed to do. The better he understands her role as a lock, the more he will realize that he doesn't want her to be a key. At the same time, a woman must recognize the role of a key and stop wanting him to be a lock. Instead of getting frustrated when her key does not think exactly like she does, she should learn to accept the key's functionality. All in all, life will be sweeter when the lock and the key learn to value each other for who they are.

It takes the combining of a lock and a key to make a true partnership in marriage. When you understand why the two of you are different, you will appreciate your mate even more. Take some time and evaluate your relationship for the sake of improving whatever is not working in your marriage. The first thing you should do is determine whether you are allowing the lock to be a lock and the key to be a key. That brings up another critical subject to explore. We know there are two in a partnership. But what's up with God making the man first?

True Headship—For Husbands Only

"The husband is the head of the wife,
as Christ also is the head of the church."

—Ephesians 5:23

We're talking about partnerships that live up to God's expectations. However, partnerships can only work if the two individuals are cooperating with God and doing what each of them is called to do. In other words, God has assigned the husband and wife different roles and if they both do their parts, they will have a true partnership.

I want to begin by discussing the specific function of the husband's role. It is extremely significant for us to understand why God created the male first. Husbands, this is something you need to take note of. Not only will there be lots of little quizzes along the way, there will also be a major test in your life on how well you carried out your role as a husband.

Congratulations, you are the one chosen by God to make the connection to the Trinity a reality in your marriage. According to how you act and the choices you make, God is going to hold you accountable for how well you handle your relationship. But, don't worry; if you follow the pattern God has laid out for you, you'll do fine. And help is on the way. Scripture points to your lifeline—which is our Lord and Savior, the head of the church. Therefore, as the head of your marriage, you are to take your direction from none other than the Master Himself—Christ Jesus.

To get you started, first let me give you a few pointers on what *not* to do. Think seriously about this question: "How do you see yourself?" In your role of headship, if you feel that you have to constantly remind your wife that you are the head of the house, it's probably because you are not acting in true headship. True headship never needs to be announced. Moreover, it is not defined by a husband ruling and reigning with no input from his wife or without any consideration of her opinion. Rather, true headship is demonstrated by a man making decisions and taking responsibility for those decisions—decisions that have been made jointly by a husband and his wife.

The choices that you make will affect your wife; therefore, her voice should be heard. Just because you are the husband and the head of the house that doesn't mean that your wife has to hand you her brain. Remember, God gave the husband and wife *co-dominion*. Real men want and expect their wives to have their own thoughts and ideas. They also want their wives to freely share their views. A real man doesn't want a "breathing mannequin." Rather, they want thinking women who will contribute to the success of the relationship. It's the way marriages work properly.

Yes, God intended marriage to be a partnership with the man having final responsibility for what takes place. That means that he assumes accountability. But it is not about him beating on his chest and roaring about his manhood. That is not what the Bible teaches. If the truth be told, most married men know that if we would listen to our wives more often, nine times out of ten we wouldn't have to hear those excruciating words, "I told you so." Unfortunately, we men hear this a lot because we don't want to listen.

Who are we to question God's wisdom? The Bible tells us that man was created first. Because God gave the man the role of leadership, the husband holds the key to success in his marriage and his household. His role was designed to be the spiritual leader of the home. That is function number one. Since Christ leads the church with love and integrity, these same characteristics are available to you by courtesy of the fruit of the Spirit. Now, you are to take your cue from our Lord and arm yourself with the equipment God has provided. You have the power of God on your side, and all of His benefits and promises, so that you can be the leader God has called you to be. This is not a time for complacency, but for diligence in working to meet God's expectations for you.

In fact, God has appointed you to be the lover and the leader of your home. Notice the play on words—it represents an important link. You are to "love her" and "lead her." In carrying out these duties, a husband assumes the role of provider and protector. That is the job that God gave Adam and the job He gave us. Let me say this, brother: God is not going to hold your wife accountable for what He has clearly given you as the husband to do. He is not going to accept any excuses from you either.

Look at what happened with Adam and Eve when they fell. Who is it that fell first? Eve did.

But when God came on the scene, notice whose name He called in Genesis 3:9.

> *"Then the Lord God called to the man,*
> *and said to him, 'Where are you?'"*

Who sinned first? Eve did.

Here's the main question. If she did it, how come God didn't talk to her first?

Now, here's the principle. God left Adam in charge. So, what did God do? He held Adam accountable for their collective failure to obey God's directive. He told Adam that they were not to eat of the forbidden fruit. So, He was expecting Adam to make sure that didn't happen.

Then, what did Adam do? Instead of owning up to his mistake, he blamed God. Listen to what Adam said in Genesis 3:12.

"The man said, 'The woman whom You gave to be
with me, she gave me from the tree, and I ate.'"

That answer didn't wash then and it won't hold up now. At the end of the day men are responsible and that's why men need to get on their knees and ask God to show them how to lead.

As the head of my household, I will have to give an account for my wife, Leslie, my sons, and all of those under my patriarchal leadership. In your marriage relationship, God is going to ask you to account for what went on in your home. It is your task to see to it that your marriage lines up with the order God has prescribed.

Consider this question: "Do you agree that God has specific intentions in mind for creating marriage in the first place?" If you agree, then you should know that the family unit grows out of that institution and is the backbone of human society. That is what makes the role of the husband so vital. God placed Adam in charge of the first family and expected him to tend to it and keep it; provide for and protect it; love it and lead it. Now God wants that same commitment from you; He wants you to answer His call and follow His instructions. Brothers, just as He summoned Adam when He needed an account of Adam's situation, at the appointed time God is going to call each of us by name and say, "Where are you?"

I have been married for thirty-seven years. After many years of intensely studying the Word of God, conducting countless marriage retreats, and counseling numerous couples—I get it. I've learned a little bit about this thing called marriage. But, because I'm human too, I may not always do everything right; nevertheless, I do know a little bit about how it's supposed to work. Now, you may say that the following observations are not true in your marital experience. I realize there are always exceptions, but there are also general principles which are valid the majority of the time. And for the most part, I find that things work a certain way. So, allow me to share some of my insights with you.

In the marital relationship, the man's role is similar to a thermostat and the woman's role is likened to that of a thermometer.

What does a thermostat do? It controls the temperature and climate within the home. The thermometer, on the other hand, simply registers the temperature that the thermostat has set. God gave the man the task of acting like a thermostat so that he would set the atmosphere, the temperature, and climate of the marriage relationship. So, men, here's a hint: When you notice that your wife seems to be a little "cold," it's because you have not set the temperature of your relationship where it needs to be for her. On the other hand, in her function as a thermometer, a woman naturally reacts to the climate in the household—whether it was intentionally set by you or it just registers at a default setting because of your neglect. This is exactly my point. You have to stay on constant watch and make a conscious decision to maintain the right temperature setting in your marriage. And remember to always keep Christ in the forefront so that you temper your environment with integrity, peace, and love.

Let me give you a good example. A brother came to me one day and said, "Pastor, it is cold in my house." I asked him if he had paid the heating bill. He said, "Yes. What I mean is that my wife is acting like an iceberg. She's as cold as ice." I responded to him, "Well, brother, you are the thermostat and she is the thermometer in your marriage. So, if it's cold in your house that's because of the temperature you've set." I then suggested to him that he go home and turn up the "heat" really high.

He called me about a week later to report, "Pastor, I did what you said and turned up the heat, but she's still acting like an iceberg." I told him, "Look, brother, if you have an iceberg living in your home and it's only been one week since you turned up the heat, don't think that it will completely melt so quickly. You have to keep the heat set on high for a long time; then the iceberg will melt and become ice water. But, if you keep that same level of heat going constantly, that ice water will in time begin to warm up. The longer you keep the climate hot, it will eventually reach the temperature that you've set it to and begin to warm you all over."

Finally, I explained to him that, as a husband, he needed to faithfully give his wife the four T's: time, tenderness, touch, and talking. I told him, "I want you to inundate her with these precious sentiments."

And, if you're not already doing these things, this is what I suggest you do also:

TIME: Give her your undivided time and attention until she is
thoroughly satisfied.

TENDERNESS: Be so tender with her that she melts in your arms.

TOUCH: Touch her with an abundance of gentleness until she wants
you to lighten up.

TALK: Talk to her so much and so often that she actually asks you to
be quiet.

A month later, the brother called me and said with great excitement,
"Pastor, you were right! I got it! I am the thermostat and it really works!"

The lesson here is that true leadership was defined by God's terms. It's
the way that, on a human level, our marriages can work in perfect harmony
just as the Trinity works in divinity.

To that end, one of two things is happening in your marriage. Make this
an opportunity to check up on your relationship. If there is no peace and
harmony in your home (and you already know the answer to that), take a
look at yourself first before you decide to place the blame on your wife or
anyone else. Then, take some action to improve your situation. For starters,
check out the practical things you can do that are found at the end of the
chapter.

If you do happen to live in a peaceful abode, it means that your thermostat is working properly. It is an indicator that your partnership is intact.
However, you may also want to go through the checklist and make some
additional efforts to keep your relationship in good shape. I believe in giving credit where it is due. So, first, give thanks to God, and then give yourself a pat on the back and keep up the good work.

Building on Solid Ground

"The righteous has an everlasting foundation."
—Proverbs 10:25

My prayer is that you have gained some inspiration and renewed passion to be the husband God desires you to be. But perhaps you need a review of the practical things that God expects of you. That is a fair assessment

because we can all strive to do better and sometimes a little knowledge is all that we need.

What, then, are the responsibilities of the husband? Well, I will tell you, they have everything to do with why God created you as a man. Furthermore, when you take the plunge and become a husband, He gives you a very specific job with several tasks. Moreover, God has in mind a particular order in which to carry out your job assignment.

First, He wants you to be the *provider and protector* of your family. Second, He expects you to be the *pastor* of your household. And third, He expects you to be a *partner* to your wife. Let's examine these roles one at a time in the order in which God set them:

1. God made man to work.

*"Then the Lord God took the man and put him into the garden of
Eden to cultivate it and keep it."*
—Genesis 2:15

The first thing God gave Adam was a job. The Bible says that God put him in the garden of Eden to "cultivate it and keep it." Notice the order here. In regard to taking care of his home, Adam's job had two parts.

His first task was to "cultivate" the garden. So, as a gardener, Adam had to raise and cultivate the crops to feed his family. That means his first priority was to be the provider for his family.

Understand that this is the Lord's doing. Consequently, there is an innate sense that He placed in the male psyche that propels him to want to work. In your main role as the husband of your household, God wants you to be a **provider** for your family. But for some men, there is a lack of ambition and the desire to work is often suppressed. For men who struggle with this, listen to what Scripture says about a man's responsibility,

*"If anyone does not provide for his own,
and especially for those of his household, he has
denied the faith and is worse than an unbeliever."*
—1 Timothy 5:8

These are some pretty strong words; but, nevertheless, it is the truth of the matter. Before a woman even considers marrying someone, she ought to be thinking this about a potential mate: *If you want to be with me, you've got to have a J-O-B. No romance without finance.* Am I right? In fact, I won't even marry a couple if the man doesn't have a job. It is ridiculous to imagine that you can take care of a wife and you're still living at home with Mama. That's what I call setting yourself up for a fall. Some may say, "But, we're in love." Well, I say you can be in love, but love won't pay the rent and the bills. Being in love cannot keep you together if the man does not have a job.

The second thing Genesis 2:15 states is that Adam was to "keep" the garden. This word indicates that part of Adam's job was to be the protector of his home. The word *keep* comes from the Hebrew word *samar*, which is a military term. In the New Testament, the Greek word for *keep* is *terao*, which means "to stand watch over." So then, a man is to be the **protector** of his home by standing guard over it.

However, the tragedy today is that the "protector" often becomes the "predator." According to the U.S. Department of Justice, 96 percent of children under twelve who were sexually abused knew their attacker and 20 percent of the abusers were fathers. For the vast majority of child victimizers in state prisons, the victim was someone they knew before the crime. Two-thirds of the victimizers committed their crime against their own child, and about half had a relationship with the victim as a friend, acquaintance, or relative other than their offspring.[3] Furthermore, the most recent statistics from the Bureau of Justice report that one third of female murder victims were killed by an intimate partner. Ninety percent of the abuse of women comes from a husband or a boyfriend.[4]

Whether the man of the house himself was the criminal who perpetrated these crimes or it happened to be someone else, these are alarming statistics that point to the fact that too many brothers are not standing guard over their families. And what is even more disturbing, all too often they themselves are the ones to be feared by their wives and children. Brothers, please pay attention to this crucial subject. God needs us to take our roles seriously. The bottom line is, our wives need our attention, our sons need our direction, and our daughters need our protection. In the role of protector, we are the key to the success of those whom God has placed under our care.

2. God gave man His word.

> *"The Lord God commanded the man, saying,*
> *'From any tree of the garden you may eat freely; but from*
> *the tree of the knowledge of good and evil you shall not eat,*
> *for in the day that you eat from it you will surely die.'"*
> —GENESIS 2:16–17

When God gave Adam His word, He was giving Adam his second role—the spiritual leader of his home. God spoke words from His mouth to Adam and commanded him to do something. He was to eat from most of the food that was present and refrain from eating only one thing. With that assignment, Adam became the pastor of his household. He was to watch over God's word to keep order in the garden.

You, brother, are to do likewise. Just as Adam was to honor God's commandment and make sure the garden stayed intact, God expects you to be the spiritual leader of your home—to watch over His Word and make sure you and your family are living in obedience to God's instructions. That makes you the **pastor** of your household. Therefore, it is up to you to study the Word of God and show yourself approved by leading your family through the godly example that you set.

3. God gave the man a wife.

> *"Then the Lord God said, 'It is not good for the man to be alone;*
> *I will make him a helper suitable for him.'"*
> —GENESIS 2:18

Here it is again. Man's third job is to be a **partner** to his wife. Eve became Adam's partner and cohabited the garden with him. She was to stand side by side with him, sharing life and everything that it means to be in a human bond. Their relationship was designed to reflect the divine fellowship of the Trinity. Isn't it so interesting that God created Eve from Adam's rib, which He took from Adam's side? That was God's way of placing them in a partnership where they were both equal. Eve was not above or beneath Adam; she was not his servant or his ruler. She was truly his partner.

And, check this out—God gave Adam a wife *after* He had given him work to do and His word to watch over. So, He made sure that Adam was well-equipped to take good care of Eve when she came on the scene. Eve was so special in God's eyes that He wanted her to have everything that she needed before He created her. Their relationship was designed in the true sense of partnership. They were literally made for each. One was not complete without the other.

And that is how God wants your marriage partnership to be today. He wants you and your spouse to operate in the roles He gave you. God is a God of order. And when things are done in order, everybody involved is positioned to prosper and achieve success in life. And, most importantly, God will be pleased.

Powerful Living

"Deacons must be husbands of only one wife, and good managers of their children and their own households. For those who have served well as deacons obtain for themselves a high standing and great confidence in the faith that is in Christ Jesus."
—1 TIMOTHY 3:12–13

Brother, there is more for you to do in your role as a husband. Now I know that you are already doing what you know to do. And in your heart you want to please God. But sometimes we may be sincere in our intentions while at the same time we can be sincerely wrong. I am talking about keeping your priorities straight. Your first priority should not be your ministry or your church—but your family.

We just discussed this as being part of the role God gave each husband. So, you need to get this right. Sometimes we attempt to get spiritual and use ministry as an excuse for not doing right by our families. But the Lord said that your work begins at home. If you are someone who thinks that you are being spiritual because you are serving in the Lord's work—but to the detriment of your family—know that you are not spiritual.

If you are thinking that you have to burn out for God all the while you are neglecting the family God gave you, God is saying to you right now, *That is not what I told you to do.* There is nothing spiritual about depriving your family of your time and attention. In fact, when you put your ministry work above your family, you are in sin. Your first responsibility is to take care of your family. How can you lead fifty people if you cannot lead five?

Your family needs your involved presence; that includes your provision, your time, your leadership, and your godly example. Whatever ministry you participate in, you should never do more for it than you do for your wife and children. When you become so spiritual that you are overlooking them, then you are too spiritual for your own good.

Here's the deal. God fellowshipped with Adam, and you can't get any more spiritual than that. However, God also decided that Adam was alone. So, He gave the man a partner. No matter how spiritual you may think you are, you can't beat walking in the garden and talking with God in the cool of the day. If you spend time with Him, you'll learn some things. And God will straighten out your misbehavior. But you must have a teachable spirit and be willing to listen—and that's one thing men struggle with big time.

If you are guilty of this, please repent right away. Purpose in your heart to change your ways and walk circumspectly before God and the wife with whom you partner. If you put His commandments first, you will be blessed. God will show you how to balance your time between your spouse, family, ministry, and career. This is what walking in the power of God and the wisdom of His Word is all about. Allow me to join the apostle Paul as he offered up this prayer for the church. The Word of God is just as alive and powerful today as it was when it was first written. So, this is for all men who are striving to live in the power of God:

> *"We have not ceased to pray for you and to ask that you may be filled with the knowledge of His will in all spiritual wisdom and understanding, so that you will walk in a manner worthy of the Lord, to please Him in all respects, bearing fruit in every good work and increasing in the knowledge of God."*
>
> —COLOSSIANS 1:9–10

God wants to fill you with the knowledge of His will so that you can focus on leading your family. This is how we get the insight from God that we need to achieve victory in our lives. Finding out God's will for your life brings you wisdom and understanding. God will be pleased and He will bless the things that you do on a daily basis. The better you get to know God and develop a personal relationship with Him, the more power you will gain to fulfill the role of leadership in your home.

You see, when you got saved, that prepared you to live in heaven. But when you got filled, that prepared you to live on earth. Being filled with the Spirit of God is what gives you the edge. Now, we have the key that strengthens every relationship—the Holy Spirit. You see, we don't have a partnership problem as much as we have a "filled with the Spirit problem." We have been equipped with the power to live right; we're just not utilizing the power that God has already given us.

The Word of God promises us that we will be blessed if we follow God's ways. Listen to what the first two verses of Psalm 128 offer:

> *"How blessed is everyone who fears the Lord, who walks in*
> *His ways. When you shall eat of the fruit of your hands,*
> *you will be happy and it will be well with you."*

My motto is, "HAPPY WIFE, HAPPY LIFE!" Husbands, the key to partnership is to walk in the fear of the Lord, follow His commandments, and have a right relationship with God and His Word. When you partner with God in this way, know that you will truly prosper while you bring much happiness to your wife. Enjoy your lifelong partnership.

Making It Happen

1. With an open and receptive heart, ask God to help you understand how to apply His reason for creating marriage as a partnership that He is pleased with. He will hear your sincere prayers and help you to transform your marriage into a reflection of His image.

2. If you and your spouse don't already have a date night, establish one. Make it a weekly event where you will look forward to spending time together. Have fun with it. To have the most positive impact on your marriage, be as creative and consistent as possible.

3. Have a meaningful discussion about the strengths and weaknesses that you and your spouse can identify about your marriage. Develop a list that you agree to work on. Then use the list to frequently check up on your improvements and setbacks.

4. Develop a plan for strengthening the areas that weaken your partnership. Be as specific as possible in identifying what actions you need to take to make improvements. Monitor your progress toward building your partnership through this exercise.

5. Include the plan as a part of your daily prayer and devotions with your spouse.

6. Celebrate each victory and record it in a journal.

7. Don't forget to give God thanks and praise for the growth and victories you see in your partnership!

Reason #3

The Perfecting
Reason
Reinforces a
Spiritual Reception

I will never forget what transpired between a former associate pastor and his wife. Sister Davis would approach Brother Davis at the end of Sunday service with her hands on her hips and attitude written all over her face. Just like a well-memorized script, she would say, "Davis, let's go, boy. I'm hungry!" Immediately, he would snap back at her, "Wait until I get through with my conversation!"

Sister Davis would then respond, "Look, boy. We've been here since 8:00 a.m. and after three services, I'm hungry. Wrap that conversation up so we can go." It would make her just that much angrier when he would coolly respond, "I said, we'll go when I finish talking with my pastor and these brothers."

Just as a reminder to him, she would stomp away and sulk within visible distance. This scenario was repeated virtually every Sunday for several years. After a while when I just couldn't take it any longer, I called her one Sunday evening and the following conversation ensued.

"Sister Davis, this is Pastor Ford."

"Hello, Pastor."

"How are you this fine Sunday evening?"

"Well, to be honest, Pastor, I'm trying to recover from my ordeal with my husband. He knows we're at church nearly six hours every Sunday and sometimes we haven't even had breakfast. Yet, after the services have ended, he has to stand around running his mouth with the fellas. Every Sunday I tell him not to do that but every Sunday it's the same thing. The worst part is that we fuss and argue from the time we leave the parking lot, we eat our meal in silence, and then go to bed sleeping back to back."

"Sister Davis, I'd like to help you change all of that, if you'll let me."

"Of course, I will let you, Pastor. Just tell him to start being more sensitive to me on Sundays and maybe that will do it."

"I don't believe that's the answer, Sister Davis."

"Well, what is it, Pastor?"

"You know, the Bible teaches that a man needs respect. Right?"

"Yes, I know that it does."

"Well, do you think he feels respected when you approach him while he is talking to other men, commanding him with your hands on your hips and calling him *boy*?"

"Now, Pastor, we call each other boy and girl on a regular basis. And—"

"Wait, please hear me out before you go on the defensive. Let me suggest that next Sunday, instead of taking your usual stance, try this instead: Don't approach him like you're angry. Walk up to him and say, 'Excuse me, gentlemen.' Then say, 'Sweetheart, may I speak to you in private for a moment?' When he says okay, put your arms around his waist, look into his eyes, and softly say, 'Baby, I'm hungry. Let's leave and get something to eat, please.'"

On the following Sunday evening, I was well into my after-hours worship services ritual, meaning I was allowing the TV to watch me. Then, my wife woke me up with an apology. She said, "Honey, I apologize for waking you up, but Sister Davis is on the phone. I told her that I didn't want to wake you but she said that it was urgent."

I answered the phone only to hear the very enthusiastic voice of Sister Davis exclaiming, "Oh, Pastor, I'm sorry for having Sister Leslie wake you up, but I had to let you know that I did exactly what you instructed me to. And I must say that we had the best Sunday we've had in years. When I said what you suggested, he said, 'Okay, Baby.' Then he turned to the brothers and told them he would talk with them later. He said, 'I have to take my honey out to eat.'"

"Pastor, we had a very pleasant conversation on the way to dinner. We also had a great conversation over dinner. Then, we went home and did something on a Sunday evening that hadn't happened in many years. So, I just had to tell you how much I appreciate your showing me how to be a better wife to my husband."

I laugh about this incident every time I think about it. Now, this story could have been a reverse situation where the husband needed some advice on how to treat his wife. But the reality is that it reinforces God's third reason for creating marriage—the perfecting reason.

The Art of Receiving

*"So the Lord God caused a deep sleep to fall upon the man,
and he slept; then He took one of his ribs and
closed up the flesh at that place.*

*The Lord God fashioned into a woman the rib which
He had taken from the man, and brought her to the man.*

*The man said, 'This is now bone of my bones, and flesh of my flesh;
she shall be called Woman, because she was taken out of Man.'"*

—Genesis 2:21–23

Did you know that as a married couple you and your mate are supposed to bring out the best qualities in each other? The third reason why God created marriage was to create a spiritual reception between the husband and wife to prepare them for just that purpose. In fact, I call it the perfecting reason.

The way in which God brought together the first two individuals was so that they would accept each other in their respective roles. In Adam's acceptance of Eve as his counterpart he fulfilled God's design for the man's role in marriage. Adam was now complete in every sense of his being. The same is true of Eve's existence. The moment God created her out of the man and joined her together with her counterpart, Eve's total makeup as a woman was complete. The couple graciously received their individual parts and the two became one flesh just as the three Members of the Trinity are one God.

Together, the man and woman became a fulfillment of God's desire for them to complete each other in matrimony. But what does it really mean for one person to complete another? And how do we recognize it when we think in terms of a marriage relationship? At first glance, two people "completing" each other sounds like the sugary words from the lyrics of an old love song. But it goes much deeper than that. It is a God-inspired idea.

When a man and woman complete each other it means they are positioned to enrich each other's lives. And that is what the perfecting reason for marriage is all about. To "perfect" something or someone means to make it or them better. God set this pattern so that what takes place in a marriage union is that the husband and wife receive each other in a physical and spiritual way. It is how He intends for us to perfect each other. You see, a husband is incomplete within himself and a wife is not complete on her own. Together they become one whole unit; they perfect each other. However, it is up to us to follow God's blueprint and reach the level of perfection in marriage that He has made possible for us.

No matter where it takes place, the ritual of marriage is done in the eyes of God. Once they are joined together, a bond is formed and the need for the couple to complete each other continues to grow until they fully perfect one another.

Let me tell you what I mean because if you want your marriage to operate in God's way, you and your spouse will need to understand the concept of being completed and perfected. The perfecting reason has everything to do with cooperating with God so that you and your mate find genuine love and fulfillment with each other. Through this chapter, I want to help you understand and come to a new appreciation of the success you can achieve together as husband and wife in the eyes of the Lord.

Let me take you back to the beginning of time for a minute when a perfect Creator put forth a perfect plan. His goal was to give man and woman every accommodation that they would need to be content as husband and wife. In a spiritual sense, Adam was an incomplete being before God created Eve. He was physically intact but something was missing from his life. He did not have everything that he needed to match the blueprint God had drawn up for the human family that He was planning to live on earth. So, God caused Adam to sleep and took a piece of his rib to create Eve. Now, Adam was half the man he used to be because a physical part of him was taken away. But God used that same part to create Eve. In His wisdom, this was all part of His plan to form a partnership so that the individual partners would not just coexist but they would actually complete each other.

Moreover, God gave the man and woman the ability to better each other's experience on earth. This is a lifelong process; it doesn't happen overnight. When you think about your own relationship, you will most likely agree that there is always room for improvement. Well, just as He did for the first couple, God made preparations for you and your spouse to develop and improve your relationship over time. Even the little things that you do when you treat each other with kindness such as anticipating her needs, rubbing his tired feet, and sending flowers for no apparent reason. These are things that build each other up. Brother and Sister Davis were doing just the opposite by being on a destructive path of tearing each other down. It only took a simple suggestion to help them turn their situation around. When Sister Davis acted on it, they both got the benefit.

The same applies to you and your spouse. You cannot find perfection in having a negative attitude toward your mate. You can only reach the kind of perfection God wants for you by showing love toward one another. This is what Sister Davis realized when she took my advice. When she began to approach her husband in a positive way, then he was able to respond favorably to her. The change in behavior that she adopted proved successful to get both of them results they were pleased with. That change took their attention away from their negativity and shined the spotlight on their love. That's what God is talking about.

Not for Women Only

There is another element to the idea of perfecting your mate. Yes, Eve completed Adam. But she also complemented him. It is important that we understand how we are to complement our mates. When operating in perfect harmony as a pair, a male and female balance each other—like a matching set of bookends. One is always ready and willing to hold up the other; when all else fails, they can rely on each other's support.

We covered the role of the husband in the previous chapter. Now, listen to this verse that directly speaks to the role of the woman in the perfecting process.

> *"And the Lord God said, 'It is not good that the man should be alone; I will make him an help meet for him.'"*
>
> —GENESIS 2:18 KJV

God created Eve for the two reasons found in this verse: partnership and perfection. The first part of the verse deals with the element of partnership that we covered in chapter 2. However, the second part of the verse, *I will make him a help meet*, is all about the woman's function of perfecting the man. It was never God's desire for the man to carry out his intended purpose on earth all by himself. Adam needed someone to work alongside him. Therefore, God brought them together so that the husband and wife's relationship could look and act like God's image of Himself—the Trinity.

From the wife's perspective, her reason for being a partner in the marriage is to perfect her husband. In today's language we would use the word *helper* instead of *help meet*. Let me explain what that means. The word *helper* comes from the Hebrew word *ezer*. Now, there are only two people in the Old Testament who were called *ezer*: God and the woman. Since we are God's created beings, we look to God as the "Big Ezer." The psalmist declared, *"I will lift up my eyes to the mountains; from where shall my help come? My help comes from the Lord, who made heaven and earth"* (Psalm 121:1–2). He asked the question and then answered it: Where does my help (or *ezer*) come from? My help (or *ezer*) comes from the Lord.

Later, the writer of the book of Hebrews declared, *"The Lord is my helper [ezer], I will not be afraid. What will man do to me?"* (Hebrews 13:6). As the people of God, we look to Him for help to overcome the pressures and challenges of life. That is what He expects us to do and that is what we should do.

But exactly why would the Bible call the woman the "little *ezer*"? The old saying "Behind every good man is a good woman" is actually full of wisdom. The word *helper* is so rich with positive meaning; notice how it suggests that the woman provides benefit, improvement, assistance, support, relief, rescue, prevention, remedy, and comfort. These are all characteristics of what a helper does. And part of God the Holy Spirit's role in the Trinity is to be our Helper. So then, the woman and the Holy Spirit share a related role. Her part in the image of the Trinity is illuminated as she helps her husband in similar ways that the Holy Spirit helps God's children overall.

So, make a note, brothers, and always keep this in your mind. The reason God calls the woman "little *ezer*" is because there are certain blessings that God has reserved for the marriage that He will only channel through the wife. When you put your wife on a pedestal, in a uniquely God-ordained way, you receive the kind of help from your wife that only she can provide. There are some times when God expects a man to submit to his wife because she has special favor given to her by God. Husbands must learn to acknowledge and accept that truth. That is why God joins a man and woman together in holy matrimony (Genesis 2:22).

Let's look at Proverbs 18:22 which says, *"He who finds a wife finds a good thing and obtains favor from the Lord."* Notice that the word *finds* suggests a passive event, which means a man is not to go out and actively look for a wife. Rather, it means that he should rest in something while that something does the work for him. Well, that "something" is the power of the Holy Spirit. And when you trust in Him, through God's power, a man finds a woman of quality that brings him abundant favor from the Lord.

I have preached many sermons on the subject of favor, and I contend that it's far better to have favor than to have money. You cannot depend on mere money because your money can run out. But if you have favor, you can always get money because you are depending on God who gives you favor. And God never runs out of anything.

Hear what Proverbs 19:14 says about finding the woman who will perfect her man. It is a blessing that only God can make happen.

> *"House and wealth are an inheritance from fathers,*
> *but a prudent wife is from the Lord."*

There is a special kind of favor that comes from a wife and flows through to her husband. Let me give you a real example of what having favor is all about. A few years ago my wife and I were preparing to go on a two-week vacation in Bermuda. We stayed in the most expensive hotel on the island and enjoyed all of its wonderful amenities. And, guess what? It didn't cost us a penny. You know what that is called? Favor! Now, don't hate—celebrate! I know that such a good thing came to us because my wife, Leslie, is a woman of God who is blessed with skill and wisdom. And I see how those benefits work out in our marriage.

Brothers, you have to get over your male-ego hang-ups to understand who your wife is in God's eyes and how she complements you. In that way, whenever the two of you come to an area where she excels, you defer to her and you don't default to a "headship" error. In other words, remember what true headship is all about and don't try to pull rank on her when God wants to bless you through her. You see, when you submit your life to living God's way, there is much benefit derived from acknowledging Him and putting forth the effort to follow His lead.

Many times I use the experiences of my wife and me as an illustration. I declare that my wife is an asset who hooks me up with something that I can't get by myself. God blesses us with special favor because of her faithfulness. Let me tell you what I am talking about. We live in a house today that we couldn't afford at the time when we bought it. My wife was a personnel director and I was a pastor. At that time, she was making twice as much money as I was. But on payday she brought her check home to me. No, I didn't club her over the head and demand that it be that way. This was something we had agreed on. I am the man of the house and I am the financier in our family. We discussed it, and based on who we are and our family dynamics, that is how we decided it would be. I also happen to be the frugal person in the family. Now, I've heard some people call it cheap but that's because they simply don't understand frugality.

Furthermore, out of her willingness to do what was best for our family, my wife sacrificed her education and her career to stay home and raise our children. After the kids got older, I regretted having to say to her, "I know that our agreement was that when our youngest turned thirteen years old you could go back to work. But now our children are being recruited by gangs. For their sake, I need you to come back home." She said, "When?" I said, "Well, give them your two-week notice when you go in today." She gave her two-week notice, came back home, and we went back to having one income.

This is a good example of what complementing is all about. I praise God for a wife who complements me and functions as the partner God made her to be. And one good thing leads to another. I had promised her when I finished school and we got stable that it would be her turn. At that point I said to her, "Now it's your turn. I'm going to do whatever God gives me to do to get you what you want." I asked her, "Do you want to go back to work?" She responded, "Well, I don't want to work." I said, "Okay. Do you want to go to school?" She replied, "Well, I don't even think I want to go to school. You've got enough education for both of us."

So, I asked her, "Well, what do you want?" She said, "I want a house. When we left Pittsburgh there were two things that I felt were sacrificed for Christ." To my question, "What were they?" her response was, "My family and my house." We had just bought a starter home and she was crazy about that house. She told me that it was hard for her to give up that house and to live in a run-down apartment. And so, I told her, "It's your time. Whatever it is that you want, sweetheart, that's what we're going to go after."

We had a friend who was always doing nice things for us. So, on one occasion my wife and I took him to dinner to show our appreciation. As we dropped him off at his house, we pulled up and I said, "That's your house?" He replied, "Yeah. Are you guys looking for a house? If you're in the market, you ought to buy this one." My wife said, "Whoa." And I echoed, "Whoa. What are you selling it for, $210,000?" He said, "No, you'd better double that and add $5,000. It's $425,000." I exclaimed, "What! Babe, we can't afford anything like that."

He asked if we wanted to see it and I said no. I had enough sense to know that it is not a good idea to show a woman something that you can't afford, knowing that she is going to want it. But, of course, my wife said she wanted to see it, which meant that we were going to see the house. (Brothers, I hope you are taking notes.) I've also learned that although you don't volunteer to let a woman see something she wants that you can't afford, you don't stop her from seeing it when she says she wants to. So, I agreed.

Our friend went in first, she walked in second, and I entered last. She looked at the living room and then toward the kitchen. Suddenly, she announced that this was her house. I don't think she meant to say it out loud. He heard her say something and asked her what she'd said. My wife said she was just talking to herself, but I repeated her words. Apparently this was something he had heard before because his reply was, "Oh, Sister Ford, if I had a nickel for every woman that said God had told her this is her house, I wouldn't have to sell it. Do you know whose house this is? Whoever gives me $425,000."

When we got back in the car, I tried to soften her disappointment as I explained that there was no way we could afford that house. She said, "You told me it was my time. That's my house. God told me. He told me that's my house. That's gonna be my house." Since I am a preacher, I then tried to handle the situation with Scripture. So, I replied, "Baby, the Bible says do not tempt the Lord thy God." Then, she reminded me of a sermon that I had preached a while back, "Tear the Roof Off the Sucker." It was about the account of the four men who carried the paralytic man. They couldn't get to Jesus because of the crowd, so they climbed on top of the house and tore the roof off the sucker! When they went through so much trouble to lower the paralyzed man down into the house, Jesus saw the faith of those men. As the account goes, the Son of God forgave the man's sins and healed him (see Mark 2:3–12).

So, my wife said to me, "Remember that? Remember how you pointed out that he was healed because of the four men's faith who carried him, not the one on the pallet?" I said, "Yeah." She responded, "Then, get on my pallet." There isn't enough room to give you all the details, but trust me, it was quite a journey from that day until we moved in. And I submit to you that we wouldn't be in that nice house today if it wasn't for the faith of my wife. I did not have the faith to believe it (doesn't this prove that pastors really are human!), and the Bible says if you don't have the faith to believe for what you want, you don't get it. Period.

God channeled that blessing to us through my wife. And this is what we realized later on. She had wanted more than anything not to leave our first house. So, we sat there and wrote in our journal that nineteen years ago she had planted the seed for her new house. And nineteen years later the fruit of the seed she had planted in faith came up. The Bible says in Luke 6:38, *"Give, and it will be given to you. They will pour into your lap a good measure— pressed down, shaken together, and running over. For by your standard of measure it will be measured to you in return."* So, know that whatever you plant grows to produce more fruit than what you initially planted. The first house that we had could fit into our new home three times over. And I said, "Baby, isn't that something. God honored nineteen years later what you gave up to serve Him."

You can't out-give God. He gave me a prudent wife who brought us the blessing of a new home that otherwise would not have been possible. This is what I mean by doing it God's way. Proverbs 19:14 became a reality for me; God's Word will do the same for you when you make up your mind and heart to obey God and line your marriage up with His pattern.

Perfecting One Another

> *"Beloved, now we are children of God, and it has not appeared as yet what we will be. We know that when He appears, we will be like Him, because we will see Him just as He is. And everyone who has this hope fixed on Him purifies himself, just as He is pure."*
>
> —1 JOHN 3:2–3

Unfortunately, many marriages have become so self-centered when they should be Christ-centered. It is a habit that reveals a serious lack of growth and spiritual maturity. Marriages in this category breed strife and division that often result in a great deal of drama.

On the other hand, couples who have grown to be mature Christians become transparent, meaning they are not wearing masks that hide under-lying ill feelings and discontent. It's easy to see their sincerity because they're not trying to cover up any ulterior motives with hidden agendas. So, it is their submission to each other that reveals the love that they nurture and share. This is a beautiful reflection of the pattern of the Trinity. At the end of the day, they can say to each other, "Since your life is transparent to me, I can see Christ in you." Listen to what Scripture says about this level of spiritual awareness.

"The mystery which has been hidden from the past ages and gener-
ations, but has now been manifested to His saints, to whom God
willed to make known what is the riches of the glory of this mystery
among the Gentiles, which is Christ in you, the hope of glory."
—COLOSSIANS 1:26–27

This is the reason I cannot emphasize enough the importance of keeping Christ in the center of your relationship. It may take some extra work to step out of your flesh and walk in the Spirit, but it is well worth it. And nothing worth having in life ever comes easy. It is worth the effort. Pause for a moment and think about whether you can see your marriage in the following ways. The love of Christ is reflected in those who are able to do these things:

- Submission—submit to each other out of your love for each other and Christ
- Communication—have meaningful conversations knowing that it is important to stay connected to each other
- Partnership—walk hand in hand through life's ups and downs and avoid breaking apart when trouble comes along

With a focus on Jesus, we see what a pure love relationship looks like. And you need to know that there is enough power in God to help you build a pure relationship. Things may or may not seem so wonderful right now, but He strengthens our hope in the future. And when times are especially rough we might even have to hope in God against all other hope. After all, our number one goal is to be like Him. If Jesus could put aside His deity and become a servant because He loves us (Philippians 2:4–5), then why can't we be determined to love our mates by putting aside our fleshly ways and following the One that we claim to love?

I'm so glad I have the wife that I have. We are in partnership together; she is my protector, and she's my perfector. She can tell when I've had a difficult and challenging day. When I go home, she'll ask me how it went. And I'll say, "Well, you know, it's just rough, baby." Then she'll rub my shoulders, pull my shoes off, prepare my salad and my salmon, bring it to me, and turn on the TV. She'll tell me, "This is your favorite program; I won't make you watch the woman's channel today."

She's a wise woman. She sits beside me and comforts me by saying, "I just want to tell you something. You know, I love you. There's nobody who could treat me like you treat me. For thirty-seven years you have cared for me the best that any man could care for a woman. You know what? You're not only the best man in the church—you're the best man in the world. There's no other man that's as good as you are. I mean it. I'm getting tired of hearing you talk about how you don't look good. You look good to me and that's all that matters. You are my Denzel. I love you."

That just pumps me up and makes me want to do better. When she encourages me, I just want to do more. I want to keep it coming. I enjoy going home just so I can get pumped up. After all, where did God take the woman from? The rib. What is a rib? A rib cage is that part of the body which has been designed by God to protect the internal sensitive organs. She's my rib. I'm the head; she's the heart. She is my helper. She completes me. She protects me emotionally. She supplies what I need. She perfects me.

I once saw a movie that illustrates how a woman perfects a man. It is entitled *As Good as It Gets* and stars Jack Nicholson and Helen Hunt. It's a good movie. Jack Nicholson played a paranoid and neurotic character with obsessive-compulsive tendencies. But he exacerbated his problem, as humans tend to do, because he wouldn't take his medication. (Sometimes we can be our own worst enemy.) Then he fell in love with Helen Hunt's character. As they were driving down the street, she told him to give her a compliment even though she knew he didn't like to give compliments. His response to her request was that he had taken his medication that day.

She told him that was not a compliment. He said that it was a compliment because before he met her he didn't care whether he took his medicine or not. But since they had met he had taken his medicine every day so that he could become the best man that he could be for her. That's powerful. He was saying that this woman made him want to take his Prozac. She made him want to be in his right mind. Her presence in his life was working to perfect him by making him do something that was for his betterment but that otherwise he would not do.

Now, as the man, I realize that I have a part in perfecting my wife too.

And my love for her makes me want to do my part. But my desire to honor her ultimately comes out of a longing to please God and to do His will. He provides the impetus for my wanting to be the best husband that I can be. And God, in His infinite wisdom, has interjected the right motivation for husbands to support their wives and to respond positively to their needs. So, when I treat my wife with the dignity that she deserves, God gives me the power to be the spiritual leader of our home. Everything falls in line when I do it God's way. The apostle Peter once offered some very sound advice on this matter:

> *"Likewise, ye husbands, dwell with them according to knowledge, giving honour unto the wife, as unto the weaker vessel, and as being heirs together of the grace of life; that your prayers be not hindered."*
> —1 PETER 3:7 KJV

It is rather humorous to me that the dynamics between a husband and wife haven't changed much over the span of history. God spoke through Peter's writings long ago and His message still stands today. The inherent differences between the male and female genders have caused many challenges in the marriage relationship. Especially when life throws a curve ball and the two of you disagree on how to handle the situation, it's rather easy to lose your way and for priorities to become confused.

God knows all about it, and He is trying to help us out by saying to the husband, *Deal with your wife according to the intimacy you have acquired by experience.* In other words, experience her. Get to know her. As the leader, this is your responsibility. The verb *dwell* means "to live." The Scripture is saying to live with your wife according to what you already know about her. This is the way to go about perfecting each other. The more you know about how your mate will react at certain times, the better you can prepare and work to smooth over the rough areas. I strongly encourage husbands to wrap their minds around this instruction from God, meditate on it, ask the Holy Spirit for help in doing it, and determine in your heart to follow it. That is your part in perfecting your wife.

This is how I put it into action. I tell people all of the time that I attend the University of Leslie. There is only one subject, Lesliology. I am ever matriculating, but never graduating from the University of Leslie. That is my job as her husband. It is similar to what I do as a pastor. I take a passage of Scripture and exegete it, meaning I study the cultural nuances, the grammatical implications, and the historical context. God expects me to treat my wife in that same way. I am supposed to exegete her like a text of Scripture so that I'm in tune with her emotionally, socially, psychologically, and spiritually. As a result of my efforts, I know what makes her tick and I know what ticks her off. It's my job to be her perfector.

Here is the benefit. Because we are believers in Christ Jesus, God looks at the two of us as heirs together with His Son, Jesus. So, if I do my part, and I do it well, the prayers that I send up to heaven on behalf of my wife and me will not be hindered—they will be heard and answered. God's favor is once again called into play. It is God fulfilling His promises to us.

This is a glorious place to be as we find ourselves in the position of the Trinity: We love together and share our hearts. We live together and share our home. We cling together and share our hopes. We labor together and share our help. We laugh together and share our happiness. We lament together and share our hurts. We remain together and will share our heritage. That is marriage as God intended—a perfect union in the eyes of God. And through it all, we thank God for what He is able to do on our behalf.

Divine GPS

> *"Trust in the Lord with all your heart and do not lean on your*
> *own understanding. In all your ways acknowledge Him,*
> *and He will make your paths straight."*
>
> —PROVERBS 3:5–6

Let me give you a practical example of relying on God's guidance to get you where He wants you to be in perfecting your mate. You see, God wants to lead you together through life's journey; He doesn't want the two of you to go it alone. Along the way, He wants to help you develop a marriage partnership that looks like His Trinity. At this point, you will have to raise your spiritual antenna and tune in to Him. And hopefully this illustration will begin to sound somewhat familiar to you.

Like many automobile models today, my car has a Global Positioning Satellite (GPS) program. Whenever I need directions, I push the GPS button. I am addressed by name and asked what I need. I announce that I need directions, state where I am, and tell the person where I am trying to go. From that point on, the GPS navigator gives me step-by-step directions. The first time I tried it, I told the guy that I was lost. He stated that I might be lost but he knew exactly where I was because I was hooked into a satellite high above the atmosphere. This man then told me my exact location and proceeded to give me directions. He also assured me that he would stay with me until I reached my destination.

As we proceeded, I was quite surprised by what the navigator was telling me. I asked him how he knew the landmarks and was familiar with areas that I passed by. His answer really made an impact on me. He said that everything was charted before him and he knew exactly where I was at all times. In fact, he could spot my car from anywhere in the world and get me to where I needed to go. Because I was feeling lost, that was extremely comforting news to my ears. And he did just what he said he would do for me.

Before we disconnected, he asked me if I had read my GPS manual. When I confessed that I hadn't, he told me about all the many helpful features that the program offers. I just needed to study it to learn about the various aspects of it. That way I could take advantage of them—weather, time, temperature, sports news—you name it. So later on I took his advice and read my manual. I even found out that the system could hook me up to my computer and receive a fax for me. I'm telling you, knowing this really opened my eyes to some great benefits.

What does this mean to you and your spouse? Many married people don't understand their roles in the way that God has designed them. As a result, their marriage is wandering aimlessly through life. If you feel like you and your spouse are going nowhere fast, you have to make use of the spiritual GPS system that our Lord has provided for you. I'm talking about God's Word and the power of the Holy Spirit working together on your behalf. The Word of God is found in the Bible; it is your Manual of instructions for properly assembling your marriage. When you want to assemble any object, such as a bicycle, for example, you have to read the manual first. Right? Well, it's no different when you want to assemble your marriage in the proper way. You have to consult with God and surrender yourself to His Spirit to avoid following erroneous directions that won't help you build a sound marriage.

I'm trying to get you to realize that you have a divine hookup. It is the power of God at work in your life. As a believer, you are connected to the Bright and Morning Star, and He's always up above you waiting for you to push the button called prayer. He is God the Son, and you can call Him by His name—Jesus. When you call on Him in prayer, God the Father receives the signal that you need help immediately. He already knows precisely where you are. So, He sends God the Holy Spirit, who, as your Comforter and Helper, is ready to guide you to peace and safety. When you feel lost and don't know how to pray, you have additional assurance because you can rely on the Holy Spirit to pray for you. He knows exactly what you need. He takes the message for you through the satellite beacon of the universe all the way to the throne of grace in heaven.

When you follow Proverbs 3:5–6, the Holy Spirit will assure you that trusting in Him with all your heart is the right thing to do. He reminds you not to rely on your own understanding about your situation, but to acknowledge Him in all of your ways throughout your journey. God knows all about you anyway, so you might as well lay it all before Him—all of your faults, failures, strengths, and weaknesses. That translates to lifting up your daily issues to God and inviting the Lord to show you how to correct your wrong behaviors and reinforce your good qualities.

He assures you that He will direct your paths. He wants you to walk down the straight boulevard because broad is the path that leads to destruction, but narrow is the gate that leads to eternal life. Ultimately, He instructs you to make a divine U-turn and surrender everything over to Him—your family and all of your concerns too—because He will get you to your destination and you can shout the victory.

And the benefits don't stop there. When you search the Manual as you travel along in life, you will find there are a whole lot of promises that you haven't discovered yet. There's healing for you in the Manual. There is the love of God for you to experience in the Manual. There's spiritual and physical prosperity for you in the Manual. There's mercy and forgiveness for you in the Manual. There's peace for you in the Manual. There are opportunities beyond your imagination for you in the Manual. When you make use of your Manual, you will gain invaluable counsel on receiving blessings that you and your spouse need but didn't know already belonged to you.

When you discover the riches of the Bible, you will better understand the depth of what salvation brings to you as a child of God. Then, perhaps, your response will be like mine. I said, "Man, I like this. I was going in the wrong direction, and the Holy Spirit told me to make a U-turn. He pointed me toward the right path. And when I obeyed Him and made that U-turn, I reached my destination by the grace of God."

So, what are you going to do? Are you and your spouse going to agree to walk this thing out together, or are you going to break out and run from each other? Are you going to break down and quit? Or, by the grace of God, are you going to break through your marital challenges and triumph in the Name of Jesus? I suggest that when the going gets hard, stop and whisper, "Father, I need more grace." I guarantee you will see an immediate and loving response from God that is the answer to your prayer.

All You Need Is Love

"May the Lord direct your hearts into the love of God
and into the steadfastness of Christ."
—2 THESSALONIANS 3:5

It is a simple prayer but it is so rich in meaning because it is the very heart and soul of your relationship. You and your spouse need each other's love to be perfected in each other and when you rely on the Lord Jesus Christ, He will get you there. When you break through all the clutter and distractions that often burden married life, what you have at the end of the day is each other. It's no wonder that God would design the husband and the wife to meet each other's needs. And He is the faithful One who will always watch over you. Living together can be a hard road to travel and you need to be steadfast and dedicated; otherwise you will give up. Jesus wants to be the Director of your heart, and you can be assured that He will teach you how to love and show you how to build up and perfect your marriage in Him.

The Bible commands husbands in Ephesians 5:25 to love their wives. That is the primary need of the woman—love. This verse was written in the imperative mood of the Greek language, and, therefore, it is a command and not merely an option for men to love their wives. The apostle Paul wanted to make sure that the husbands knew that their duty was to meet the needs of their wives in every way that is humanly possible. When you are seriously committed to doing that, the question to constantly ask your wife is, "Do you need anything?"

On the other hand, it is interesting to note that nowhere in Scripture is there a command for the wife to love her husband. Now, Titus 2:4–5 speaks to women and strongly encourages them to love their husbands and children and to exhibit behavior that is proper for women in general. However, that is not a command to women; rather it is an exhortation for them to make sure their behavior was a model for their community and brought honor to God. It was not written as an imperative for women to love their husbands; it is really saying that it's the right thing to do.

Since God has given us His love, it is the strength and power of His love that helps us to perfect each other. But there is a stark difference in how He designed men and women to show their love. Women express love by *nature*, and men demonstrate love by *nurture*. God made women to naturally show love by the loving nature that is inherent in them. For instance, the natural bond between a woman and her child will cause a woman to love that child without reservation because her spirit is open and receptive to the transference of her love. Conversely, men were designed to put their love into action through physical ways. For example, doing such things to benefit their families like teaching a child how to play baseball or working to provide food and other necessities is a concrete form of love that they can relate to. These are the characteristics of a nurturer. That is why men need a special commandment from God to express their love in the many subtle ways that appeal to their wives.

Here are seven basic ways that a woman needs her husband to demonstrate his love. So, brothers, pay close attention to the following list. It will help you to understand how you are to perfect your wife:

1. Love and affection

What's love got to do with it? Love has everything to do with a woman's makeup and motivation. She is either driven by love or the lack of it. That is why God created the woman to be loved by her husband. When a man understands that his wife shares a part of his own flesh, he should be compelled to love her as much as he loves his own self. Paul explains it this way, *"So husbands ought also to love their own wives as their own bodies. He who loves his own wife loves himself; for no one ever hated his own flesh, but nourishes and cherishes it, just as Christ also does the church"* (Ephesians 5:28–29).

Although this may seem like a sacrifice for you, know that a woman who is given sufficient love will not reject that love; rather, she will be naturally motivated to embrace it. When you are sincerely meeting a woman's primary need for love, she will feel an overall sense of security in that love. If your love is motivated by God, she will know it, and it will be reflected in the climate of your relationship. Genuine love will satisfy all of her other needs.

2. Spiritual leadership

God gave the man His word in Genesis 2:16. So, by default, the husband is the spiritual leader of the home. As the patriarch of the family, it is the man's responsibility to make sure the family goes to church, attends Bible study, has regular devotion time, and prays together regularly. It is his duty to point out the difference between right and wrong and make sure that his children choose righteousness. As she supports him in these efforts, a woman needs to know that she can rely on her husband to provide spiritual direction for her and her family.

Overall, she needs her husband to assume his role in being the head of the family and leading by example. Otherwise, the family structure is out of order and the pressure is upon the woman to make up for his lack of responsibility. She may feel constrained to take it upon herself to keep her family grounded in the Word. But know that this could become a distraction from giving her full attention to her own responsibilities as a wife and mother.

3. Conversation and quality time

Although there is much debate over the subject of men and women and the number of words each gender uses daily, it is commonly noted that men engage in conversation considerably less than women. According to neuro-psychiatrist Louann Brizendine, "The numbers vary, but on average girls speak two to three times more words per day than boys."[1]

When you have to discuss typical family matters such as children, food, school, television, sports, and even sex, it helps to communicate effectively with your mate about these things. Otherwise, misunderstanding one another can often cause serious problems. Having a good perspective on this subject, Dr. Brizendine also states: "We've learned that men and women have different brain sensitivities to stress and conflict. They use different brain areas and circuits to solve problems, process language, experience and store the same strong emotions."[2]

As a result, it is beneficial to be in harmony with each other's various modes of communication as much as possible. A husband who can be in tune with how his wife thinks and can anticipate her needs will have a more successful conversation. Brothers, whether you are in the mood for talking or not when your wife approaches you, this would probably be a good time to press on and give her your undivided attention. Let her know verbally and through your body language that you are interested in what she wants to convey. Talk to her; tell her that you love her, and remind her of how important she is to you over and over again. Some loving cooperation can go a long way when you dwell with your mate according to what you already know about her communication habits.

4. Financial support and stability

Now, think about this very carefully. A couple recites their marriage vows and promises to remain together in times of sickness and health, for richer or poorer, and for better or worse. But, trust me, even though a woman may have said these things, she wasn't anticipating the part about being poor. No one wants to be poor, and she doesn't expect to be deprived because of financial constraints. She didn't marry you with the belief that you could not provide a stable home and future for her.

I guarantee you that a lack of financial planning on your part was not in her perceived future. Instead, most women look on the positive side and believe that their spouse is prepared to take good care of the family that you plan on building together. In fact, when the apostle Peter used the phrase *giving honor to the wife* in 1 Peter 3:7 (NKJV), what he was saying is that the wife is worthy of money. The word *honor* in this verse is *timdao*, which is where we get our word *tomato*. In the Greek language this word means "money." In other words, Peter is reminding husbands that their wives are valuable and should be treated as such.

5. To be number one in her husband's life

A wife needs to know that she is cherished and that her husband delights in her. In fact, there is no stronger human bond than that between a husband and wife. She should have her husband's constant attention—even when they are apart. She needs you to stay in contact with her; call her several times a day just to tell her that you love her. It is the husband's duty, I repeat—duty, to make sure that his wife knows beyond a shadow of a doubt that he puts no other human being above her. He does this through his actions, by giving her his time, talk, tenderness, and touch to the point that she gets it. Because he is consistently showing her in various ways, she understands that she is loved by him and holds a place of prominence in his heart.

6. Protection

Men mostly think in terms of providing physical protection for their wives. But there are other areas where a woman needs protection, particularly in her times of weakness. You are also supposed to reassure her and make her feel safe when she feels intimidated and vulnerable. What about emotional, social, intellectual, and financial protection? All of these areas are important to a woman. For example, if a man is not a good steward of his money, then his wife does not feel protected and her sense of security is affected. When that happens, a common reaction is for a woman to find ways to protect her own interests by building her own savings. But in a marriage relationship, there isn't supposed to be his and her accounts. However, if she feels that he can't handle his business, her natural instinct is to insulate herself from the threat of financial lack. That is the beginning of a separation and a rift in the bond between them. A lack of protection on his part can manifest itself in many ways and can become a slippery slope as one act of division often leads to another.

7. Family commitment

A woman needs to know that she can trust her husband to create a safe and secure environment for her family. She needs a mate whom she can depend on to be a good father to her children. The best thing a man can do for his children is to love their mother. She will cherish the stability that you provide, knowing that you are fully invested in your family. She can rise to do her best when there is a shared sense of values that is fostered by your loyalty and dedication to your family.

Brothers, I am telling you that this thing is powerful. Please take ministering to your wife's needs into serious consideration. You have to pay attention to the well-being of your wife. She is your most valuable asset. Understand that you can't expect to have a summer wife when you bring home winter weather. That's impossible; it just doesn't work that way. Remember, you are the thermostat. If you bring coldness or harsh feelings into your home, you will get that in return. It is your responsibility to set the climate in your household. You are the key to the success of the home. Try repeating this over and over to yourself: I'm the man. I'm the man. I'm the man.

Protect Your Partnership

Brothers, when you are determined to make your marriage a success, these issues will matter greatly to you. But you need help. It's time to turn once again to the Bible to find out what God says that you should do. The more you invest in your relationship, the better results you will enjoy. A sound marriage is based on mutual love—it is the backbone on which your relationship is built. And love demands respect. The part of the Bible that has the most to say about the subject of love is what I call the love chapter: 1 Corinthians 13:4–8. You will gain an insurmountable advantage in your marriage when you take my summary of this message to heart and put it into action in your marriage partnership.

Love is patient and kind. When you get this, you will not be in a hurry for everything to happen all at once. You won't have a perfect marriage overnight, but you will realize that love covers a multitude of sins. Real love does not get envious of its partner. Love doesn't belittle its spouse and have an attitude that tells the world that you think you're "all that." Love is not selfish; it doesn't demand that everything goes its way. Love doesn't have a temper that flares up at a moment's notice.

Love doesn't want to see his or her mate stumble and fall and then gloat about it. Love never exposes the frailties and weakness of its mate. Rather, love will make you support your mate and protect the love you share. Love gets happy when it witnesses the truth prevailing over lies and deception. Love can hold up under pressure and doesn't buckle under when times get rough. Love is always willing to give the benefit of the doubt and stays ready to believe the best of each other.

Love will endure whatever the marriage encounters in life. Love will always hope for the best outcome in any situation. Finally, those who believe God's Word also know that you can't go wrong when you choose to follow love's prescription for life. And love will never fail them.

Winning the Ultimate Battle

Yes, love can hold your marriage together, but there are some times that marriage will hold your love together. Furthermore, married people who love the Lord should want to do everything that they can to avoid the pitfalls in marriage that could lead to destruction. When you both understand it is God whom you must ultimately please and you then work to develop His character in you, your marriage will reap the benefits. That's when it will begin to look like the Trinity.

Someone once said that you can view marriage as having three rings. First comes the engagement ring, next comes the wedding ring, and then comes the suffering. The bottom line is that certain attitudes and behaviors work against your partnership. If your marriage has fallen on bad times, take a closer look to understand why. Marriages don't deteriorate in one day; rather, relationships tend to break down in six phases. Everybody needs a checkup once in a while. To avoid winding up in a trap that could potentially lead to its demise, evaluate the phases where your marriage could be in jeopardy.

The Bible speaks about God's people being destroyed because they lack knowledge. If you see you and your mate in any of these phases, or if you sense that the climate of your marriage is reflected here, it's time to do something about it. Taking action to protect your marriage is the goal, and procrastination can only make things worse. To win the battle for your marriage, you first need to know about the signs to be aware of.

Phase 1

The Spiritual Phase. The health of a marriage deteriorates in the spiritual realm first. It occurs because of a failure to keep Christ and His Word at the center of the relationship. That is the first mistake many people make. Too many times we focus on the two flesh and blood partners in the marriage and leave the most important component out. There is no way that a marriage can fail with Jesus Christ as its focal point. When a couple is focusing on Jesus they will be in tune with His Spirit. And He will keep them in tune with each other. So, the tie that binds it all together is Christ.

Therefore, the key to the success of a marriage is submission to Christ first and then to each other. The Bible says that a threefold cord is not easily broken (Ecclesiastes 4:12). And so it is Christ, your mate, and you—because you can't maintain a strong marriage without Christ as the equalizing factor in your relationship. I use the example of a clear plastic glove to represent believers in a relationship with God. That relationship makes their lives transparent. If I placed my hand inside the glove, you could plainly see my brown hand, which represents a believer being filled with Christ. This is a picture of what we need in our marital relationships: two individuals so filled with the love of Christ that it's all they see when they look at each other.

Here's why. We can't pick and choose what we want God to be involved in and expect to have strong marriages. There should be nothing in the relationship that we should be reluctant to bring God into. If people would seek God before their problems arise in the way that they do when they seek God after their problems occur, generally they wouldn't have to seek God with any problems. But the problem is that we use God like a spare tire. We mess the marriage up, and then we want God to fix it up. The wonderful thing about the grace of God is that He will do it. He will fix a broken relationship if you give Him all of the pieces. He absolutely will. But God wants us to understand that, to reach the goal of functioning like the Trinity, we must be committed to Him before the marriage and committed to Him in the marriage.

Singles often ask me how they can know that a certain person is the one they are supposed to hook up with. My response is: Start running for Jesus and run as fast as you can. When you look over and see somebody that is also running for Jesus and keeping up with you, that's your spouse. You'll be in a better position to build a strong marriage when the two of you keep Christ at the center of your relationship.

Phase 2

The Reality Phase. After the marriage ceremony is over and the honeymoon soon becomes a fond but distant memory, the reality of being married begins to settle in. What does the word *honeymoon* mean? It means "sweet month." It is temporary, and when it's over you actually begin to see the person that you've married. Then, you start to realize what living with that person will be like for the rest of your life. You don't really see it when you are dating or even when you are engaged. This is the phase where those things that you thought were cute about each other while dating now get on your nerves as you realize you have to deal with it on a permanent basis.

When people don't take the time to build a strong relationship by getting to know each other before they plan a wedding, they only know what they've got once they have the papers. That's when you find out that he's not who you thought he was. You find out that his breath stinks at 6:00 a.m. and his feet stink at 6:00 p.m. You find out that she isn't all that you thought that she was. She's not Sleeping Beauty; she just doesn't want to get up out of bed.

My suggestion is, if you haven't already done so, the first thing is to begin a serious prayer time. You're going to need it to get you through some difficult situations. It takes commitment to God's Word and determination to make your marriage survive. And for that you will need to lean heavily on your communication with the Lord to help you make the adjustment to married life.

Phase 3

The Transition Phase. The problem with a lot of marriages is that some married people don't realize that they are married. They're still trying to live like they're single. NEWS FLASH: You're not single anymore. In too many marriages people are living single but they are actually married with children. Hmmm . . . sounds like good titles for TV programs. They haven't learned that there is a transition that has to take place. Some brothers talk back to their wives saying, "You're not my mama, I don't have to check in with you." I beg to differ with you. You owe her an explanation because you are married to her. To the women who say, "I can spend what I want to because I have my own job," I beg to differ: You are married to him; it's no longer your money. Money is an asset that two married partners are supposed to share.

You don't get to do what *you* want to do anymore. All of those wrong attitudes have to be changed when you are married. The two of you are now "one", and you have to learn how to live like it. Single life is over. Yes, you should know who his friends are because he is your husband. Yes, you need to know where she's going because she is your wife. Where you spend your money and what you spend it on becomes the business of both of you.

When your plans cater only to your personal needs, it will cause detrimental results to your relationship. It's a sign of immaturity when you think that your marriage is all about you. There are some newlywed couples who are prone to saying really immature things like, "I want her to work because she has to hold up her end. It's fifty-fifty." I just want to know what Bible they've been reading. Marriage is not fifty-fifty. If that were so, where do you draw the line? How would you know when you've done your 50 percent? No, marriage is 100 percent. It is not give and take like a business proposition. Marriage is give, give, give, give . . .

Phase 4

The Romantic Phase. This phase is in jeopardy when the couple's talk, time, touch, and tenderness have diminished. It happens when they become insensitive to each other's needs, including the area of sexual intimacy. In fact, intimacy is very important. In my marriage seminars, I utilize a survey that covers twelve aspects of intimacy. It is designed to be completed by both the husband and wife separately. It encourages them to talk and share with each other. They are to come together to compare their answers and discuss the areas in which they disagree. They are to break down the reasons they think the various aspects of intimacy are working or not working in their relationship.

To get the most out of this exercise, the couple is supposed to really roll up their sleeves and commit to finding resolutions for their areas of weakness. Then an action plan is used to target a particular problem in the marriage; the couple is to evaluate the ideas that are suggested for improvement and thoroughly exhaust each one until they reach a solution. The idea is to help your marriage survive by putting forth the effort to restore romance in your relationship. It may take some hard work to turn your marriage into the loving relationship God would have it to be. But the good news is on the way when you take each other's suggestions and intimacy comes alive!

Phase 5

The Retaliation Phase. This is when the proverbial "war of the roses" takes place. Instead of living like June and Ward Cleaver, the couple lives like Homer and Marge Simpson. Or, worse yet, Al and Peggy Bundy. Resentment and bitterness have set in, and the couple begins to damage each other intentionally. It starts with a breakdown in communication when you begin to talk *at* each other and *about* each other instead of talking *with* each other. Spouses start to retaliate by saying things that undermine the relationship. They find themselves having bitters feelings and start to shut down in opposition.

If the situation escalates, couples start to get even against each other. Often they end up being very vulnerable and open to having affairs. If you're constantly telling him what a dog he is and he can't do anything right, somebody at work may be telling him that he's the sweetest person they've every met. When other women compliment him on his personality, he will begin to think that his wife doesn't appreciate him. Or, when a woman feels like her husband doesn't appreciate her and frequently reminds her that she is overweight and out of shape, someone else might tell her that she is a soft and cuddly pillow that he would love to lay his head on. My point is that people can find themselves being swayed by outside attention when they grow weary of verbal and emotional battles with their spouses.

Phase 6

The Rejection Phase. Extramarital affairs often occur when a marriage is broken. If a spouse has resorted to having an affair, it is a form of serious rejection. Separation or divorce can be an unfortunate result.

Negative communication then becomes a key factor in the fall of any marriage. It all starts with words. Words are powerful and once they have been spoken, there is no taking them back. Certain words are extremely detrimental and can undermine a person's self-esteem. And causing harm is exactly what they are meant to do.

The Bible says that "death and life are in the power of the tongue" (Proverbs 18:21). Knowing this led me to rethink that old phrase, "Sticks and stones may break my bones, but words will never harm me." That is a false statement, which I have reworded to state the truth: "Sticks and stones may break my bones, but words can break my heart." Words are powerful; they can break your heart. Words will destroy your relationship. No matter how tough someone might think they are, people cannot continue to be rejected without it taking a toll on them emotionally.

For instance, a wife may say to her husband, "Honey, I was thinking that I want a business of my own." She starts to describe the kind of business she might envision when her husband interrupts and says, "That's the stupidest thing I've ever heard in my life." Well, you can forget about hearing her dreams again. Or, a husband might tell his wife, "Baby, I'm thinking about going back to school to get a degree in engineering." If her reply is, "What? You? . . . " That dream just died.

The point is that harsh and insensitive words can kill a marriage by sabotaging the partners. The bottom line is, no one is happy when a marriage fails. There is no winner; everyone loses something because a spiritual separation breaches God's reason for marriage. But do not dismay; God has a prescription for keeping marriages together that will hopefully bring some illumination to your situation.

It's All Connected . . .

Brothers, this discussion is mostly for you. Don't think that I'm picking on you. I'm not the designer of the marital relationship. However, as a fellow brother, I want you to be aware because your marriage is serious business to God. Remember, it was God's idea to create the man first and give him primary responsibility for the health and well-being of the marriage bond. As a result, in our pursuit of perfecting the marriage relationship so that it lines up with the Trinity, there is an underlying theme and a connection that I will explain here because God doesn't want us to miss this.

Without the power of God working behind the scenes, we don't have the right equipment and, therefore, no chance to realize God's vision for the union of marriage. However, God is the author of matrimony and marital relationships, and He really wants you and your spouse to succeed. If you've been thinking all along that God is indifferent to your situation, think that no longer. He is both able and willing to help your marriage realize its full potential.

This is what you need to know. I often say that we don't have a relationship problem, we have a "filled with the Spirit" problem. When we cooperate with Him, the Holy Spirit produces fruit in our lives. It is no secret: If you practice love, joy, peace, longsuffering, kindness, goodness, faithfulness, gentleness, and self-control, you and your mate are on your way to victory in your marriage. And when you depend on God's power He will develop His fruit in you. That is a sweet path to take that brings about good results. My friend Brother Davis responded to his wife in a sensitive way once she allowed God's fruit to come forth and be a blessing in their relationship. Love, gentleness, and self-control were already there, someone just needed to point out to her that she was overlooking the powerful change that would take place for her and Brother Davis when she relied on them.

Here is the prescription for perfecting our marriages. Test it and see for yourself. Particularly in my own experience, with the chronic health problems that my wife faces, sometimes there can be enormous pressure to deal with. This is a major area in my life where the Holy Spirit benefits me immensely. I rely on the fruit of God's Spirit to help me deal with the challenges of caring for my wife and all other family concerns, along with the demands of being a pastor. After all, God's wisdom and power supersede anything we could accomplish on our own. When you think about your own relationship, what situation comes to mind first? What do you want the Lord to work with you on so that the problem will be fixed?

But before you can expect God to help you unravel the difficult things that put a strain on your relationship, you have a choice to make. You must decide whether to choose the path of unrighteous or follow God's way. This matters greatly to your marriage because it determines whose influence you will follow. Take a self-examination moment and consider the two contrasting descriptions that the apostle lays out here. Which camp best describes your behavior?

"Now the deeds of the flesh are evident, which are: immorality, impurity, sensuality, idolatry, sorcery, enmities, strife, jealousy, outbursts of anger, disputes, dissensions, factions, envying, drunkenness, carousing, and things like these, of which I forewarn you, just as I have forewarned you, that those who practice such things will not inherit the kingdom of God.

But the fruit of the Spirit is love, joy, peace, patience, kindness, goodness, faithfulness, gentleness, self-control; against such things there is no law.

Now those who belong to Christ Jesus have crucified the flesh with its passions and desires.

If we live by the Spirit, let us also walk by the Spirit."

—GALATIANS 5:19–25

This Scripture passage is drawing a stark distinction between the only two paths to follow in life. One is narrow and the other is wide. One leads to destruction and the other leads to eternal life. The wide path seems easier to follow because there is so much room to maneuver about. But the problem is that we wind up indulging in our fleshly desires. Everyone has them; the question is, "Do you take the easy way out and give in to whatever your flesh wants you to do?" Just look at the long list detailing the deeds of the flesh. Anybody who has lived on this earth for a while should know that it doesn't take any power to give in to sin. That's the easy way.

On the other hand, when you take the narrow path, your life will produce good fruit. When you got saved, Jesus' work prepared you to live in heaven, but when you got filled with the Spirit, He prepared you to live on earth. You have the power to choose. The Holy Spirit gives you the ability to embrace the things of God so that you can live like the child of God that you are. The Word of God promises that you can crucify your fleshly passions when you belong to Christ. That's not an empty promise—it's the truth.

Walking the narrow path changes everything from unrighteousness to righteousness. When you are a child of God, you have a new life, a new chance to live right. He just wants to help you acknowledge the truth about yourself, give up your old ways of immorality, angry and abusive behavior, whatever it may be; acknowledge that truth about yourself; and begin to walk joy, peace, and goodness in your daily life. In other words, if you know that you are a child of God—then act like it. Put yourself on a steady diet of God's Word and be determined to obey God.

You see, the devil would have you be ignorant to who you really are. He wants your flesh to dominate your behavior instead of allowing the Holy Spirit to guide your actions. He wants to lure you into thinking that, in the big picture of life, your place in this world is virtually insignificant. But that is not so. The cause and effect that you generate through your personal choices matter even into eternity. Life is a series of connected events that affect everyone and everything else in your sphere of influence. The people around you are watching you. And, although you may not readily see it happening, the way that you conduct yourself and the climate you set in your marriage then spreads beyond your immediate boundaries and touches others in ways that may be difficult to imagine—yet, they are very real.

So, that is what the fruit of the Spirit is for—it is the power in your relationship that keeps your connection to God strong. Think about the benefits it will bring if you tap into the abundance of love and affection that may be lying dormant in your heart. When you allow the love of God inside you to bubble up, it will help you to be patient and kind toward your loved ones and everyone else that you meet. You will remain faithful to God, your wife, and yourself when you demonstrate the fruit of self-control. When the Holy Spirit directs your life, you will be able to live in the peace of God.

To illustrate what I'm talking about, I want you to read on to see the dramatic impact that a man has on his marital relationship and even the world when he chooses to live without the Spirit of God. Then, you will also see the outcome a man will bring about when he chooses to walk in the Spirit of God and allow the fruit of God's Spirit to work in and through him.

Here is a summary of what Dr. Tony Evans says about the significance of a man's role and the impact it has on the world: If you've got a messed up man, you have a messed up marriage. If you have a messed up marriage, you have a messed up family. If you have a messed up family, then you'll have a messed up church because families make up churches. If you have a messed up church, you have a messed up city because it's churches that comprise a city. That's a problem because the church is the thermostat in the world. If we have a messed up city, then you have a messed up state because states are comprised of cities. If you have a messed up state, you have a messed up country because countries are comprised of states. If you have a messed up country, you have a messed up continent because continents are comprised of countries. If you have a messed up continent, then you have a messed up world because the world is comprised of continents. And so, *"Righteousness exalts a nation, but sin is a disgrace to any people"* (Proverbs 14:34).

So then, the reverse is also true, and this is where we need to focus our efforts. We can't afford to miss this. If you want a better world, then you've got to have better continents. And if you want better continents, then you've got to have better nations. But the only way you can get better nations is if you have better states. But the only way to get to better states is to have better cities. And the only way to get better cities is to have better churches because they are filled with people who love God. And the only way you can have better churches is to have better families. And the only way to get better families is to have better marriages. And the only way to get a better marriage is to have a better man.[3]

To build a better marriage, you've got to go back to basics. Remember, this thing starts with the man because God started with the man. But it's up to the man and whether he chooses to master his God-given role. If you want to get it right, brothers, you have to follow His pattern. When the thermostat (the man) and the thermometer (the woman) register at the right temperature for your marriage, everything that concerns your relationship is given the opportunity to fall in line.

Now, let me warn you, it won't be perfect, because there's no such thing as a perfect marriage. Yet, our goal is to mirror the Trinity. Even as we strive to do that, we are still human and as such we have flaws. God knows this but He expects us to do nothing less than our very best because He has given us His best. The sum of perfection in our present human state is manifested when we *"press toward the mark for the prize of the high calling of God in Christ Jesus"* (Philippians 3:14 KJV). When we press on, we find perfection in Him.

God is calling men and women to take their roles in perfecting their partnership seriously because He is seriously looking for His children to be a reflection of His Trinity. And when you have the kind of relationship that God has in mind, you are connected to God's Trinity. That puts you in the position to enjoy marriage and your family as God intended. And your ultimate reward will be waiting for you in heaven. Trust Him, it's all worth fighting for.

Making It Happen

1. With an open and receptive heart, ask God to help you understand how to apply His reason for creating marriage as a means to perfect your marriage partnership. He will hear your sincere prayers and help you to transform your marriage into a reflection of His image.

2. Married couples need to spend quality time together doing things that they both enjoy. However, this area of the relationship is often shortchanged because of the demands of day-to-day life. Choose something that you will both enjoy. Putting forth the effort is well worth it because this can be valuable time that has the ability to bring a husband and wife closer together. Although there are some who do, many women don't consider watching a football game or other sports programs as spending quality time with their mate. If your wife happens to be someone who is not interested in sports, it's not fair for you to expect her to enjoy watching a game with you.

3. To facilitate your desire to improve your relationship, it would be helpful to view the Word of God as an instruction Manual that will lead to blessings and favor when you do what it says. The fruit of the Spirit is *love, joy, peace, patience, kindness, goodness, faithfulness, gentleness, and self-control.* Before your next scheduled quality time, list three ways that you have observed your spouse demonstrating each fruit of the Spirit. Share your list with each other.

4. For your marriage to really work and to please God, you have to reach the point that you both embrace your God-given roles as husband and wife and, by the grace and mercy of God, live them. Why do you think God decided to give each partner different roles to play in marriage? What can you do as your wife's partner to improve your performance? What can you do as your husband's partner to improve your performance?

5. In your own words, what do you think it means to perfect your mate? What are some of the things a man should do to perfect his mate? What are some of the things a woman should do to perfect her mate? Name some ways that you plan to improve yourself and become a better spouse.

6. How does your partnership measure up? What things can you do to make it better? Keep this simple question in mind and ask your mate

often, "Do you need anything?" Making this a practice will put you both in a mind-set of meeting each other's needs and knowing that your primary concern is taking care of each other.

7. Do you believe marriage partners should be transparent to each other? You will see the Trinity at work when you look at each other up close and personal. It is completely possible because God has made it so. Jesus said it best, *"The things which are impossible with men are possible with God"* (Luke 18:27 KJV). Have a meaningful conversation about this question and share with each other qualities that you appreciate in your partner. Include as many intimate details as you can.

8. Effective communication is one of the greatest assets a couple can possess. Discuss the seven basic ways that a husband should demonstrate his role as the protector of his wife. Have a similar discussion about the wife's role as protector of her husband.

9. To win the battle for your marriage, discuss each phase of marriage breakdown. Identify areas where you are having difficulty and focus on ways to strengthen your relationship.

10. A woman needs her husband's undivided attention on a consistent basis. So, the two of you need to find an activity where both of you are fully engaged. Show her that you enjoy being with her. Marriage is all about compromise and this is an option that should not be overlooked as you choose how to spend time together. The time spent is significant only when both of you find enjoyment in your shared time.

Reason #4

The Procreation
Reason
Fulfills a
Spiritual Requirement

The day had finally arrived. George and Sarah were thrilled that their son was born at last. It had been a rather difficult pregnancy, really touch-and-go for the past three months. But Sarah and little Alex came through the delivery with flying colors.

Well, that was fourteen years ago and now George and Sarah were faced with some unexpected challenges, like so many parents today. They talked about it often; they thought they had done all the right things. After all, Alex didn't want for anything. He went to the best schools, had all the latest gear—cell phones, video games, MP3 players, a computer— you name it. Besides that, he looked the part, wearing all the latest styles. But somehow it wasn't enough to keep him out of trouble.

Sarah got regular phone calls from the school disciplinary office. She was frustrated and didn't know what to do. They talked about it all on a regular basis. "I don't understand. He seems angry all of the time," George told the counselor one day. "We give him the best of everything, but it doesn't seem to make a difference in his attitude."

"Maybe that's the problem, Mr. Smith. Alex is overloaded with things, but is he getting enough of what he really needs? Does he have your attention?" George paused for a moment in contemplation. He didn't seem to have a clue that he hadn't been giving his son enough of himself.

Later at home, when he and Sarah talked about what the counselor had said, they reacted in defense. "Yes, Alex is rebellious. But isn't that normal? Don't kids just turn away from their parents as they grow up?" Sarah was quick to defend how they had raised their son. The way she saw it, she was a good mother and felt that she was giving Alex enough love for both of them. George worked hard and long hours to provide them with a decent lifestyle. After all of their rationalization, one question remained on both of their minds: "Wasn't that enough?"

The Lord Will Increase You . . .

> "God blessed them; and God said to them,
> be fruitful and multiply, and fill the earth."
> —GENESIS 1:28

In very commanding words, God said to Adam and Eve, "Have babies and fill the earth." By pronouncing this blessing on the man and woman, He enabled them to populate the earth with human life. Traveling down the ages, we find that same blessing extended throughout future generations to come.

But does this mean that God wants us to have babies just for the sake of having babies? Absolutely not! God said, "Be fruitful and multiply" because He has a particular reason for the reproduction of human life. And He specifically selected those in a marriage partnership to carry out that purpose and commanded them to do it. Overall, God's reason for procreation is to fulfill a spiritual requirement. But we need to understand the importance of that requirement and why He would make procreation one of the seven reasons why He created marriage.

Let's start with the question, "Why does God want the earth to be replenished?" The answer points directly back to what the Trinity of God proclaimed two verses earlier, *"Let Us make man in Our image, according to Our likeness"* (Genesis 1:26). This is God's plan for procreation. It should be man's desire to cooperate with God to bring forth a reflection of His image many times over. Therefore, it is through the process of nurturing our offspring that they are transformed into His likeness. For those of us who have been blessed with children, biologically or through any other means, this is our reasonable service—to meet God's spiritual requirement.

Now, I am fully aware that every married couple does not have children and there are as many reasons why as there are married people. However, God wants those who have no biological children to know that it is possible to participate in His reason for procreation. There are many children who need spiritual guidance but have no one to provide it. Everyone can reach out with an open heart to help develop godliness in a young person who is in need of assistance and tender loving care. Community service, adoption, foster care, and even mentoring programs can all be avenues to help fulfill a spiritual void in someone's life. In whatever way they come into your life, know that children are a gift from God.

Through His gracious benevolence, God simply loves to bless His people. Scripture tells us that *"children are an heritage of the Lord: and the fruit of the womb is his reward"* (Psalm 127:3 KJV). What this means is that children provide a legacy for us. Furthermore, we who have been blessed to have them hold a great responsibility. They have been entrusted into our care, and it pleases God when we take His gift seriously. The reason is that He wants our babies to grow up and be faithful, mature Christians who will love Him and serve Him wholeheartedly.

In the Old Testament, the word *heritage* used in Psalm 127 is the equivalent of the word *stewardship* that is found in the New Testament. It comes from a Greek word that means "household management," which means the responsible care of something entrusted to someone. God intends the parents to whom He rewards children to provide and care for His gift in a caring and responsible way. He loaned our children to us and trusts us to do the right thing by them. Now, I know that some of you might be thinking, *I sure wish He would come and get what He loaned me.* But seriously, we need to find out exactly why God gave us the precious gift of parenthood and what He expects us to do with the children He has placed in our care.

In fact, we are to handle the job of stewardship of our children by keeping the image of the Trinity in mind. As children of God, we are God's offspring and He has given us an inheritance (Romans 8:17; 1 Peter 1:3–5).

The Bible tells us that *"a good man leaves an inheritance to his children's children"* (Proverbs 13:22). We, in turn, are to follow God's pattern and pass on an inheritance to our children. This legacy often comes in the form of a material inheritance and, of course, that is a good thing. But even more importantly, we should pass on to them a spiritual inheritance by teaching our children about the wonderful gift of salvation that God has provided. To make that happen, we have to apply diligence in our parental responsibilities because it is tantamount to the success of our children. Through spiritual guidance and proper home training, the best gift you can give your children is to encourage them to believe in Christ Jesus and receive His gift that will last forever. Beyond knowing they have a personal relationship with Christ, it is a beautiful and satisfying thing to see your children witness to others.

God Is a Seeker

Do you know that, ultimately, our heavenly Father wants us to give our offspring back to Him? He is looking for believers who have been brought up in the fear and admonition of the Lord. His main objective is for us to produce godly seed, and He wants to be well pleased with the children that we bring into this world. We know this because as a Father Himself, He showed extreme pleasure with His Son, Jesus, and publicly declared it when Jesus was baptized (Matthew 3:17). God loves to boast about His children.

Procreation ensures that God has the seed that He desires. The question then becomes, "Why is this seed so important to Him?" A godly seed ensures that God's plan of salvation for mankind will be fulfilled. Everyone born into this world will need to have the opportunity to be saved and live eternally with God. So, God is seeking those who will labor with Him to spread the Good News throughout the earth. He wants to see His reflection when He looks at His human creation. And the only way that can be possible is for man to be restored to right standing with God through salvation in His Son, Jesus. Therefore, children should be trained in godly ways so that they can deliver the Gospel to those who are lost.

By virtue of the fact that we are all the product of God's creation narrative, every believer has involvement in the plan of salvation. To describe what procreation means for all believers, two explanations come to mind.

1. For those who have children or are contemplating having them, it is necessary for you to evaluate how well you understand God's expectation that comes along with parenthood. God wants you to take seriously the task of raising your children so that they will reverence Him and walk in His ways.

2. Whether you have biological children or not, understanding the reason for procreation will give you an informed perspective on what God will accomplish through godly children and the impact they will have on the world.

Through procreation, God created us with deliberate intentions in mind, and He is looking for those who have a desire to answer His call. Let me turn your attention to some very specific kinds of people that God was seeking in the Bible and why He sought them. You should also know that God is still seeking these same kinds of people today. That means you have a place in what God is looking for too. And you should be able to find yourself in some of these descriptions.

1. God seeks sincere worshippers who will diligently seek after Him. Scripture announces, *"But an hour is coming, and now is, when the true worshipers will worship the Father in spirit and truth; for such people the Father seeks to be His worshipers. God is spirit, and those who worship Him must worship in spirit and truth"* (John 4:23–24). The word *seek* means "to be after something, to be on it" like white on rice, like a duck on a june bug, like a flea on a dog. The all-wise, all-knowing, always-present God of the universe is worthy of our worship. He didn't have to create us, but He did. In return, He deserves our praise and worship continually. Pause for a moment and think about this: God is looking at your heart at this very moment. Does He see a true and sincere worshipper?

2. God seeks those who will be watchmen; those who will serve Him with faithfulness and steadfastness. He says, *"I sought for a man . . . [to] stand in the gap"* (Ezekiel 22:30 NKJV). He's seeking for a watchperson to pronounce His Word and warn people not to stray from God. In the Old Testament, the prophet Ezekiel was a watchman for God. God

held him accountable for delivering His message to the children of Israel. In the New Testament, the leaders of the church take on a similar role and are given the charge to watch over God's people by instructing them in the Word (Acts 20:28; Hebrews 13:17). God is seeking people who will lead by example and be accountable to Him.

3. God is seeking the lost in this world. Jesus said, *"The Son of Man came to seek and to save that which was lost"* (Luke 19:10). We come into this world as sinners. But Jesus came to bring salvation to us. In His own words, He said, *"It is not those who are healthy who need a physician, but those who are sick; I did not come to call the righteous, but sinners"* (Mark 2:17). He cares so much for His creation that God made a way for man to be reconciled back to Him. He doesn't want anyone to perish in their sins. Yet, if people don't repent and receive salvation, sadly, that will be their end. As followers of Christ, we have the ability to think and to speak so that we can communicate His Word and share the good news of Christ with the world.

4. God is seeking diligently for godly children. Procreation is God's way of producing a continuous flow of believers for generations to come—*"that he might seek a godly seed"* (Malachi 2:15 KJV). It is referring to those who received the baton of faith through a strong line of spiritual parents and grandparents. There are people whose parents passed down a legacy of faith to their children, and their children passed it down to their children, who promise to pass it down to their children. This is what it means to dedicate our children to God. The idea comes from the word *train*, which literally means "to dedicate." It's very interesting to note that we receive our children from the Lord, and then we dedicate them back to the Lord. So, much of walking with God and acknowledging Him is a reciprocal relationship. God seeks us and we seek God.

By being the sincere worshippers God is looking for, our hearts should be willing to stand watch for God, to proclaim His truth, and to encourage one another in the faith. This is the sum of reaping a just reward when we put God first; that is, ahead of all the "things" that we desire to have. God's response is,

"For all these things the nations of the world eagerly seek; but your
Father knows that you need these things. But seek His kingdom,
and these things will be added to you. Do not be afraid, little flock,
for your Father has chosen gladly to give you the kingdom."
—LUKE 12:30–32

God has set this whole thing up for us to succeed and we must follow the pattern to reach the goal of victory in our lives. We know when we have done right by God when we see a reflection of God instilled in our children and our children's children. The Bible gives us a good perspective to think about: "*Grandchildren are the crown of old men, and the glory of sons is their fathers*" (Proverbs 17:6). For generations to come we want our seed to partake of God's goodness. It is up to us to put them on the path of blessings by the way in which we prepare them for life. This is how we truly honor God and our legacy becomes a testament to Him. He chose to give us children so that we get the benefit and He gets the glory. This is what I call a win-win situation.

Got Kids?

As parents, we have been given the responsibility to be an example for our children and lead the way for them. God wants us to fully embrace His plan for our children and raise them up to be powerful witnesses for the truth of God's saving grace. The psalmist recognized this and was inspired to draw an insightful comparison to the job that we have in preparing children for the work of the Lord. The Bible tells us that "*as arrows are in the hand of a mighty man; so are children of the youth*" (Psalm 127:4 KJV). To break this Scripture down, let me share my friend Pastor Kenny Grant's perspective on this subject:

"Arrows are made, not born. You don't go out and pluck an arrow off an arrow tree. Scripture says that arrows are in the hand of a mighty man. First of all, you have to craft the arrow to produce it. Once you produce it, you have to polish it. And then, once you polish it, you have to sharpen the end and shape it into a point. Then when you've

shaped it, you've got to propel it. The direction in which you propel the arrow is the direction it's going to go in. So then, when you have shaped and sharpened them, you shoot them at the enemy. That's what an arrow is for."[1]

God places so much emphasis on procreation because of its extreme importance to His agenda. As believers, we automatically become soldiers in God's army, and He has a profound work for us to accomplish in this world. There is a battle going on for the souls of people who God wants to be saved and the enemy wants to destroy. Ultimately, there are only two choices in this life: death or eternal life. So then, according to this biblical analogy, we are to train our children to be tools in the hands of the Lord. When they learn to do God's work, He can send them out to win souls.

This is the way God would have it to be; He gets the glory from lives that follow His pattern and become a reflection of the Trinity. Earthly parents typically are pleased when their children look like them and grow up and reflect the values they have instilled in them. It is the same with our heavenly Father; in fact, that is where we get this idea. More importantly, it should be our heart's desire to see God's character reproduced in our children. Don't you just smile when your children do something that pleases you because you know that it pleases God too?

But our ability to produce children that reflect God's image brings praise and honor to God only when we raise them properly. We have to arm them with the right tools that will equip them to live in this world without being a part of this world. Now, let me just say this, and I am indicted as well: How can we raise up godly children when we allow them to watch MTV and BET? Such entertainment is not intended to glorify God.

We are not supposed to give them to the enemy by allowing worldly influences to dominate their ideas and shape their impressions. Rather, we are to shoot them at the enemy—armed with the sword of the Spirit. And before we can shoot them at the enemy we have to teach our kids to fight with all the ammunition that God has provided for His children. Give your children all the encouragement they need to be godly students of the Word, to love the Lord, and to follow good role models—like Daniel, for instance.

Daniel was a young man in biblical times who was firmly rooted in God and would not back down or compromise on his belief in God. The Bible says that he determined in his heart that he would put God before anyone else, including the king. As a result, God gave Daniel favor with the people in authority over him. Young people can learn from his example of how to stand for what is right. They have to be able to say no when everybody else is saying yes. It's going to take a lot of faith for them to stand firm in the evil day. So, tell your children about the power of prayer and show them how to pray in faith. How else will they be able to mature into responsible Christian adults who are guided by the Spirit of God and will, in turn, train their own children to do the same?

Parents can't expect for everything to simply fall into place when it comes to rearing their children. You need a strategy. From the time that they are babies until they grow up to be young men and women, parents are to focus on molding their children into individuals whose lives will be pleasing to God. They are to be shaped and formed into what God's Word says that believers should be. That is what a godly seed is all about. God has given us sufficient information about what He wants of our seed—He wants them to become His seed by living a life that other people can observe and see God in. God wants our children to look like Him.

This is what George and Sarah didn't quite understand. There are far too many negative models of parenting that distract otherwise well-meaning people from knowing what it really means to train their children properly. They thought it was sufficient to make Alex conform to this world's standard by giving him all the material things our culture says we should have. But they overlooked the fact that he wasn't being molded into God's standard; they weren't giving him spiritual guidance and teaching him that he has a heavenly Father that he will one day have to give an answer to for his life.

On the other hand, it is very possible to guide a child's development so that in the end he or she is living up to your expectations and what you have taught them about God. When it comes to raising their children, there are many couples who take God's idea to heart and dedicate their lives to keeping children on the right path. Beyond being faithful in attending church and Bible study, they live the Word of God in their homes. Their children see positive role models when they look at their patents. That is not to say that they do everything perfect, but children can even learn from the mistakes they observe if parents are honest and take advantage of teachable moments.

For example, one couple in particular is getting it right; together they have built a strong family foundation that resembles the Trinity. I have no doubt that God is pleased with Donna and Bryan. They took an opposite approach from George and Sarah in raising their children. Their three children are now young adults. The youngest is attending a prestigious university and in the third year of getting his bachelor's degree; the middle child graduated from a highly respected Christian college last year and is now working on her master's degree and teaching school; and the oldest daughter has dedicated her life to becoming a doctor. She is currently a resident in training at a prominent medical school.

Now, you may think that this family must be very affluent and well able to afford all of this education; but that is not the case. They haven't had any more advantage than any other average working couple could offer. What they do have are two parents who love God. Donna and Bryan have enough faith in Him to believe that God will provide for them. And God is showing His faithfulness to them. They took the responsibility very seriously of training their children in a way that glorifies God. If you look closely, what they are doing is reflected in God's Word to husbands and wives and their families. That is Donna and Bryan's prescription for success and they are proving that it works.

Home Is Where the Heart Is

"Wives, be subject to your husbands, as is fitting in the Lord.

Husbands, love your wives and do not be embittered against them.

Children, be obedient to your parents in all things,
for this is well-pleasing to the Lord.

Fathers, do not exasperate your children,
so that they will not lose heart."

—COLOSSIANS 3:18–21

These verses form a picture of the procreation story that was authored by the Spirit of God. They are a formula for engendering family relations that bear a reflection to the relationship of God the Father, God the Son, and God the Holy Spirit. Sometimes we tend to make things harder than they need to be. God would say to that, if we do what He tells us to and follow the pattern He has given for families in Ephesians 5:22–33, Ephesians 6:1–4, and Colossians 3:18–21, we would be very satisfied with the results.

These three passages tell us that each family member has a role to play that was defined by God. Donna and Bryan decided to create a home environment where they could prepare their children to step out into the world and take their place in society firmly grounded in their Christian beliefs. Their children thrived in a safe environment where they were trained to develop their spiritual maturity. All of them emerged with a desire to build on the training they were given at home. All parents should take a similar stand and view their home as a training ground for their children. They will be giving their children a launching pad to learn how to do their part in building the kingdom of God here on earth.

The Word of God has a lot to say about husbands and wives. They are admonished to love each other in the way that God outlined for them. It becomes much easier for children to obey their parents when they see the mutual exchange of love between them. Living in a peaceful environment encourages young children to be considerate individuals because Mom and Dad are not constantly bickering and striving against each other. Rather, their behavior should show their children how to live together in love and harmony. Moreover, parents have to model integrity so that their children will know what it looks like; otherwise, they can't be expected to choose right from wrong if they haven't been taught the difference. Home is where the heart of a child is developed. It's up to parents to mold their children's hearts in a way that pleases God.

Much can be said about the profound impact a mother has on her children. It is immeasurable and invaluable. Mothers, such as the one I just described in Donna, play a tremendous part in creating a nurturing environment. One of the most important jobs a mother has is to teach her children what it means to have respect for themselves and everyone else.

I know this can very often be a difficult thing to do with the many challenges facing families today. Not only are there a number of negative influences outside of our doors, but many enticements have made their way inside the home as well. I'm talking about things that can compromise the Word of God such as television programs, video games, and computers and the Internet. The level of demonic influence is increasing all the time. The media seems to be in competition over who can push the envelope the furthest. Most TV shows make fun of doing the right thing and instead glorify the wrong—all of which undermines the family unit. Beyond that, many video games and movies reinforce evil doing—not to mention the fierce level of debauchery that can be viewed on Internet websites. These are reasons why it is so important to monitor your children's activities and what they can be exposed to through these potentially destructive avenues.

Children are given many reasons to rebel against the morals and values that their parents are determined to instill in them. George and Sarah seemed to have missed an opportunity to teach their son from an early age about the principles of life. As the one ordained by God to assume the role of headship, all of this made George's role even more critical at a time when he was busy earning but also neglecting to set aside occasions to teach his son how to choose good behavior over bad.

Sarah needed to know that God did not arbitrarily define the roles in the family by throwing darts at a dartboard. The love she had for her son could not replace the love and direction Alex needed from his father. The roles God has given us hold spiritual meaning that cannot to be taken for granted. Unfortunately, too many people often do just that. They don't realize that following the instructions described in God's Word should not be ignored. And we wonder why so many children are being led astray.

Times are tough. Today, the efforts of two dedicated parents are often met with strong opposition in a battle for their children's welfare. Single parents face an even greater challenge as they try to counteract the lure of ungodliness that tempts their children. My heart goes out to parents everywhere who struggle to keep their homes intact and their children on the right path. This is no joking matter.

Getting to the Root of the Problem

What does the word *husband* mean to you? Well, I can tell you that it means "he who bands the house together." The Anglo-Saxon word for husband is the combination of two archaic words: *hus*, meaning "house" and *bonda*, meaning "band." The *husbonda* is the "master of a house," the one who bands the house together—as in house-band, or husband, which is the word that we recognize today. This word also denotes the idea of a frugal manager—a position that carries a lot of weight in today's economy.

So, brother, you need to know that you have been chosen by God to be the one who bands your family together. There are countless distractions in the form of false gods that come against the family dynamic—people and things that would take God's place in your children's hearts if allowed to do so. It is your responsibility to see to it that God is given first place and being served faithfully in your home. A good way to keep this in the forefront of your family is to adopt Joshua's promise: *"As for me and my house, we will serve the Lord"* (Joshua 24:15).

However, there is a crisis going on, and this is what's at the root of the problem. There are situations where maintaining a wholesome family life can become extremely difficult. When the father is absent from the home, for whatever reason, there is a void that even the most dedicated mother cannot fill. This is nothing against her; a mother has her own equally important position in the family. My point is, when the husband/father is not present, family unity becomes challenged. A woman is forced to step out of her role and take on both parental roles to try to make up the difference. She was not designed to assume the role of a father figure. Although many women succeed in producing godly seed by the grace of God, this is virtually impossible for so many others, no matter how hard they may try. Nevertheless, in today's society when a woman finds herself in this position, she deserves all the credit in the world for trying. But what she really needs is the support of a worthy counterpart to share the responsibilities of raising godly children—to complete the model of the Trinity that has been broken.

Let me give you some statistics on fatherless homes. This data was compiled from the sources indicated below and reported on the Center for Children's Justice[2] and the Dept. of Health and Human Services[3] websites. The absence of a father in the home poses a critical problem and is the cause of the following disturbing information:

- 63 percent of youth suicides are from fatherless homes (U.S. Department of Health and Human Services, Bureau of the Census)
- 71 percent of all high-school dropouts come from fatherless homes (National Principals Association Report on the State of High Schools)
- 90 percent of all homeless and runaway children are from fatherless homes
- 85 percent of all children that exhibit behavioral disorders come from fatherless homes (Centers for Disease Control)
- 85 percent of all incarcerated youth grew up in fatherless homes (Fulton County Georgia jail populations; Texas Department of Corrections, 1992)
- 71 percent of teen pregnancies are to children of single parents (U.S. Department of Health and Human Services.)
- Teenage girls without fathers in their lives are two and a half times as likely to get pregnant and 53 percent more likely to commit suicide (1999 Report of the Department of Health and Human Services)

These alarming statistics show that the negative effects of a father's absence can be measured by the lack of authority and protection in the home. It's relatively easy to produce children but much harder to be a father to those children. So, a man is the key to a family's well-being.

However, there is good news to report as well. On the other hand, the benefits of following God's Word are immeasurable for a man who decides to be a good steward over what God has given him. Listen to what Psalm 128 says about such a man:

"How blessed is everyone who fears the Lord,
    Who walks in His ways.
When you shall eat of the fruit of your hands,
    You will be happy and it will be well with you.
Your wife shall be like a fruitful vine
    Within your house,

Your children like olive plants
   Around your table.
Behold, for thus shall the man be blessed
   Who fears the Lord.
The Lord bless you from Zion,
   And may you see the prosperity of Jerusalem all the days of your life.
Indeed, may you see your children's children.
   Peace be upon Israel!"

Do you hear the blessings pronounced over the one who steps up to the challenge of being a husband and father? If you fear the Lord and walk in His ways, notice the benefits He says you and your family will receive:

- *You will eat from the fruit of your labor.* That means God will bless your finances.
- *You will be happy.* That means you will have great feelings.
- *It will be well with you.* That means you are securely in God's hands and your future will be assured.

Then the story really gets interesting as it describes the relationship between a husband and wife. In the King James Version verse 3 explains what causes your children to flourish like olive plants around your table, it says: *"Thy wife shall be as a fruitful vine by the sides of thine house."* Now, how does a vine grow? First, you have to take that vine and give it somewhere to cling to, which means your wife needs a home that you have prepared for your family. You are the fence, the stable structure where you plant your wife right next to you. When the vine begins to grow, it will cling to the fence post.

Situations in life are designed to make you cling together. But you have to understand that in order to flourish, a vine (that's your wife) has to have something to cling to. It can't cling to a fence (that's your role) that has fallen down, and it cannot cling to a fence that isn't there. On the other hand, when conditions are right, a vine will begin to climb. Guess how high the vine climbs? It will climb as high as the fence so that the vine and the fence can live together side by side. Before you know it, that vine begins to cluster and produce fruit all over it.

Do you know what happens to the fruit? The husband and wife press the fruit of the love they have produced together and make fine wine. You know, they say that wine will make a sad man glad. Maybe that's what Solomon was thinking about when he wrote to the brothers, *"Rejoice with the wife of thy youth . . . and be thou ravished always with her love"* (Proverbs 5:18–19 KJV). The word *ravished* means "intoxicated." Here it means to get drunk on the love of your wife. Man, don't you like that picture?

Overall, you are a blessed man because your family is stable. It's difficult to think of anything better than a stable living environment. That has an impact on the future.

My point is, as the leader of your home, God helps us to prosper when we do it His way; but it's up to every individual to allow Him to be your leader. If you follow the blueprint of the Trinity that is laid out for you, you and your family will be blessed of the Lord, living in peace and prosperity.

Teach Your Children

"Children, obey your parents in the Lord, for this is right.

Honor your father and mother
(which is the first commandment with a promise),

so that it may be well with you,
and that you may live long on the earth.

Fathers, do not provoke your children to anger,
but bring them up in the discipline and instruction of the Lord."

—EPHESIANS 6:1–4

Notice here that the Bible has instructions for everyone in the family unit. But, as head of the household, the husband/father is to lay the groundwork of the family structure. You can help your children succeed in life by giving them a strong foundation. Parents like George and Sarah are deceiving themselves when they mistake propping up their children with material things for giving them a sure base to build upon. To be most effective, you've got to give it to them straight from God's Word in their formative years. A really good place to begin is with Ephesians 6:1–4 because these verses deal with parent/child relationships. They are not only principles to live by, they are commandments to obey.

Begin by teaching your children to love and honor God first while you model that behavior for them. I believe the most important thing that you can teach your children is to obey. Most kids readily understand the concept of being rewarded so when you point out that they will receive a reward for their obedience you are motivating them to honor you and value your authority. Open up your Bible and point it out to them. Tell them what the Word says, if they want to live long and satisfying lives, they have to give you the reverence that God asks of them.

The fourth verse speaks directly to fathers and commands dads to not irritate their children and provoke them into doing wrong behavior. Fathers (and mothers too, for that matter) do not serve God or their offspring well when they take their authority for granted and rely on the proverbial sentiment, "Don't do what you see me do; do as you are told." Children immediately see the hypocrisy in this attitude, and it compromises parental authority. Young people have no motivation to simply do as they are told when they observe you doing just the opposite. They have to see the proper behavior modeled for them. And, believe me, they are watching you from a very early age.

When you spend quality time with your children doing even the simplest of activities, they will appreciate you for it. It says to them that they matter to you. Your actions will validate them, and in return they will affirm you as a parent. Teach them to show others the kind of concern that you show them. These are valuable lessons that will last a lifetime.

The Word of God offers more sound advice that you should pass on to your young people, *"Hear, my son [or daughter], your father's instruction and do not forsake your mother's teaching"* (Proverbs 1:8). But the flip side is that parents should treat their children with due respect so that they will want to obey. God did not give you authority for you to abuse it by provoking and/or ridiculing them. Jesus said to treat others the way you want to be treated.

Yes, you have to establish rules that will keep your house orderly. However, be careful about being so strict that you discourage them from trying to follow your orders. Sometimes rules that were intended to rein your children in do just the opposite and drive them further from you. When you invite the Holy Spirit to show you the way to handle your parental responsibility, He will give you the spirit of power, love, and sound wisdom to make it all happen the way that it should. Remember, you want to show your children God's love so that they will carry that love with them wherever they go.

So, take your cue from Him and care for your children with the same love and kindness that your heavenly Father grants you. God doesn't hassle you or mock you. Rather, He regards you with the utmost patience and long suffering.

All of this is saying to you, brother, fear the Lord and follow the law of God. Do you know that the law detailed extensively in the Old Testament comes down to a single directive that was given by Jesus in the New Testament? He said that the greatest commandment is—love. Listen to Jesus' words:

> *"'You shall love the Lord your God with all your heart,*
> *and with all your soul, and with all your mind.' This is the great*
> *and foremost commandment. The second is like it, 'You shall*
> *love your neighbor as yourself.' On these two commandments*
> *depend the whole Law and the Prophets."*
>
> —MATTHEW 22:37–40

Everything points back to love—loving God, loving your wife, loving your children, loving yourself, and showing love to everyone whom you encounter. If you're a man, the key to a happy wife and a happy life is that you walk in the love of God as Jesus defined it. In other words, have the right relationship with God and His Word.

Now, I am not so naïve as to think that all children fall in line with a gentle nudge or an occasional reprimand. There are no two ways about it; some kids are just "hardheaded," as the saying goes. Under these circumstances, you are required to use the proper discipline to help them correct their bad behavior. By now, we should all know the biblical answer to this situation. The Bible says, *"He who withholds his rod hates his son, but he who loves him disciplines him diligently"* (Proverbs 13:24). Perhaps you may be more familiar with the simplified version: "Spare the rod and spoil the child."

If you don't use appropriate levels of discipline when they are young, they will grow up to be lawless individuals that do not have respect for anyone or anything. Notice the verse says to be diligent when you apply discipline. That means you should be consistent in correcting bad behavior. Otherwise, you can send mixed messages that only add to any confusion that already exists in their minds. So, choose your battles wisely. Recall the wise words of Proverbs 22:6, *"Train up a child in the way he should go, even when he is old he will not depart from it."* The goal is for parents to train their children so that they will grow up to be well-behaved, positive contributors in society who, most of all, love the Lord. The ones who appreciate the values and training their parents gave them are better equipped to succeed in life.

A mother eagle understands the principle of training her eaglets to leave the nest and become strong eagles that can stand on their own. So, here's what the mother eagle does. She'll shake the nest. Now, the eaglet that's been paying attention and watching his parents will try its wings and begin to fly when the nest is shaken. But somehow there's always an eaglet that won't fly even though the nest is being shaken. So, guess what the mother eagle does? She turns the nest over, takes her eaglet to the edge of a high cliff, and pushes him off.

Did you get that, mothers—she pushes him off. When the eaglet tries to flap his wings but can't make it, she swoops down and catches him before he hits the ground. Then, she takes him back up and dumps him off again. When he flops down, she picks him back up. She will continue to do this until that little eaglet can start flying on his own. The moral of this story is: There is a time to cut the umbilical cords off your children and teach them to fly on their own. When children grow older they will not forget the lessons you instilled in them during their developmental years.

Principles for Parenting

To that end, let me offer you some biblical principles on parenting. If you haven't already done so, you may find these ideas useful to consider in rearing your children.

Principle #1:

Children are valuable. God expects parents to foster their children with the highest sense of love and regard. They need the kind of nurturing and guidance that will put them on the right path to be mature and responsible Christian adults with a desire to serve the Lord. The following are reasons why children are to be regarded with loving care:

(a) Throughout biblical history children were considered to be a blessing and a most welcome gift from God (Genesis 25:21; 1 Samuel 1:1–28). Children are given to us by God, and He has a plan for them. I know that this is a fundamental rule, but it is important just the same. So, take it as a reminder. Children must be nurtured and treated with respect on all levels, including their spiritual, emotional, and physical well-being.

(b) Not only are they a gift from God, children are made in the image of God—after the pattern of the Trinity (Genesis 1:26–27). Consequently, children are not to be taken for granted. When you recognize this truth, it makes you realize how truly important your children are. Understanding what the Trinity means to us helps to put into perspective our job in rearing children to be a godly seed that God can use to help build His kingdom.

Principle #2:

Children are unique. It is unfathomable to grasp how God designs each child in a unique way, yet He does just that. In His infinite wisdom God makes decisions that dictate how each person's DNA is hardwired. Knowing how to handle children can be a challenging effort, but I cannot encourage you enough to respect the uniqueness of your children. It is where a child's strength and talents are found that can lead to his or her destiny. Help your children to develop a healthy sense of self-worth by recognizing the following points so that they will have a strong sense of self-appreciation:

(a) Each child is unique physically. Within the same family there may be some similar traits between siblings; however, every child has his or her own distinct physical characteristics. Even in the case of twins each child will have a distinguishing feature. For example, Genesis 25:25–26 describes the physical distinctions of Isaac and Rebekah's twin sons. Esau's complexion was red and his skin was very hairy. On the other hand, Jacob describes his appearance in Genesis 27:11 as being a smooth-skinned man. As parents, we have to be careful to avoid showing favoritism based on the differences in our children as such behavior can have a negative impact on a child's self-worth.

(b) Each child has a unique personality. Personality traits are so exclusive to an individual that the complex attributes of one persons existence cannot be duplicated in another human being. The Bible says that Esau was a skillful hunter, a man of the field while his brother, Jacob, was a mild man who was content with dwelling inside the tent (Genesis 25:27). This was a direct contrast between the sources of the two brothers' interests. Clearly, their individual self-image had not been stifled by their parents; they were free to be themselves. It is important to allow your children the freedom to develop their personalities but at the same time give them the necessary guidance.

(c) Each child has a unique set of skills. God instills distinct talents and gifts within every person He creates, which essentially sets them apart from one another. In the case of the two brothers Jacob and Esau, Genesis 25:29 shows a further differentiation between them. Previous verses drew comparisons to Jacob's inclination to stay near the home and Esau's preference to being a man of the field. By stating that Jacob had been at home and "cooked a stew," his domestic tendencies were apparent while Esau, the hunter, came in from the field tired and weary from hunting. To encourage a sense of self-competency in children, help them to recognize and develop their abilities. This will give them the edge that they will need when they have to compete with other children. Whether it is a musical ability, mathematical skills, or a knack for working with their hands, children having an opportunity to develop their talents is vital to their success in life.

Principle #3:

Children need to be taught how to make proper choices. It is a behavior that is learned from their parents' instruction. Parents aren't perfect by any stretch of the imagination, but God does expect us to be diligent in preparing our children to succeed in life. A huge part of this relates to learning to make the best decisions. Perhaps that was the biggest mistake that Isaac and Rebekah made in rearing their sons. Esau made a hasty decision that cost him big time. His younger brother Jacob tricked him out of his very birthright when he offered Esau some food to eat in exchange for a priceless blessing that rightfully belonged to him. The poor guy thought that he was so hungry that he was about to die and Jacob seized the moment. He took advantage of his brother's weakened state of mind and Esau gave up a promise from God that could not be regained (Genesis 25:30–34).

As a concerned parent, you want to prevent your children from making costly mistakes whenever possible. The best way for children to learn the art of using good judgment is to provide opportunities in which they can exercise their decision-making skills. As you strive to teach them to develop this aptitude and provide opportunities for them to practice the ability to judge wisely, consider the following ways that you can help them:

(a) Allow your child/children to perform age-appropriate tasks. Use your wisdom in identifying useful and safe jobs around the house that will instill a sense of responsibility in them.

(b) Ask them to express their opinions about various considerations that will affect your family. Include them in some of the plans that will affect them personally. When they find that you respect their ideas, they will be encouraged to cooperate more fully with your decisions.

(c) Acknowledge their successes. To reinforce their desire to excel in life, it is very important to underscore the positive achievements they make. Acknowledge them with appropriate awards for what they have accomplished.

(d) Adjust expectations to their abilities. Strike a good balance between providing positive challenges while at the same time setting goals that are achievable for them to reach. In other words, set them up to win and not lose. For younger children, you might try making up games to complete household chores such as setting the dinner table, sweeping the floor, or washing and putting away dishes.

(e) Activities that you provide can bring enjoyment as well as instill values they need to learn. To teach them the importance of honesty in competition and fair play, involve them in after-school and weekend programs, sports competitions, exercise programs, etc. Remember, children learn their value system from their parents, so you will be the first example they will follow.

Principle #4:

Children should be treated equally. When siblings notice their parents showing preferential treatment of one child above the other, their self-esteem is greatly undermined. Scripture tells us that Isaac and Rebekah were guilty of another no-no in dealing with their children. Genesis 25:28 explains that Isaac loved his son Esau; he was the one that hunted game. Apparently, Isaac was very impressed by his son's great ability to capture the game that his father loved to eat. On the other hand, Rebekah loved their son Jacob most likely because Jacob stayed close to home; she knew that she could rely on him because he was always near. Undoubtedly, these two brothers were well aware of their parents' disposition to favor one of them over the other.

Parents sometime underestimate their children's ability to pick up on even a subtle display of favoritism shown to a brother or sister. This attitude is unhealthy because it puts a child's perception of his or her self-worth at risk. They can start to wonder if there is something wrong with them when they feel overlooked or ignored because a parent shows a preference for a sibling. There are two ways that you can focus on that that will help you avoid this kind of situation:

(a) Avoid comparisons of your children. God places good qualities in every person He creates. It is best for you to know your children so well that you recognize their strengths and weaknesses early on. There is no need to play favorites when you focus on each child's talents and highlight those strengths. When you make each child feel special, it will foster a healthy relationship between you and each individual. By doing so, you are letting your children know that you share an equal amount of love for them and no one is more loved than the other.

(b) Avoid interjecting competition between your children. Children should never feel as though they must compete for a parent's love and attention. A minimal amount of sibling rivalry is considered normal since it is a natural desire to be the best. However, your job is to channel that spirit of competition among your children in a positive way. Give each one of them positive reinforcement equally as you guide them in learning to appreciate each other. This will teach them to love each other with a strong family bond.

Principle #5:

Children need unconditional love and affirmation. This is the most important reason not to compare your children or encourage them in competition with one another. Above all, it is a parent's job to help their children know that they are blessed. Through this expression of love they will see a reflection of God's Trinity. Our heavenly Father is a God of forgiveness. When we make mistakes and ask Him to forgive us, God does just that. God expects us to imitate His actions when it comes to our own children.

Moreover, the best way to show love is through affirmation. Children aren't perfect, but they need to know without a doubt that their parents validate them through positive reinforcement. Growing up is a difficult process under even the most favorable circumstances; subsequently, they do not need to endure emotional scars brought about by parents who failed to cover their children with the strength and power of their love.

Principle #6:

Children need their parents to set a good example for them. When your behavior doesn't line up with what you are trying to teach your children, it becomes confusing to children when they are expected to distinguish between right and wrong practices.

Parents have a God-given obligation to set the proper example for their children to emulate. But we can learn from the example that Rebekah set for her son Jacob. She was quite instrumental in formulating the plot to rob her son Esau of his blessing as the firstborn. Rebekah went as far as to engage Jacob in deceiving her husband into thinking that he was conferring a blessing on his older son when in fact he blessed the younger one instead. She actually encouraged her son to lie to his father (Genesis 27:8–29). Can you think of a more horrible act for one parent to commit against another by teaching her son to commit such a deceptive deed?

Principle #7:

Children need discipline that affirms. Have you ever witnessed a child cry-ing out for discipline? It is quite amazing to observe a child's behavior when they are having a temper tantrum. If you watch closely you will detect that he or she is expecting an adult who is witnessing the act to step in and reprimand him or her. You can just tell that they are just waiting for someone to take au-thority over them and insist that they stop misbehaving and straighten up. When someone does, it reinforces the child's knowledge of good and bad behavior and the realization that restraint is in order when they step out of line. Disciplinary action should include the following considerations:

(a) Guidelines should be set and communicated to avoid any misun-derstandings. Use this as an effective lesson in teaching your children to obey instructions and authority. Since this is about setting the rules that will help you and your children enjoy a mutually satisfying relationship, in-sist that they participate in the process of creating the guidelines. This will give you the opportunity to affirm their good behavior or correct their mis-behavior because they will know your clearly communicated expectations. It will be their guide in knowing what you consider good conduct and where they stepped out of line.

(b) Standards should be set. The standards that you establish will help you determine whether your children are measuring up to your expecta-tions for what you will and will not tolerate. Make sure that your standards are based on the Word of God, and tell your children that they are ac-countable not only to their earthly parents but to God our Father in heaven. Setting standards also allows you to clearly identify the rewards and conse-quences for your children's actions. As such, it would be a good idea to write them down and review them with your children on a regular basis.

(c) Discipline must be equal with the offense. Administering punish-ment should be used as a means of preventing a child from repeating his or her mistake. But there is nothing worse in a child's mind as being punished unfairly. This calls into play a use of sound judgment on your part when you strike a good balance between the offense committed and the punish-ment you give. It will make a big difference in whether the resulting punishment will be a valuable tool for correction or whether it works against your authority in your child's mind.

For example, consider the following. Would you administer the same punishment in these situations: (1) your child takes a snack without your permission after you have specified not to do so; (2) your child leaves home without your permission; (3) your child gets into serious trouble at school. If you do not choose an appropriate discipline in each of these cases, it could send the wrong message and distort the impression that you are trying to make. Depending on the offense, punishment that is too harsh or too soft will not be as effective as it needs to be. In other words, the punishment you give should equal the seriousness of the offense.

(d) Discipline should be consistent. A particular fault that many parents are guilty of is to send different messages when a child repeats the same mistake. Be consistent in controlling the consequences of their actions. For example, every time a child repeatedly does not clean his or her room, give the same punishment that you have established for that offense. It will serve as positive reinforcement in the child's mind that you mean business, and it keeps the integrity of the standards you have set.

(e) Discipline should not be done in anger. This principle should be obvious since anger is an emotion that needs to be kept in check. Scripture admonishes us to "be angry, and do not sin" (Ephesians 4:26 NKJV). Therefore, God acknowledges that anger is sometimes an expected reaction in some circumstances. However, in regard to our children, we must control our anger over a child's misbehavior and not allow it to overtake us. If a parent punishes a child while he or she is angry for whatever reason, there is potential to do much more harm than good.

On the other hand, the worst thing we can do is to allow our children to grow up without understanding the value of discipline. The world is full of immature adults who, as children, didn't have the benefit of receiving consequential treatment for their actions.

Principle #8:

Children need parents who can admit their faults. One of the best things you can do for your children is to set an example of excellence that they can follow. Your children are constantly watching you, so, it is not possible for you to hide all of your indiscretions from them. So, it's best to admit that you are human and you have faults too. Through your sincere behavior as you try to live your life by pleasing God, you will lead them on the right path to victory in life. Some of the ways to accomplish this all-important lesson for them is to do the following:

- Don't cover up your mistakes.
- Don't rationalize your mistakes.
- Don't use your authority to excuse your mistakes.

Of course, as they grow older children have to make their own decisions in life, and sometimes no matter how good of an example you've set or how much discipline and guidance you give them, problems still arise. When there is an unruly child in the home who is rebellious and does not want to obey, even after you have expended your efforts trying to correct him or her, it's time for serious intervention. In the Old Testament days, such situations weren't taken lightly. Listen to the following description,

> *"If any man has a stubborn and rebellious son who will not obey*
> *his father or his mother, and when they chastise him, he will not*
> *even listen to them, then his father and mother shall seize him,*
> *and bring him out to the elders of his city*
> *at the gateway of his hometown.*
> *They shall say to the elders of his city, 'This son of ours is stubborn*
> *and rebellious, he will not obey us, he is a glutton and a drunkard.'*
> *Then all the men of his city shall stone him to death;*
> *so you shall remove the evil from your midst,*
> *and all Israel will hear of it and fear."*
> —DEUTERONOMY 21:18–21

It's a sobering thought to imagine having to stone a child to death, but intolerance of misbehavior was intended to deter young people from going astray. Of course, this is a drastic measure by today's standards. But one has to wonder how much better it is to see a young man or woman being hand-cuffed and thrown into prison because their rebellious ways led them astray.

My point is, disciplinary action is a necessity; but love, guidance, and encouragement are equally important. Finding a good balance of these elements is a wise approach even as you always keep the Lord in the midst of your child rearing efforts.

The Tragedy of Divorce

Unfortunately, there are some grave dangers aimed at the plans God has for marriage and procreation. One leading cause of concern that poses a challenge is an unfortunate situation called divorce. Many people have invested enormous energy in their families and their futures, yet, in some cases, marriages fail anyway. There are endless reasons why this happens. And the sad truth is that divorce has great potential to reap havoc in the lives that it touches.

But the Word of God has something to say about the heartbreak of divorce. There is no better way to prevent it from happening other than when you apply God's Word to your situation. No one has enough strength within themselves to avoid every pitfall that may surface in life. Only God's Word can make a lasting difference in anyone's efforts to hold their marriage together. You need it; we all need to rely on it. God alone has the power to overcome a mountain of human obstacles that would stack themselves against your efforts to protect your marriage and the precious seed God has given you.

You are probably familiar with the saying "Knowledge is power." Well, know that the power of God is totally against the tragic event of divorce taking place. These two things together can prevent divorce:

• Know why God is against divorce.
• Rely on His power to build and strengthen your marriage.

Divorce is a major problem. Now, understand this dialogue is not about divorcing for reasons of abuse of any kind. That is another area altogether, which is beyond the scope of my discussion here. What I am addressing is an overwhelming trend where people continue to jump in and out of marriage unions without grasping the full extent of their actions. Perhaps their disregard for God's wishes is due to ignorance or plain old selfishness. Whatever the case may be, I would recommend that they listen to what God says about it:

> *"'For I hate divorce,' says the Lord, the God of Israel, 'and him who covers his garment with wrong,' says the Lord of hosts. 'So take heed to your spirit, that you do not deal treacherously.'"*
> —MALACHI 2:16

> *"But to the married I give instructions, not I, but the Lord, that the wife should not leave her husband (but if she does leave, she must remain unmarried, or else be reconciled to her husband), and that the husband should not divorce his wife."*
> —1 CORINTHIANS 7:10–11

God hates divorce, and He's not so thrilled with those who carelessly break their marriage vows. From what God expressed in Malachi 2:16, it is clear that He detests divorce and takes it quite personally. Notice the severe warning God issues; He is emphatically saying not to deal with marriage in an unfaithful, disloyal, and deceitful way. Divorce is a spiritual affront to God. Whether they are aware of it or not, when people marry and then break up for so many frivolous reasons, it shows a lack of faithfulness to God and the commitment to marriage that He embedded in the covenant.

In the 1 Corinthians 7:10–11 passage, the apostle Paul has a very specific message on marriage. For a woman who leaves her husband, there are two options. She must either remain unmarried or she must reconcile with her husband. To the husband, Paul simply says that he should not divorce his wife. That is pretty straightforward talk from the Word of God about this highly unpopular subject—at least it is unacceptable from the Bible's perspective.

The word *divorce* is derived from the Hebrew word *kerat*, which means "to cut off." This is exactly what divorce does to a man and woman; it cuts off the marriage covenant and separates two partners that God joined to-gether. Consequently, they leave behind yet another broken relationship and that breaks the heart of God. Since divorce is so common in our soci-ety, one might be lulled into thinking that it's no big deal. But let me tell you that God considers every situation that ends in divorce a severe matter. He is not happy when people throw their marriage vows away. Every believer should be sensitive to the things that have meaning to God; it will help us to reverence the things that He holds dear. That is why it is so important for husbands and wives to hold God close and keep the Spirit of God at the center of their relationship. He will help them keep their priorities straight.

In a spiritual way, marriage and procreation come together to form a human reflection of the Trinity. According to Genesis 2:24, when two peo-ple consent in matrimony they are no longer free to act independently of each other. In the essence of their humanity, they have become "one flesh." As a result, when divorce enters the picture, it does two things:

- Divorce severs a relationship and has devastating effects on the lives of the two individuals that are caught in it. God took the vows they exchanged very seriously; He did not in-tend them to be divided. Moreover, Jesus asserted that no one is to separate the partners because God has put them together in a covenant of marriage and that agreement is not to be broken (Matthew 19:6).
- Divorce has the potential to interrupt a godly seed from tak-ing its place in the building of God's kingdom. As such, it is a deterrent to God's reason for procreation. The truth is, the bearing of offspring may be the most important reason for marriage in God's sight. Without this crucial component of the marriage union, future generations of God's seed would not be possible.

When challenged by the Pharisees on the subject of divorce, Jesus an-swered them in Mark 10:4–12. He explained that the only reason God allowed it in the first place was because of the stubbornness of the people—the hardness of their hearts. He followed up that declaration by giving the only valid grounds on which God would allow it; that is, when sexual sin is committed by a spouse (Matthew 5:31–32). The apostle Luke recorded Jesus' words on getting a divorce for anything other than sexual sin, *"Everyone who divorces his wife and marries another commits adultery, and he who marries one who is divorced from a husband commits adultery"* (Luke 16:18).

Marriage is something that God loves. And divorce is a direct challenge to God's affection for it. This leads me to believe that sincere Christians, who profess to love God and the things of God and who are contemplating marriage, should take the time to understand why God detests divorce. As a result, they would be better prepared for the pursuit of their mate.

For those who are getting ready to be married, know what you're getting into. There is a whole lot to be gained from studying God's Word and using it as a road map to prevent believers from making big mistakes that could later on cause deep regret. We're about to find out what effect divorce has on God and those who find themselves in this category.

A good place to start is found in Malachi 2:10–17. This passage presents a historical background of divorce in the Old Testament. But know that God feels the same passion about it today. To get the most from the following breakdown, you may want to read along in your Bible. This is a summary of God's reasons for why He hates divorce:

a. Divorce rejects Yahweh's command (vv. 10–12)
b. Divorce robs us of our spiritual blessings (v. 13)
c. Divorce wrongs the partner to whom the covenant promise is made (v. 14)
d. Divorce ruptures the covenant we established with God (v. 14)
e. Divorce ruins the continuity of a godly seed (v. 15)
f. Divorce is repulsive to God. He said that He hates it (v. 16)
g. Divorce refuses to honor the permanent nature of marriage (v. 17)

In the days of the prophet Malachi, God was not happy with the men who sought to divorce their Jewish wives simply because they wanted to marry pagan women. These men were from the tribes of Israel; they were

God's own people and that was their justification for divorce. Through the prophet Malachi, God addressed the issue of men who turned their backs on His marriage covenant. These people were treating God with an irreverent attitude, and the things of God had no real meaning to them. They rejected God's command by blatantly rejecting their spouses.

Their hearts had turned cold as they acted in contempt of God. Consequently, God brought a curse upon them. He withheld blessings from them for disobeying His commands. These disobedient men missed out on some blessings that God would have given them through their wives. But when they put their wives away in divorce, those blessing were cut off.

Today, this still holds true. Men are robbed of precious blessings whether they understand it or not. Some brothers who have kicked their wives to the curb are not doing so great, but their wives are doing quite well without them. It's because God will bless those who are obedient to Him.

The Bible is clear about why God objects to this rebellious action and finds it offensive: *"The Lord was a witness to the covenant made at your marriage between you and the wife of your youth, against whom you have dealt treacherously and to whom you were faithless"* (verse 14 AMP). God is not pleased when we refuse to love and honor the spouse who has been wronged in the case of divorce. Having an indifferent attitude toward your marriage vows and duties speaks of betrayal to God and the spouse that's left out in the cold. This is because the covenant of marriage is made between a man, a woman, and God Himself. When the covenant is violated, God sees that as the marriage partners turning their backs on an agreement in which He Himself played an active role.

Someone once told me that he was preparing to get a divorce before I taught on this subject. Subsequently, he decided to wait on God. God convicted this man by His Spirit, and the brother realized that he should not go against Him. Your struggles may cause you to sometimes question God; you may even attempt to stray away from Him. But hold fast to the lifeline that the Word of the Lord offers you, *"'Return to Me, and I will return to you,' says the Lord of hosts"* (Malachi 3:7).

If you are giving divorce consideration, I sincerely hope that you will pray earnestly and wait on God. He will show you the way to overcome every situation in your life. God is the greatest marriage Counselor; He will never disappoint you.

Beware: Domestic Violence

There is another situation today that is a critical problem because it undermines God's reason for procreation. The presence of widespread physical and emotional abuse that is found in many broken families contributes greatly to the cause of divorce and why we should do everything possible to put an end to it.

Domestic violence is a serious assault by any measure and, therefore, a major enemy against the sanctity of marriage. Tragically today, the one who is to be the protector in the home—a trustworthy man who is to be revered and respected as the leader of the home—has often become the predator. As the majority of such violence is directed toward a woman and her children, here are some alarming statistics about the plight of far too many families today.

- One third of pedophiles committed their crime against their own children, and 50 percent had a relationship with the victim as a friend, acquaintance, or relative other than their offspring.[4]
- The U.S. Department of Justice reports that females are more likely than males to experience nonfatal intimate partner violence.[5]
- Intimate partner homicides make up 40–50 percent of all murders of women in the United States. In 70–80 percent of intimate partner homicides, no matter which partner was killed, the man physically abused the woman before the murder.[6]
- 80 to 90 percent of children are aware of the domestic violence in their families.[7]
- Approximately 1.3 million women are physically assaulted by an intimate partner annually in the U.S.[8]

- Boys who witness their fathers' violence are ten times more likely to engage in spouse abuse in later adulthood than boys from non-violent homes.[9]
- In the United States, 63 percent of young men between the ages of eleven and twenty who are serving time for murder have killed their mother's abuser.[10]

All of these heartbreaking facts can make a woman's home more dangerous for her children than the city streets. God never ordained that anyone should submit themselves to any kind of abuse and harm. If you are experiencing domestic violence, please separate yourself from it. Although I am not talking about divorce, I am talking about removing yourself and your children from an abusive situation. This may not seem like a simple task, but with the help of God it can be done. The first order of defense is to seek protection for yourself and your family.

Remember, when God has rewarded you with children, He wants you to be a good and faithful steward so that your precious seed will grow up to be mighty warriors for God. That means nurturing and protecting them; and, sometimes it means fighting for them and yourself by using the sword of the Spirit, which is the Word of God. As you remove yourself and your children from a violent situation, the power of God will be with you.

If you are asking the question, "How do I know that I'm in an abusive relationship?" let me give you some insight from the book of Judges, chapter 6 that could be very helpful to you. It is based on the story of Gideon and how God used him to deliver his family from oppression. By obeying God, Gideon overcame adversity in his life. God is no respecter of persons. Gideon found courage in God to get the victory over his shortcomings—and so can you.

The people of Israel were crying out to God because they were being oppressed and abused by their enemies, the Midianites. They had been the cause of Israel's plight for seven years (Judges 6:1). Gideon was an average person living during this time. In fact, he didn't think very much of himself and had pretty much accepted what he thought was his fate in life. He was content to merely stay alive. Like many others, Gideon and his family were just trying to survive under the oppression of their adversaries. Under his dire circumstances, Gideon thought that he was doing all he could. He spent his time working to preserve wheat for food and protect it from the enemy so that his family could eat.

When the Angel of the Lord visited him one day, the messenger from God delivered a word of affirmation to Gideon. It is a fact; depending on how they are used, words are powerful instruments that can do either harm or good. Well, God wanted Gideon to realize the power he had to accomplish something great. In spite of how weak and inadequate Gideon felt, God called him a *"mighty man of valor."* You should be aware, God will use reassuring words to let you know that it is His strength working within you to do what may otherwise seem impossible.

But even before the Angel affirmed Gideon, He said something very powerful to him. He greeted Gideon with the comforting words, *"the Lord is with you,"* (Judges 6:12 NKJV). This is the greatest source of encouragement—to know that the presence of God is with you and nothing can break through His protection and overpower you.

In a different situation, when the angel Gabriel greeted Mary, the mother of Jesus, he spoke the same words to her, he had come to tell her that she was carrying the Savior of the world (Luke 1:28). Can you imagine? What an awesome task! Yet, Mary sensed that she had the strength to handle her situation when she heard that the Lord was with her. What comfort these words should bring to you. When you know that the Lord is with you, you should also know that you can overcome any situation because God's got your back.

Back to our story. Gideon struggled at first and questioned whether he was capable of doing anything to deliver his people. He wasn't quite convinced until he heard that God was with him. He needed to know that God thought of him as a man who possessed the strength to fight for what was right. God understood where Gideon was; but He had plans for him nevertheless. He was going to use Gideon to deliver His people from their enemies. Initially, Gideon responded to his assignment by claiming that he was the *"least in his father's house"* (Judges 6:15 NKJV). You see, Gideon didn't think very much of his ability; he didn't see the potential that God saw in him. But God assured him that he would not be alone in doing what God wanted him to do. He said in so many words, "Don't worry about it. I will be with you, and you will defeat your enemy by yourself" (verse 16 paraphrase). In the end, Gideon cooperated with God and God defeated the abuser of His children.

Now that you know Gideon's story and the successful outcome that God orchestrated for him, I pray that God will speak to you as you consider the following points about abusive situations.

1. You know that you're in an abusive relationship when the relationship takes away from you instead of adding to you. The Midianites were abusing Gideon and his people. They were encamped against Israel and constantly destroyed their produce, *"leaving no sustenance for Israel"* (Judges 6:4 NKJV).

    When an abusive relationship is holding you hostage, you will experience lack. If even the most basic material necessities that we often take for granted are scarce or unavailable and you know that you are doing your best to meet the needs of your family, something is working against your efforts to provide. You may feel like you cannot get ahead because what you really need is always missing; there is never quite enough.

    If this sounds familiar to you, first look around you and assess the situation. When you know who or what is causing the lack, then pray to God specifically about that so He can address your problem.

    Above all, know that you have spiritual riches that no one can take away from you. God wants you to realize your potential to do great things. He will help you rise above everything that challenges the victory that you will find through your faith in Him. My prayer is that you will break through the oppression that surrounds you.

2. When you are in a relationship with someone who is keeping you from realizing your God-given potential, you are experiencing abuse. The thing that was keeping Gideon from realizing his potential was his enemy, the Midianites. But, the Angel of the Lord appeared to Gideon and called him a mighty man of valor.

God wants you to only answer to the names He has given you and not the negative names that the enemy wants you to answer to. You are none of those things, and you never were. Something inside of you dares to believe that you have more to offer in life but you are being held back. You may have a heart's desire to do something that you know will make a positive difference for you and your family. God will be your partner in reaching your goal. He sees you as the valuable person that He created you to be. He thinks good thoughts about you. God has plans to give you a prosperous future. He wants you to live in peace.

When you search His Word you will be amazed to find God's promises to you and what He calls you. Wherever you find words that will bring something good into your life, substitute your name and personalize God's message to you. For example, the angel said to Mary, "*Rejoice, highly favored one, the Lord is with you; blessed are you among women!*" (Luke 1:28 NKJV). Know that you are God's child and you belong to Him. He wants you to realize that you have the favor of God on your side. When you look in the mirror, tell yourself that of all the women in the world—you are blessed!

3. When you are in a relationship and your self-esteem is sabotaged, you are being abused. Gideon had low self-esteem and he was intimidated by those who were oppressing and abusing his people. When you are in an abusive relationship, the image of your self-worth has been severely damaged. Many women submit to abuse because they somehow believe that they deserve to be mistreated. A woman can mistakenly believe that even through the physical and mental abuse that she endures that her abuser actually loves her. There is no such love, and to believe that is to believe a lie. That is a product of warped thinking and low self-esteem. No one deserves to be abused.

Allow me to let you in on a secret. Did you know that Jesus Christ Himself is sitting at the right hand of the Father in heaven making intercession for you? He is providing you with mercy and love on a daily basis. How else do you think you make it through?

He wants you to know that you are loved and nothing in life has the ability to separate you from His love. No adversity—even the trials and tribulations that you experience in your life—can take God's love from you. Rather, those things should make you depend on God's love to see you all the way through and bring you out. God will send you the help that you need as you receive the truth of God's Word into your heart. It is there for the taking. With the help of God you are able to end your abusive situation. You must believe that you are more than a conqueror because He loves you (Romans 8:37).

4. Abusive situations can temporarily rob you of your hope and faith in God. If you feel you're in a hopeless situation, know that God is a God of hope and He does not change. The apostle Paul offers some encouraging words on the importance of having hope: *"Hope does not disappoint, because the love of God has been poured out within our hearts through the Holy Spirit who was given to us"* (Romans 5:5). It is so important to know that the power of the Holy Spirit will see to it that your hope and faith will work all things together for your good because you love God and He has called you according to His purpose (Romans 8:28). You see, just as He had something for His servant Gideon to do, God has something for you to do.

   You may be thinking that you are not capable or qualified for God to deliver you from bondage. But the Bible tells us that the Spirit of God helps our weaknesses. In those times when you don't even know how to pray about a situation, Romans 8:26 assures you that the Spirit intercedes for you. In other words, He helps you out by praying for you. Then the Father hears the prayer of faith on your behalf and responds with the blessings you need.

   Protecting the seed that God has placed in your care is what this is really all about. It is the spiritual requirement that is connected to God's reason for procreation. So, I urge you to walk in the wisdom and the love of God and rely on God's power to deliver you. Even as He delivered His children many years ago, God will free you from oppression and abuse even now—if you trust Him and believe that He can do it. Jesus will say to you just as He told His followers when they thought that a situation was hopeless, *"Do not be afraid any longer, only believe"* (Mark 5:36).

The Word Is the Answer

There is one thing to always keep in mind: No matter what the problem is in your relationship, there is something in the Bible that can help you overcome whatever it may be. It's about tapping into the right source. But the trouble with many of us is that instead of reaching for the Source from whom all answers to life's dilemmas and from whom all blessings flow, we listen to Oprah, Dr. Phil, Montel, and so many others. Moreover, we listen to friends who have all kinds of problems of their own instead of listening to God who has no problem but is able to fix ours.

When you've tried everything else and still haven't reached a place of peace in your life, it's time to turn it over to God. Psalm 55:22 says, *"Cast your burden upon the Lord and He will sustain you."* God is ready and willing to bless marriages to reach their greatest potential. But it has to be done in Him and through His Word. It's the only way to make my prayer for you a reality in your life:

> *"The Lord shall increase you more*
> *and more, you and your children.*
>
> *You are blessed of the Lord who made heaven and earth."*
>
> —PSALM 115:14–15 KJV

Making It Happen

1. With an open and receptive heart, ask God to help you understand how to apply His reason for creating marriage as a means of producing godly seed. If you have no children, ask God how you can be a blessing and provide spiritual direction to a child or a young adult in need of guidance. By being a blessing to others, He will hear your sincere prayers and help you to transform your marriage into a reflection of His image.

2. Parents are responsible for monitoring their children's behavior and activities to ensure that their children are not involved in any inappropriate behavior. If you have a teenage child, do you believe that it is your responsibility to periodically search through your child's personal belongings such as closets, dresser drawers, diaries, cell phone text messages, Internet sites visited, etc.? If so, what approach would you take if you happen to find something of which you don't approve? Or, what advice would you offer a parent in this situation?

3. It is important to lay down ground rules for children of all ages. Once you thoroughly explain to a child that certain items are off limits in your home and are reasonably sure that the child understands, if your young child broke an object that you treasured, how would you handle the discipline? Or, what advice would you offer a parent in this situation?

4. It is one thing to monitor your child's behavior within your own home, but when they are exposed to other people's home environments it becomes more challenging. If you give permission for your child to stay overnight at a friend's home and their standards are quite different that yours, what would you do if you find that they watched television programs that you do not approve of? Would you allow your child to visit overnight a second time? Or, what advice would you offer a parent in this situation?

5. Comparing one sibling to another can undermine a child's self-esteem and confidence. When a younger child has the same teacher that his older brother or sister had in that same grade, how would you handle it if the teacher pointed out that the younger one isn't doing as well as the older child did? Or, what advice would you offer a parent in this situation?

6. As food for thought to help you evaluate your parenting skills, take time to give some consideration to your parent/child relationship. Ask yourself the following questions in regard to how you interact with your children and write down your thoughts as you reflect.

1. Do you give your child/children your undivided attention by setting aside quality time for listening to them?
2. Do you consider your child/children's feelings?
3. Do you give your child/children sufficient recognition for the accomplishments they make?
4. Do you accept your child/children for who they are as individuals?
5. Do you avoid comparing them with others?
6. Do you handle disciplinary actions in a private manner and not in front of your child's siblings or friends?
7. Do you allow your child/children an appropriate amount of privacy?

Reason #5

The Pleasure
Reason
Provides a
Spiritual Romance

"We want to get a divorce!" The words startled me as they assailed my ears. I would even consider them oxymoronic considering their source—divorce and the Smith name in the same sentence? Absolutely not! After all, the Smiths were the ideal pair— most couples in the church wanted to emulate them. Mr. and Mrs. Smith had been married twenty-seven years and were blessed with three children. She was a serious student of the Bible and a very popular Sunday school teacher as well. He was a dedicated father and solid provider for the family. They were both faithful members of our assembly and lovers of the Lord Jesus Christ.

I asked them why they wanted to get a divorce and was taken aback when I heard their answer. They were having problems in their sex life. Even though they had three children, Mrs. Smith admitted that she never enjoyed sex. Immediately, I began to wonder about that. Generally, when that situation exists in a marriage relationship it means one of the partners had been abused or misused by someone. Typically, a family member or a very close acquaintance is responsible for the abuse.

However, as I continued to listen to their story, I found that was not the case in this instance. As it turned out, Mrs. Smith's mother had greatly influenced her daughter's concept of sex, and that had helped to shape her attitude about it. In her mother's view, sex was for procreation only and not for pleasure; she actually believed that sex was "nasty." This woman had never enjoyed sex with her husband, revealing to her daughter that she had only endured it.

Prior to coming for counseling, the Smiths hadn't had sex in almost eight months. I directed them to the Word of God where Hebrews 13:4 declares that the marriage bed is to be undefiled. I reminded them that God views sex as an act of worship. I knew that I was "preaching to the choir" because she knew the Word as well as I did. I proceeded to make several futile efforts to help resolve the issue, but to no avail.

Mr. Smith said that he would not stay in a marriage without sex, and a few months later they were divorced. Of course, I'm sure there were other issues that precipitated the demise of their relationship. But clearly they didn't understand that they should have given priority to God's reason for pleasure in their relationship. One of God's reasons for creating marriage is to provide a spiritual romance for married couples. When God gave us sexual pleasure in the context of a marriage, He said it was good. In fact, when He commented on intimacy in marriage, He went even further and said it was *very* good! Amen! God, I agree with You!

The truth of the matter is, the Bible speaks of three kinds of love. And you should know that marriage needs all of them:

- AGAPE is unconditional love. This is the kind of love that God has for His people. It is a spiritual love that God infuses into our hearts. We are to emulate God and demonstrate this type of selfless love that asks for nothing in return. Because it comes directly from God, He expects us to share it with everyone that we touch in life. The most profound definition of agape love is found in 1 Corinthians chapter 13.
- PHILOS is affectionate love. This is a special kind of love that is shared between friends. It is the foundation of a successful relationship because it involves a spirit of give-and-take between two people. This is a good place to begin a relationship because it has the potential to become a healthy marriage partnership.

- EROS is erotic love. This is the kind of love that displays strong romantic feelings and sexual desire. It is a self-benefitting act of love which means that it primarily serves each individual in a personal way.

A Spiritual Romance

"For this reason a man shall leave his father and his mother, and be joined to his wife; and they shall become one flesh. And the man and his wife were both naked and were not ashamed."

—Genesis 2:24–25

Were you aware that God has a purpose for pleasure? Did you know that sex is a spiritual experience first and then it is a physical act? Within the framework of marriage God masterfully designed sexual attraction to be at the very core of that union. It is called romance. In doing so, He formed the strongest bond that could ever exist between a man and a woman.

God created a spiritual romance to be a uniquely human experience. Furthermore, it is as old as human history. We learn from Scripture that Adam and Eve were joined together as one flesh. And the Word also suggests that God caused them to engage in sexual relations (Genesis 2:24). Because God called everything good that He had created, the man and woman were not ashamed of their nakedness. They were free to enjoy the purest form of pleasure known to man. There was no shame in Adam and Eve's game. There was no blame in their game. They were naked and it wasn't a big deal. God even placed them in an environment where everything that surrounded them reflected His goodness.

Therefore, from the beginning it was all about a spiritual romance. Adam and Eve were comfortable with their lives and their blissful surroundings. It was all good in the garden because their lives and everything they represented was in alignment with their Creator. And so it was under these circumstances that the God of all wisdom and knowledge ordained the marriage covenant.

Yet, He didn't stop there. God shared in the experience and became an intrinsic part of the state of matrimony. By appointing Himself as the One who watches over the vows made between a husband and wife, He sanctifies the couple by setting them apart to enjoy each other's presence. Ultimately, God's plan is for the union of a man and woman to become an exclusive reflection of the sacred communion that is shared between the three Persons of the Trinity. You should consider yourself immensely blessed when you and your spouse hold romantic pleasure in a sacred and prominent place in your marriage. In God's eyes, you look like the image that He created you to be. When your relationship includes a healthy dose of romance you have created a climate that will strengthen your marriage and enable it to thrive.

In the Beauty of His Holiness

The Bible further speaks of the wonder of the sexual act and compares it to the mysterious nature of various things that are found in the human experience. One writer described it this way:

"There are three things which are too wonderful for me, four which
I do not understand: the way of an eagle in the sky, the way of a
serpent on a rock, the way of a ship in the middle of the sea,
and the way of a man with a maid."
—Proverbs 30:18–19

As humans, we are instinctively compelled to find ways in which we can relate to what we have come to understand as the work of God's hands. In other words, we recognize the things of nature as exquisite and beautiful. For example, most people find pleasure in gazing upon an exquisite flower, an exotic bird, a brilliant sky on a sunny day, the vastness of an ocean, and so on. Although we cannot readily understand all that God has done, we can appreciate it just the same because we know that God is the ultimate Creator whose creations demand our admiration and respect. Thus, when God sanctified the sexual act and fashioned it around a spiritual romance, He filled it with a sense of splendor and deep intimacy where marriage partners could enjoy each other in His presence. It is a thing of beauty.

Allow me to emphasize this point because you and your spouse need to really get this: With God at the center of your marriage, you are living under the auspices of His blessings. Scripture sends a comforting message to those who have the wisdom to keep the Lord close to them. As a result, you and your spouse would do well to acknowledge the presence of God in your marriage. Listen to these words of divine inclusiveness that are sure to bring great rewards.

"You will make known to me the path of life; in Your presence is fullness of joy; in Your right hand there are pleasures forever."

—PSALM 16:11

This is what makes sharing a life together so incredibly good. When you put your focus on God, you will understand that wherever God is, the path of goodness and mercy will follow and lead you in building a sound marriage. All married couples need the goodness of God and His enduring mercy. In fact, I cannot even imagine how a marriage can be successful without the constant exchange of genuine love and affection that is also devoted to loving God.

And part of that overall experience is to find pleasure in each other. This is what I tried to convey to Mr. and Mrs. Smith. With all that she had in her favor, she didn't recognize that God has given each of us the capacity to absorb a great deal of pleasure over the course of our lives. And for that we should be thankful. Mrs. Smith needed to understand that God looks at the beauty of the sexual act and considers it an offering to Him. That offering then becomes a sacrifice of worship.

When we worship Him, we are giving God His rightful place in our lives. It is the highest form of reverence and devotion. Scripture speaks of worshipping the Lord in the beauty of holiness, giving to God something that is due only to Him (1 Chronicles 16:29 KJV). Brothers and sisters, this is serious business to God. The Lord placed such a distinction on the act of lovemaking that nothing else on earth compares to it. If you really want to honor God with your marriage, you need to consider sexual pleasure as a special act of kindness from God. In return for God's favor, give your spouse the highest level of love and devotion.

Faithfulness Is a Virtue

This is where the Smiths missed it. I am sure Mrs. Smith would object if she were told that she was being unfaithful to her husband. But Mr. Smith would agree because faithfulness also involves the understanding that they were not to deny each other sexual pleasure. It is evident that this is a serious matter; it is what destroyed their marriage.

Instead of giving thanks for the mate whom God had given us, so often we easily misuse this sacred gift. If Mrs. Smith had put God's desire for her marriage above her mother's teaching, she could have learned to overcome her inhibitions. I want to offer this suggestion: Do not fail to cherish your loved one any longer. Sex is a ministry to your mate; you and your spouse should regard it as such and treat it with the dignity and respect that it deserves. In doing so, the two of you will bring glory and honor to God. It sounds so simple; it's what some call a "no-brainer." Even so, we all too often make it so hard. Accordingly, Scripture issues a wise warning:

> *"Stop depriving one another, except by agreement for a time, so that you may devote yourselves to prayer, and come together again so that Satan will not tempt you because of your lack of self-control."*
>
> —1 Corinthians 7:5

Here Scripture is cautioning a husband and wife against denying each other the pleasure they are bound by their covenant to give each other. We are warned against practicing abstinence for long periods of time because it can have a detrimental effect on the relationship. However, many couples tend to take each other for granted and somehow the initial sexual attraction begins to wane over a time of consistent neglect.

Moreover, it is actually the duty of a husband and wife to keep each other satisfied sexually. This is God's method of preventing either spouse from wandering outside their union. You've heard of this kind of behavior; it's commonly referred to as "looking for love in all the wrong places."

But the good news is that when a couple remains faithful to each other, God smiles; He is pleased. And the two will reap the benefits of keeping their marriage vows sacred. King Solomon wrote of beautiful principles that were designed to guide us successfully throughout the temptations and challenges that may come our way. He was a wise individual, who long ago described how a husband should relish his wife all the days of their existence:

> *"Let thy fountain be blessed: and rejoice with the wife of thy youth.*
> *Let her be as the loving hind and pleasant roe; let her breasts satisfy*
> *thee at all times; and be thou ravished always with her love."*
>
> —PROVERBS 5:18–19 KJV

This verse begins with the commanding verb *let*, which means "to allow something to happen." It implies that you are in control; you can exercise your will to make a satisfying marriage become a reality for you and your spouse. In other words, you have the power to choose blessings for your relationship. The next command is exhorting you to rejoice and share a joyous union with your wife. Also, here the word *ravish* means "to be intoxicated, to get drunk on love." When a person gets drunk, he or she can become so consumed with what is being ingested that it can soon be an overwhelming experience. That is how the sexual relationship within the confines of a marriage is supposed to work. The pleasure that it brings a husband and wife is a holy, beautiful, and overpowering thing to behold and enjoy.

Pleasure Talk

This may sound strange, but a couple can get hung up because communication has a strange way of breaking down. And suddenly there's trouble bridging the gap to reach a mutual understanding and clear up those unspoken issues. Instead of avoiding an escalating argument a husband and wife can get more and more tangled up in it.

Does this sound familiar to anyone but me? I don't know what it is, but there's something about human nature that gives us a tendency to single out the wrong and overlook what is right. This is where the "I dos" in the marriage vows turn into "you don'ts." So, ladies, allow me this opportunity to apologize on behalf of all husbands— but you have to actually tell us what you want and need for us to do. In the majority of cases we'll do what is within our power to make it happen.

Please don't get me wrong. It's simply that when the subject of communication between the sexes is considered, there is a very fine line where misinterpretation and misunderstanding can creep in. And, trust me, I'm not trying to cross that line. I am just trying to be very real about addressing one of the most serious subjects on this side of heaven—the problems that we need to overcome in marriage so that we can find real pleasure in each other.

You see, God wants all men to know how to please their wives. And positive communication can bring His desire about. It is a main contributor to the success of a marriage. God has made man to be a pragmatic being and a problem solver. So, when you lay it all out in clear terms like a, b, c, and 1, 2, 3, then we can work through that and turn it into a solution. However, sometimes it appears that a woman is under the impression that a man can read her mind to determine what she needs. Then, when he doesn't succeed in performing this unachievable feat she often becomes frustrated because she's not getting what she needs. And that's a problem that must be solved.

This may just be my opinion, but there seems to be a huge difference between how men and women process thoughts. Marriage is a two-way street, and my point here is that it always helps when wives tell their husbands what they need because we may interpret the same situation in a different way. I'm not saying either gender is right or wrong; we're simply different. But since God has given husbands the responsibility of taking care of every aspect of our wives' concerns, understand that this is a major undertaking and we want to get it right.

So, sisters, beyond making fundamental provisions to sustain our families, we don't know what more you need us to do unless you tell us. That's why I ask my wife to tell me what she needs so that I can give it to her. But a woman might say something like, "Well, if I have to tell you, then you won't be doing it because you want to. You'll be doing it because I told you to." That sentiment must mean something to the female psyche, and I respect it. But for men, that's not the heart of the matter. We just need to know so that we can accommodate. In fact, we could help each other out if we tell each other what we need. When you talk about perfecting a relationship, it would make us so much more compatible if we could agree on this. After all, it is God's will for us to enjoy the provision of pleasure and satisfaction that He expects us to find in each other.

Of course, there are always exceptions, but there is often a breakdown in experiencing God's pleasure when couples are engaged in intimacy. A man will typically tell his wife what he wants—how she can give him pleasure. But a woman generally wants her husband to guess or somehow instinctively know what pleases her. Mrs. Smith shared with me that she found it very difficult to give of herself, and Mr. Smith was denied the opportunity to persuade her to open up to him. It was a frustrating situation for both of them. If she wanted him to hold her, then, he would need her to tell him so because surely he couldn't read her mind.

Moreover, ladies, when you simply want to talk, tell your husband that he needs to turn the TV off. Let him know that you need to share what is on your heart so that he will give you his undivided attention. Please don't think that when a man is watching a game and his woman happens to walk in the room, he will immediately understand that she needs his attention. Believe me, it takes more than that for a brother to get it. Remember, men focus best on one thing at a time, and when that thing is the game, nothing else readily penetrates the mind.

The fact of the matter is, if you assume that he will know what you desire without informing him, disappointment is surely on the way. Tell him that you need him to comfort you, reassure you, show you his love, and hug you—whatever is on your mind. Let him know how much it means to you; wrap your arms around him. If the brother has any sensibilities, he will turn the TV off to show you that you're more important to him than any game. The average man will respond to you when you let him know what your needs are. On the other hand, if a man is inconsistent in dealing with his wife's needs and affections, a woman can easily misinterpret his intentions at any given time. That's when a brother can come up short. So, we need to learn how to strike the right balance in keeping our wives satisfied.

I am sure of one thing—knowledge is power. And that means half of the battle is won when you know where the problems are hiding. Then, you can use the other half to fix the problems once they have been identified. So, the more a husband and wife know about what each of them expects from the other, the more a marriage can stay on the side of good. The best thing to do is ask God to empower you to bring pleasure to your spouse and peace to your marriage. Rest assured, you will both reap the benefits.

It is a fortunate thing when verbal communication easily transitions into physical communication, particularly when a man and woman are both on the same wavelength; it enables them to respond to each other with the same level of loving intentions and intensity. A woman should tell her man and then show him what makes her feel good. And, rest assured, he'll tell her that she's got the kind of love that will make him call in sick. Discover what satisfies your mate and spend time building each other up. At the end of the day, something deep inside of a man and woman knows that when we do what God tells us to do we please each other—and God is pleased too. And we all want to feel His pleasure.

High Yield Dividends

There is a lot of truth in this statement: The average man will give romance to get sex, and the average woman will give sex to get romance. When you consider sex and romance, it is no secret that God made men and women to have different needs. For example, in the case of the Smiths, perhaps if Mr. Smith would have taken more time trying to find out how he might please his wife, they could have possibly avoided divorce. Inherently, we think differently, and that has a direct effect on our actions. Mrs. Smith obviously had difficulty thinking on the level of pleasing her husband sexually, but with a little more help from him she may have overcome her inhibitions. Within the context of establishing the man as the initiator and the woman as the responder, God would expect Mr. Smith to take the lead in finding the solution to their problem. However, husbands and wives cannot solve every problem without Him. And nothing is too hard for God to fix when we turn our struggles over to Him.

To illustrate this point, think of a woman as an emotional bank. Whatever you deposit in her, you will receive that same sentiment in return. If you deposit affection, you will receive affection. She will take it, allow it to influence her thoughts, decisions, and behavior in a positive way, and then give it back to you. As a result, you will end up getting more than you initially invested. That's what is called making dividends. But actually, it is the law of sowing and reaping, which is God's principle for giving and receiving.

However, be aware because this process also works in the reverse. If you give a woman trouble, she'll take it, allow it to influence her thoughts, decisions, and behavior, and give it back to you as double trouble. Furthermore, if you are getting marital bounced checks because you haven't made any deposits but you keep trying to make withdrawals anyway, those requests will be returned to you marked "insufficient funds." They can often be described in four decisive words: *I have a headache.* That means you have overdrawn your account, and when you try to make a withdrawal the only thing you will get back is a declined request.

Now, I am the first one to admit that I'm not a perfect husband. But I've been married long enough to have discovered some things over the years. Let me tell you what I've learned. My wife was in a terrible automobile accident. When she recovered, she wanted to go and visit her sister. She was gone for two weeks. When it was time for her to come back home, I went to pick her up from the airport. I got myself ready to greet her. I dressed in one of her favorite suits and tie and put on her favorite cologne. Then, I went and bought two bouquets of flowers and headed to the airport.

It was a busy day and there were a lot of people waiting for flights. However, I was the only one standing there dressed in a suit and holding two bouquets of flowers. When I saw her coming toward me with her suitcase, I rushed to meet her. I greeted her with kisses and gave her the flowers. When she thanked me, I complimented her by saying they were nothing compared to her beauty. I took all her bags in one arm and her hand in the other and we walked toward the exit. An older gentleman looked at us and called us newlyweds. I thought that was something worth noting and so I flattered her by saying, "Isn't that something, baby. We've been married over thirty years and that man thought we were acting like we just got married."

Notice that all the while, I'm making emotional deposits. I'm trying to impress her and show her that I'm all man by continuing to use one hand to carry everything and holding on to her hand with the other. Finally, she asked me if it wouldn't be easier for me to use both hands to carry the bags, but I said, "No way." I told her that it was important for me to touch her because I'd been missing her touch.

Here's the icing on the cake, brothers. When we got into the car, I switched to my feminine mode. I started asking her questions about her trip. You know, the way that one of her girlfriends would do. Now, I know what you're probably thinking. But men and women communicate in such unique ways that most of the time we are not even close to being on the same wavelength. We don't connect through our body language and tone of speaking. So, during the ride home I wanted to know all about what had happened on her trip. I asked her what had been exciting, where they ate dinner, and so on. To show that she had my undivided attention along the way, I interjected at the right moments and made the proper comments such as, "Is that so?" etc.

All through the time we ate lunch, I made some more deposits. After that we sat up for a long time just talking and sharing. Finally, the time was right and I made a withdrawal. You see, I had deposited enough in her emotional bank to even enjoy multiple withdrawals.

So, brothers, here's the secret. Before you want to make a withdrawal, you have to make ample deposits. Get up early in the morning and make her breakfast in bed. When you go to work, call her several times throughout the day and tell her that you miss her. You can bank some high dividends when you make consistent deposits into your mate's emotional bank. And sometimes when you've made enough deposits, it's like getting free money because you can even make an occasional unexpected withdrawal.

What's Love Got to Do with It?

For brothers who are serious about making their marriages strong and want to know how to unlock the mysteries of a successful marriage, you need some good examples of how to treat a woman with love and respect in the manner and language that she comprehends. When you approach a woman in the right way it makes her want to respond positively to you.

In my first book entitled *When a Man Loves a Woman*, I present an example based on the biblical account of Jacob and Rachel. When Jacob first met Rachel, you might say that it was a case of love at first sight. Through the Lord's help, he found and eventually married the woman of his dreams. But before they wedded, Jacob invested heavily into Rachel's emotional needs. Through his actions he showed her that his commitment and loyalty far exceeded any obstacles that crossed their paths.

Read on and see what can be learned from Jacob's pursuit to win over and please the woman of his dreams. If you are familiar with the story in Genesis chapter 29, Jacob wanted to marry Rachel, but her father insisted that he first had to work seven years. When Jacob agreed to Laban's proposition, his willingness to serve her father in order to marry Rachel *confirmed her identity*. He cared so deeply for her that the time seemed to fly by. As such, his dedication to winning her hand in marriage *assured her security*. When he kissed her hand, *he affirmed her*; it said to her that *he appreciated her*. Then, *he showed her his compassion* by allowing himself to cry before her. Not only that, it didn't matter to him that there were men standing by and watching.

Finally, *he solidified his association* with Rachel. The time came when he fulfilled his end of the bargain; yet, Jacob was found still wanting. After he had met his obligation, he found out that he was essentially tricked into marrying Rachel's older sister, Leah. The two women's father had the audacity to suggest that Jacob work another seven years for Rachel to be his wife. At that point, Jacob *established an even closer bond* to her by recommitting himself to work the additional years for Rachel's hand in marriage. I could almost hear Rachel saying, "What a man, what a man, what a mighty good man. Oh yeah, I sure will marry this man." Now, clearly, the brother worked hard to get the woman he wanted.

The Power of Pleasure with a Purpose

Yes, the state of pleasure can definitely be a place of physical and spiritual fulfillment for you and your spouse. However, there are other aspects attached to the definition of pleasure that reach far beyond sensual gratification. Most people tend to think mainly in terms of sexual pleasure, but God has a multifaceted description of what pleasure is all about.

What is more, God intertwines the element of pleasure with the entity of purpose. He has placed a sense of purpose in each of us that envelopes our entire being and gives every individual his or her own specific reason for living. So then, there is another level of reaching your full potential to experience pleasure in God. In discovering your purpose you will find pleasure because there is something specific that God wants you to do with your life. But know that you cannot do this alone. If you are married, fulfilling your purpose automatically involves your spouse. Remember, the two of you are now one flesh.

Even more importantly, as you consider what having a purpose is all about, you will find no greater example than when you look at the life of the Lord Jesus Christ. What did He do? He lived according to His purpose. As the Son of God, His primary function was to come to earth and redeem man from his sins. In the book of Matthew, the angel of the Lord declared to Joseph, *"And she [Mary] shall bring forth a son, and thou shalt call his name Jesus: for he shall save his people from their sins"* (Matthew 1:21 KJV).

With these words, the angel announced the purpose that our Lord was preparing to fulfill. Think about it. Jesus never had an army; He never even wrote a book, but when it was all over He was satisfied with His life because He had accomplished His purpose. Consequently, He could say that it was finished; that is, His purpose for coming to earth was completed. He had given of Himself, died on the cross, and paid the penalty for our sins. As a result, the writer of Hebrews was prompted to write these inspiring words that enable us to press on in life:

> *"Fixing our eyes on Jesus, the author and perfecter of faith, who for the joy set before Him endured the cross, despising the shame, and has sat down at the right hand of the throne of God."*
> —HEBREWS 12:2

Through it all—Our Lord and Savior felt the Father's pleasure because He was intently focused on His purpose. This is truly a manifestation of pleasure with a purpose. Jesus returned to heaven and took His rightful place because He completed His assignment. In anticipation of His triumphant life, we also find that the Father in heaven experiences pleasure, and He found it in His only begotten Son. At the time of His baptism, our heavenly Father affirmed His Son, Jesus, by saying, *"You are My beloved Son, in You I am well-pleased"* (Luke 3:22). That's pleasure.

So, when it comes down to how God regards His children—pleasure and purpose go hand in hand. And guess what, as a reflection of the holy Trinity, we have an opportunity to express our pleasure in living out our purpose as well. Remember, we are made in the image and likeness of God. Therefore, when we are doing the thing that God uniquely placed inside of us to carry out, we have the opportunity to feel an extreme sense of pleasure in a spiritual way. However, what one does with their God-given purpose is yet another story because people are on various levels in their discovery and awareness of what God wants them to do. Consequently, if you ask a number of persons what their purpose for living is, you will get as many answers as the number of people that you ask.

Allow me to further explain the concept of pleasure with purpose using the following example. There is a powerful line in the film *Chariot's of Fire* that exemplifies this idea. The story goes that the sister of one of the main characters was urging him to return to the missionary field in China. She couldn't understand his decision to leave his missionary work and take another direction in his life. But this multitalented individual had decided to leave his ministry to go and run in the Olympics. He explained to his sister that God had given him more than one purpose. He also had the talent to excel as a runner. In so many words, he tried to help her understand how this principle applied to him. He summed it up with a declaration: ***when he runs, he feels an exuberant display of God's pleasure.***

That is a powerful thing because what he was conveying to her was that God had given him more than one gift. He would not have been an excellent runner if God had not given him that ability and expected him to use it. And when you exercise any gift that God has given you, you cannot help but feel pleasure because you are doing what He created you to do. The pleasure you will experience becomes, in reality, a spiritual fulfillment of God's purpose for you.

Let me give you another example. God has given both the male and female sexes a purpose that is specifically relative to the characteristics of each respective gender. In other words, men have a general purpose that is distinct from women. The reverse is also true. But understand that, as I am a man, the duty of a man toward his woman is a subject very dear to my heart. So, permit me to focus here on the man's purpose because if men were to get this right, I guarantee you that so much of what concerns both men and women in life would fall into place.

I'm speaking to both partners now. But it all begins with the man because God began the creation of human life in this way—by creating Adam first. And who are we to try and question the Master's design?

Building a solid family life is like assembling the pieces of a puzzle together. For instance, if the final product is to be a beautiful picture of a scene of nature, every piece must fit into its proper place so that the puzzle will depict the complete picture it was designed to be. Well, imagine life as a puzzle where all the pieces represent a different piece of your life. As a married man with a family, your puzzle would have a man-piece, a woman-piece, perhaps several child-pieces, a home-piece, some automobile-pieces, one or two job-pieces, etc. You get the picture. (Sorry, but the pun was intended here.)

Well, in this particular puzzle—the puzzle of your life—God is saying that you have to begin with the man-piece if you want all the other pieces to fall into the proper place as He intended. Life can so easily get out of balance; that is why we must be careful to follow God's plan and do it His way. He is the great equalizer; we need to depend on Him to maintain the delicate balance that is so important to successfully living out God's purpose for marriage and the family structure. It is through understanding and applying this process that we find true pleasure in life.

Now, recall an earlier discussion of Proverbs 18:22 about how a man should go about finding a wife. Along his journey in life, he finds a good thing and gains favor from the Lord because he allowed God to lead him to his wife—the love of his life. This is truth that goes back to the beginning of creation and the roles that the man and woman were assigned. Once again, when God made Adam first, He made Adam the spiritual head from the start of humanity. This is also the premise that makes the man the initiator in the relationship. The fact is, God made the first woman figure, Eve, so special that before she came into existence, He made sure everything she would need was already provided for her.

How did God provide for her? Provision was ordained to come through her husband—the very being God used to bring her into existence. Now, she is in the position to be the responder to the one who provides for her. Therefore, the moral of this story is that the husband and wife who live out

their God-given roles will find their sense of pleasure and purpose by coming together in synchronization with the Almighty God, their Creator.

Now, ladies, please allow me to speak to you on behalf of men. I want
to let you in on a little secret. Men feel the greatest sense of contentment, satisfaction, and peace when we know that we are fulfilling the purpose for
which God has called us. God has so designed us that when we do what He
wants us to do for our wives and families, we feel His pleasure. That is the
deep part of what makes a man go out and work. His drive and ambition to
work reflects his connection with the purpose God gave him to care for and
stand guard over his home. These are the things that make a man feel good
about himself as the provider and the protector. He gets fulfillment out of
knowing that he works to put a roof over his family's head, food on the table,
and clothes on their backs. It makes him feel God's pleasure.

However, brothers, be aware: there is a flip side of this great phenomenon.
God said that a man should not eat if he does not work (2 Thessalonians
3:10). So, in effect, He also joined the man's purpose with his self-worth.
This explains why a man who is not working has low self-esteem. In particular, a man who has not found a way to provide for his family is not living
up to the fundamental purpose God gave him as the head of his household.
To turn that situation around, he must redirect his attention to God's Word
to first get an understanding of where he is and then find out what he needs
to do to correct the problem. Listen to what God's Word also says about
this:

> *"But if anyone does not provide for his own,*
> *and especially for those of his household,*
> *he has denied the faith and is worse than an unbeliever."*
> —1 TIMOTHY 5:8

No one who professes to be a believer wants to be found in denial of his
faith in God. Besides, deep inside of every man God has placed the desire
to work and be a provider. Yes, times can be hard on a brother. But if this is
your struggle, the first step toward a positive change is to face the reality of
your situation. If you are feeling down and out, this is no time for excuses;
it is a time for action. God will transform a willing heart and infuse it with

a determination to make the necessary changes in your life. For anyone who has a downtrodden spirit, know that He will build you up. But you have to first surrender your prideful will and lay it all before Him.

That is why having an intimate relationship with the God of all wisdom and power is so important to your survival. By His Spirit, you will discover that God can help you find your purpose in Him. To become the man of God that you are destined to be, He wants you to recognize that you need the Holy Spirit to lead you in the process of discovering your purpose. As you become a diligent student of God's Word, He will show you the appropriate steps and give you the grace to take some action to make good things happen. It's a step-by-step process, and once you begin to trust God, He will begin to unlock the door to the blessings that you need. When it starts with the leader, your enthusiasm will become contagious and success will be on the way. You will find the courage to step out in faith and take your loved ones to a level in God that will be satisfying to you and spread throughout your entire household.

Brothers, finding your purpose in God is your main responsibility to your family because that is how you will find pleasure and satisfaction in life. The burdens of the house are on the man, and we know we're accomplishing our purpose when we go out and provide for our wives and children. Brothers, you ought to be saying "Amen." We can only be satisfied when we feel we have done what God has built us to do—and when we are fulfilling that purpose.

The Pleasure of His Company

"My beloved is mine, and I am his."
—SONG OF SOLOMON 2:16

If you are ever looking for a book that tells the story about experiencing marital pleasure, look to the Bible. The book of the Song of Solomon highlights an exceptional picture of the passion and romance shared by two married lovers. Written as a type of love song, it is a biblical tribute to human sexuality expressed within the context of marriage. Most importantly, this beautiful account of a godly romance stresses the importance of a marriage that is covered by the blessings of God. A brief discussion of their intriguing romance is warranted because it speaks directly from the Bible about how God created two sexes, joined them together in matrimony, and made sexual intimacy the highest form of their expression of love.

One thing stands out very prominently in the elaborate description that King Solomon and his bride, the Shulamite woman, give to each other— they are deeply in love. Notice from these passages the passionate relationship they shared:

> *"You have made my heart beat faster, my sister, my bride; you have made my heart beat faster with a single glance of your eyes, with a single strand of your necklace. How beautiful is your love, my sister, my bride! How much better is your love than wine, and the fragrance of your oils than all kinds of spices! Your lips, my bride, drip honey; honey and milk are under your tongue, and the fragrance of your garments is like the fragrance of Lebanon. . . .*
>
> *"I have come into my garden, my sister, my bride; I have gathered my myrrh along with my balsam I have eaten my honeycomb and my honey; I have drunk my wine and my milk. Eat, friends; drink and imbibe deeply, O lovers."*
> —SONG OF SOLOMON 4:9–11; 5:1

We peer into their bedroom on their honeymoon night as they give themselves to each other unreservedly. This is intimacy at its best: romantic, sensual, and sexual. There is talking, touching, tenderness, and teaching going on. They are experiencing the exhilaration of the exploration of each other's bodies and enjoying the journey toward mutual orgasm (yes, he is waiting for her).

In case we've forgotten, Proverbs 5:18–19 reminds us that mutual satisfaction should be our goal in giving each other pleasure. That means we men need to make sure we follow the direction of Solomon. He is describing to every man the kind of man that his wife wants him to be—a man with a slow hand and an easy touch! Take your time!

The Master's Stroke

"For it is God who is at work in you,
both to will and to work for His good pleasure."
—PHILIPPIANS 2:13

Ultimately, we were created for God's pleasure. That is why we are compelled to honor Him with our lives and give Him alone all of our praise. Let me give you another practical explanation. Not too long ago, I was informed that the piano at our church was broken. To make matters worse, we were preparing for a concert pianist to play for us the following Sunday. When he arrived, I suggested that he use the keyboard because the piano had some broken keys. His response to me was, "Brother Ford, I am a skilled pianist and quite proficient at what I do. I will use the piano because I have enough skill to adjust the music and play it the way that I want it. They won't even know that the keys are broken."

As I listened to him, I started taking notes. He then asked me what I was writing. I told him it was my closing illustration for the next week's sermon. He said, "You got an illustration out of that?" And I replied that I most certainly did. He asked me to share it with him. So, I told him, "You see, I am a piano in life and God has called me to play a melody in my marriage. But I have broken keys. There are some things I cannot do because of who I am as a man. I just don't have all the answers. But I have a Master who is able to come and play my life. He can transpose the notes of my life, and He is able to make beautiful music in my marriage. When people see it, they won't even know that there were broken keys—because the Master played me."

That's the way it is for all of us. You might as well admit that you have broken keys. God is the One who created you, and He can do things in us that normally we could not do. He can minister to our spouses, not because of us, but in spite of us, as we allow Him to work through us. And then we will be able to receive pleasure from acknowledging the Master of our lives and give Him the praise that He so rightly deserves. We can join the psalmist and honor God by proclaiming, *"Let the Lord be magnified, who has pleasure in the prosperity of His servant"* (Psalm 35:27 NKJV).

Making It Happen

1. With an open and receptive heart, ask God to help you understand how to apply His reason for creating marriage to be a spiritual romance. He will hear your sincere prayers and help you to transform your marriage into a reflection of His image.

2. Get up half an hour earlier than usual and meet with the Lord. Ask the Lord to fill you with His Spirit so you can be empowered to fulfill His purpose.

3. When a man has fellowship with the Lord, it enables him to do for his wife what the Lord has done for him. When there is trouble between you and your spouse, as the man, your ability to make things right will depend on how you minister to your wife. Ask God to show you ways in which to fellowship with your wife and make her feel special.

4. Make sure you spend appropriate amounts of quality time with your wife. Use the following ways to give your wife your undivided attention.
   - Call her from work two to three times a day just to see how she's doing.
   - When you come home from work, take the first half hour or so just to talk to her.
   - Help her with dinner or whatever she may be doing.
   - After dinner, help her with the dishes instead of watching the game. Invite her out for a drive to get an ice-cream cone and just talk to her.

5. To sharpen your communication skills, read Dr. Gary Chapman's book *The Five Love Languages*. Also, for additional inspiration, read the Song of Solomon in its entirety.

6. The word *knowledge* means "intimacy acquired by experience." The more you communicate with your wife, the more you will understand what makes her tick and what ticks her off. Ask the Holy Spirit to show you how to please your wife and keep her content. My motto is "Happy wife, happy life!"

7. Plan as many vacation getaways as you can. Being alone together will give you time to practice your intimacy without the usual interruptions of life.

Reason #6

The Reason
for Purity
Facilitates a
Spiritual Responsibility

Once there was a king who invited all of his subjects to come to his palace for a banquet. The whole town got excited and gathered together because the king was having a banquet. When they came into the vestibule of his palace, he said to them, "Listen, I'm going to prepare this wonderful banquet for you. I want you to wait here and don't do anything until I come back."

He went away and the people waited and waited. Of course, after it was taking so long and it seemed as though the king wasn't coming back any time soon, they started looking around. Then one person noticed that there were already tables set up with cloths covering them. Out of sheer curiosity they lifted up the cloths and saw that underneath them there was food already prepared. Someone reminded them that the king had said not to eat anything until he returns. But another person said that he was hungry and couldn't wait any longer. Then, all of the people decided they would just go ahead and eat.

So, they ate and ate until they were stuffed. When the king returned, he opened the doors of the banquet hall and showed the people all of the delicious cuisine that he had for them. There was lobster, filet mignon, and all kinds of delicacies. He told them to come on in and eat. But they were already full. When the king noticed that they weren't enjoying themselves, he said to them, "Why aren't you eating? Are you already full?" to which they replied, "Yes, we are stuffed. We don't need anything else."

Then the king said, "Wait a minute. What do you mean you're already full? I told you not to eat until I came back!" They said, "But all of this food was here. We saw it when we removed the cloth that was over it and we just filled ourselves to capacity." The king said, "You ate the food that was under the covers?" And they admitted, "Yes, we did." He exclaimed, "Oh no, you filled up on garbage! We were going to give that to the dogs."

A Spiritual Responsibility

The Bible tells us that God has given His children some very special gifts. One of the things He has reserved for those who marry is a beautiful thing called sex. And when we partake of it under the direction of the King, it's a wonderful banquet to behold. But for those who can't wait until they are married to engage in sex as God intends, all they will receive for their impatience is garbage instead. In effect, they spoil the gracious gift of God because sex outside of marriage is the opposite of His blessing, and, therefore, it becomes a hex.

But some people don't realize that there is a hex on sex when it is misused. For that reason, they need to know that Scripture reveals the mind of God and His concern for sexual morality. Listen to what the apostle Paul explains about the importance of refraining from sexual impurity:

> *"For this is the will of God, your sanctification; that is, that you*
> *abstain from sexual immorality; that each of you know how to*
> *possess his own vessel in sanctification and honor."*
> —1 THESSALONIANS 4:3–4

Every believer should understand that God is the God of all wisdom and knowledge. Because He is the Creator of life, His forethought about every detail that pertains to it cannot even begin to be measured by human standards. That is why, as believers, we must put all of our trust in God—the One who knows what is best for us. It is also our duty to serve Him with reverence and obedience. In return for our faithful commitment to His ways, He provides for our every need, protects us from all harm, and gives us eternal life with Him.

With His divine insight and understanding, the God of all holiness watches over every aspect of His creation. Since He highly regards the relationship that we call marriage, He is determined to protect the sanctity of it. As a result, the marriage bed is designed to be a preventive measure to sexual immorality. In the following passage it is clear that the apostle Paul understood this principle and urged the church not to engage in sexual activity outside of the confines of marriage. Listen to his words,

> *"But because of immoralities, each man is to have his own wife,*
> *and each woman is to have her own husband.*
> *The husband must fulfill his duty to his wife,*
> *and likewise also the wife to her husband."*
>
> —1 CORINTHIANS 7:2–3

Scripture says that it is God's will concerning you and your spouse to remain faithful to each other. This is so important to God that He made it a spiritual responsibility for a couple to maintain a pure, wholesome, unadulterated relationship. When He gave married people the important duty to protect each other in this way, it was intended to keep them from venturing outside their marriage to find sexual pleasure.

God is a holy God, and, because we are made in His image, He wants us to live holy too. This is yet another way in which a marriage relationship reflects the relationship of the members of the Godhead—the Trinity. The problem is that we often make it hard on ourselves. But there is no excuse; we must first know that the Lord Jesus freed us from the power of sin—and then act like we know it.

He wants us to understand that we can live sexually moral lives, married and single people alike. But it's up to us to rely on the Holy Spirit who operates in us to make the difference. He gives the power to fight off the temptation to do what we know is wrong. The Word of God informs us that we must yield ourselves to the Spirit of God to keep from being a victim to the fleshly desires that can so easily sway us. As a matter of fact, the only power that we should allow to have control over us is that of the Holy Spirit.

Sexual Immorality—What Is It?

Once I was asked, "Pastor, why is sex outside of marriage wrong? And, why can't people have sex with someone other than their spouse?" These questions were asked of me at a marriage seminar. They clearly indicate that some individuals have more than curiosity—they've got issues. I explained to the group that sex is the fence around marriage. Generally, if you won't stay outside the fence before marriage you won't stay inside the fence after marriage.

I further explained that marriage is a covenant. And a covenant is an agreement based on a relationship ratified by blood. So, God's ideal is a relationship that comes together with a virgin man and a virgin woman who get married. When they consummate their marriage with the sex act, the hymen is broken, the blood is shed, and the covenant is sealed. Sex then becomes like the ordinance of communion. It is a reminder of the covenant that you made with your spouse. Each time you have sex you renew the covenant.

Furthermore, sex is one of two cords that are designed to hold marriage together. It is commenced by the vow that initiates the covenant. For example, in my marriage it went like this:

I, James Ford Jr., take you, Leslie Ann Moore, to be my lawfully wedded wife. In sickness and in health, in poverty and in wealth, until death do us part.

Since sex is the act that establishes the covenant of marriage, a failure to remain faithful in the marriage covenant can be biblical grounds for divorce. According to Matthew 19:3–9, adultery is a violation of the "one-flesh commitment" made to your spouse before Almighty God, the Lord Jesus Christ, and the Holy Spirit. Therefore, the sexual act is more than physical; it is spiritual because God designed it be the Velcro that fastens two souls together.

So, let's be clear. We need to know what sexual immorality is lest we fall prey to it due to a lack of awareness of what it really means. This is no time to act as if we don't know any better. Because sexual immorality is a direct contradiction to God's commandment, it is a sin against God. When a marriage is at risk because someone has been unfaithful, the stakes are high and there is too much on the line. I'm talking here about the difference between living with sin in one's life and living in a way that is pleasing to God.

The subject of practicing purity is so very serious in God's mind that the Bible has a lot to say about it. When Paul wrote about sexual immorality, he used a Greek word from which we get the word *pornography*. This term covers a wide range of sexual activities that God abhors including premarital sex, lust, homosexuality, and adultery. So, let's talk about each one to get a better understanding of why God is not pleased with these sinful behaviors.

Premarital Sex

For singles who desire to please the Lord through their lifestyle, avoiding fornication is of paramount importance. Fornication distorts God's reason for purity. The Webster's Dictionary definition of this word is "consensual sexual intercourse between two persons not married to each other." The description is about as clear as it can be. If you find yourself within the words of this definition, it's time to repent.

Single people need to be aware that those involved in premarital sexual activities are putting their future marital relationship in grave danger. This type of immoral sexual conduct includes: masturbation, Internet porn, porn magazines, etc. These behaviors have the potential to frustrate an individual psychologically because of the effect it has on the imagination. When a person engages in these activities and then gets into a marital relationship it may be difficult for the marriage partners to be satisfied sexually because of the individual's previous perverted sexual experience.

Furthermore, since we know that God preserved sexual relations as one of the greatest benefits of marriage, within this context, pleasure is a privilege given by God as a part of the framework of marriage. That is why I tell single people that God is not keeping sex away from them; He is keeping sex for them. Although sex is to be reserved for marriage, many unmarried couples ignore this truth and make sex a necessity in their minds. They think they cannot live without sex and over prioritize the need for it.

But, I am here to tell you that you're getting yourself involved in more than you expect. If you are single, sex should not be a priority for you. Your first priority should be maintaining a strong personal relationship with the Lord so that He can help you keep all of your other priorities straight. Yet, some people will argue that they have to try sex out before they make a marriage commitment. Their reason is that you don't buy a car without testing it first. Well, first of all, this isn't about driving a car. This is about building a sound relationship. When you look at that logic, it doesn't make sense. How many people move into a home and then later sign the mortgage papers? You don't go to a restaurant and tell them you will eat their food and then decide if you want to pay for it.

The point is, God wants you to set the right priorities in your life. The life of Samson typifies a good example. His story is found in the book of Judges. Within the span of three chapters Samson went through three relationships. Clearly he didn't have his priorities straight. Sex had controlled this man until it dominated his attention. Finally, he came across a woman named Delilah who did him in. But we need to understand that his problem didn't begin with her. Instead, his problem led him to Delilah. They were not married, and they had no business being involved sexually. But, since he had made sex such a priority in his life, she used her feminine wiles against him and was able to completely deceive him. Unfortunately, Samson allowed sex to essentially destroy his life.

If you could ask Samson, he would tell you—sex can fool you. There are many people who were actually in lust when they thought they were in love. That's because sex doesn't belong in a premarital situation. There are many people who hooked up with somebody and had sex only later to find out that the relationship was based on a superficial reason because sex cannot keep a relationship together. No matter how good it is. If you don't believe it, talk to somebody who has been in that type of relationship. You will find out that such relationships are empty and they soon grow old and tired.

Lust

These are some extremely sobering words from the mouth of Jesus: *"But I say to you that everyone who looks at a woman with lust for her has already committed adultery with her in his heart"* (Matthew 5:28).

Just in case anyone is confused and so that there is no misunderstanding, our Lord was making it clear that a person can mentally commit adultery simply by looking at someone with a desire to engage in sex with the individual. And in the mind of God, that is equivalent to performing the act.

Jesus made it very clear that lust and adultery are very close friends. But, lusting after someone is something that can be controlled because it begins in one's mind. However, if you don't find a way to overcome it, you have to deal with the serious repercussions of following after every whim of your flesh. When you allow your mind to feed your flesh you will lose every time. That is why it is so important to live every day with a determination to follow the Holy Spirit. You have to wake up in the morning and make a conscious decision that you will obey God *this* and every day. But that in itself is not enough; it is just the starting point. You must do something really radical: take out your Bible to renew your mind and feed your spirit with the Word of God.

The apostle James explained how lust and temptation lead to sin and death and ultimately destroy a person. Let me caution you, this is risky business; so beware.

> *"But each one is tempted when he is carried away and enticed by his own lust. Then when lust has conceived, it gives birth to sin; and when sin is accomplished, it brings forth death."*
>
> —JAMES 1:14–15

Do you see the progression of the effect lust has when it is allowed to take its own course? When you give the Spirit of God control of your actions, you don't satisfy the lust that is waiting for an opportunity to take you down the dark path of destruction.

Homosexuality

What does our Lord have to say about homosexuality? It is a sin. It goes against the very nature that God created for the male and female genders. Consequently, when people give in to unnatural displays of passion, God unequivocally condemns their actions. As Paul's words graphically describe the seriousness of the sin of homosexuality, notice he asserts that there is a penalty involved for those who choose to participate in homosexual activity:

> *"For this reason God gave them over to degrading passions; for their women exchanged the natural function for that which is unnatural, and in the same way also the men abandoned the natural function of the woman and burned in their desire toward one another, men with men committing indecent acts and receiving in their own persons the due penalty of their error."*
> —ROMANS 1:26–27

Paul then goes on to proclaim that God's righteousness will prevail in the end. God will not be mocked or tricked into compromising His standard for holiness.

> *"Or do you not know that the unrighteous will not inherit the kingdom of God? Do not be deceived; neither fornicators, nor idolaters, nor adulterers, nor effeminate, nor homosexuals . . . will inherit the kingdom of God."*
> —1 CORINTHIANS 6:9–10

Here God's Word is asking a direct question about a fundamental knowledge that we must absolutely be clear on. It is a challenging question, to say the least, but Paul knows what is at stake for anyone who falls into the category of people who will not inherit God's kingdom. In other words, God has promised us, if we live in the righteousness we have through His Son, Jesus, we will be a part of the program He has established for our future with Him. We should be confident when we act in obedience to God's Word and submit to His will that God will bless us indeed. This is not just a good idea; it is the path to victory in life. No matter your age or station in life, God is looking to believers to be an example for others to emulate. You may never know how your chaste words and actions could have a positive influence on someone who is living on the edge of sexual immorality.

To that end, God would have all believers follow Paul's instructions: *"In speech, conduct, love, faith and purity, show yourself an example of those who believe"* (1 Timothy 4:12).

Adultery

Jesus pointed out that adultery is the only reason that God permits divorce (Matthew 19:9). The reason God allows divorce in this instance is that adultery is extramarital sex; meaning sexual activity that takes place outside of a marriage. As much as God hates divorce, He detests adultery because it is a serious offense against the sanctity and purity of marriage. That is why our Lord was very specific in saying that divorce for any other reason puts the former marriage partners at the risk of committing adultery when they engage in sex with new partners. Listen to the commandment of God:

> *"You shall not commit adultery. . . . You shall not covet your neighbor's house; you shall not covet your neighbor's wife."*
> —Exodus 20:14, 17

In today's society, believe it or not, it has become rather fashionable in some circles for husbands and wives to have extramarital affairs. What is an affair? An affair is an addiction to another person that begins to take control over the two involved. A wife or a husband who has an affair allows the devil to launch an attack on that marriage. Proverbs 6:32 (NKJV) asserts that an adulterer doesn't understand what he is getting into. It goes so far as to issue a warning that whoever commits adultery "destroys his own soul." That's why God says don't enter into it.

When it comes to indulging in affairs, marriages are at the risk of becoming yet another divorce statistic. But God wants us to maintain sexual

purity and preserve our marriages. That is why His Word clearly states in 1 Corinthians 7:2 that *"every man ought to have his own wife and every wife
should have her own husband."* For this reason, we must make a commitment to faithfulness and behave according to this instruction. But for those
who are still not convinced that we should take God's Word seriously, listen to the counsel we have been given as the Bible makes the case against
adultery:

> *"Drink water from your own cistern and fresh water from your
> own well. Should your springs be dispersed abroad, streams of
> water in the streets? Let them be yours alone and not for strangers
> with you. Let your fountain be blessed, and rejoice in the wife of
> your youth. As a loving hind and a graceful doe, let her breasts
> satisfy you at all times; be exhilarated always with her love.
> For why should you, my son, be exhilarated with an
> adulteress and embrace the bosom of a foreigner?"*
> —PROVERBS 5:15–20

Moreover, bringing an affair into one's marriage not only breaks the
bond between husband and wife, it severs the relationship with God and
places the adulterer outside of fellowship with Him. To that end, the apostle James was tough on the subject of adultery:

> *"You adulteresses, do you not know that friendship with the world
> is hostility toward God? Therefore whoever wishes to be
> a friend of the world makes himself an enemy of God. . . .
> But He gives a greater grace. Therefore it says, 'God is
> opposed to the proud, but gives grace to the humble.'"*
> —JAMES 4:4, 6

James is asking a very pointed question here to cause believers to think
before they do the wrong thing. However, there is hope for people who go
astray; the Word of God has the power to transform anyone's misguided actions. He is reminding us that we have a weapon called grace that God freely

supplies. When we are confronted with temptation, grace gives us the power to side with God. James goes on to tell us how to do it in verse 7: *"Submit therefore to God. Resist the devil and he will flee from you."* The secret is in drawing closer to God and, in turn, God promises that He will draw closer to us. And, guess what? The closer you are to God, the farther away the enemy will be from you.

In fact, looking at Jesus Christ as the supreme example we see the epitome of purity. We are the bride of Christ and, rest assured, Jesus does not commit adultery on His church. When anyone chooses adultery, they are siding with the ways of the world. They not only reject their spouse, they are turning their back on Christ. Our Lord would say to the guilty ones, "You are married to me; how dare you jump into bed with the world? You are My wife, how dare you uncover yourself for somebody else?" My question is, "How do you look Jesus in the face and answer those charges?"

The Body Is the Lord's

Because we belong to God, we cannot allow sex to hex our destiny. Through our association with Christ, believers have been set apart from sin, and engaging in illicit sex will only interfere with our fellowship with God. The Bible says we should abstain from premarital and extramarital relationships and remain pure in our relationships. I don't know about you, but I'd rather fulfill God's plans for me rather than any ideas I could dream up on my own. Our finite minds are so limited, but God knows the beginning from the end. For a few fleeting moments of pleasure, trust me, it's not worth spoiling the joyous banquet God has planned for us in the end. It's only a matter of waiting on God's timing that will allow us to partake of His promise that we will spend eternity with Him.

Scripture gives several reasons to avoid sexual immorality. These are found in 1 Corinthians, chapter 6.

1. Sex has the power to control you

As I mentioned earlier, God gave sex a specific purpose. Therefore, it is against God's law for unmarried people to get involved in sex before marriage and for married people to engage in sex outside the marriage. For either group, there is an equal amount of danger in playing with it. Think of sex as a heavy-duty power tool. If you use it for anything other than its intended purpose, you run the risk of causing much harm. And so many people are messed up because they entered into premarital sexual relationships. As a result, they gave sex the potential to control them. When an unmarried person is involved in sexual activity they are taking advantage of a powerful tool that God intends to be used only within the confines of marriage.

On the other hand, so many marriages have been devastated because a married person has no business engaging in sex with anyone other than their spouse. They are giving sex power over them that it must not have. I say that sex is the Velcro of the soul, but Jesus explained it this way: *"The two shall become one flesh."* However you put it, it is a serious matter; a married person who is involved in extramarital sex has joined themselves with someone else. Now, sex has the power to destroy that marriage.

But God has a desire for purity that will prevent this kind of control from wreaking havoc in the lives of believers when we adhere to His instruction. Let me give you some background into Paul's teaching on the subject of purity. He was addressing the Corinthian church at the time but his message applies to all believers—both married and unmarried:

> *"All things are lawful for me, but not all things are profitable. All things are lawful for me, but I will not be mastered by anything."*
>
> —1 CORINTHIANS 6:12

The church at Corinth was in a sexually obsessed culture. The situation was so extreme that on the Acropolis at Corinth there was a temple dedicated to Aphrodite, the goddess of fertility. Part of the ritual for worshiping her was indulging in sex. In fact, the city had one thousand temple prostitutes whose entire purpose was to service the male worshippers. In this verse, Paul was responding to the argument that the people gave for justifying their sinful behavior. They had created an atmosphere where everything was acceptable; it was a "do your own thing; do whatever feels good" kind of society. But Paul argued that even though he was free to choose, he would not be mastered, or controlled, by anything—including sex. And they should not be either.

A little later in chapter 7, Paul responded to another group of people in the church who had an opposite view. They believed that everything related to the physical senses was evil. Some of the wives were following this erroneous teaching, which suggested that practicing celibacy was the more spiritual way. As a result, these misguided wives had a perpetual "headache" when it came to having sexual relations with their husbands. So, when a wife would say that she had a headache, her husband would go up on the mountain to "worship." The men argued that God made man a sexual being, and, subsequently, man was free to exercise his sexual prowess.

But the apostle told them that they were both wrong. In 1 Corinthians 7:3, he instructed these wives to give themselves to their husbands. He also said that the husbands should give themselves only to their wives so that the devil would not have an opportunity to interfere in their marriages. Paul was warning them of the danger of not fulfilling each other's sexual needs.

What the Corinthians really didn't understand, and what you need to know, is that whenever people decide to enter into a sexual relationship, they are essentially creating a soul tie. Sex is like cement because it seals the marriage vows. The sexual bond is a controlling factor and once that bond is created it is not to be broken. God designed sex so that married couples could enter into a uniquely intimate experience, and He reserved it for marriage. He made it that way so that individuals would have a desire for their spouse alone. God expects it to be an exclusive relationship where the partners not only treat each other with mutual respect but also engage each other sexually—something they are not to do with anybody else.

There was another common saying of the people in the Corinthian church that Paul mentioned in 1 Corinthians 6:13: *"Food is for the stomach and the stomach is for food."* By this they meant that just as eating food was a necessary part of life, having sex was also. They thought there was no difference—food and the stomach were made for each other. So, they used a similar comparison to sex being for the body and the body for sex. This is how they justified their freedom to have sex outside of their marriages. God had given them the ability and the equipment, and they wanted to use it. And as long as it felt good they thought they should be able to do it.

Paul was trying to correct their faulty thinking. He pointed out that God did not make their bodies for immoral purposes; rather, God made their bodies to reflect His own pattern of purity. He warned them that what they were doing was, in fact, immoral and following after their erroneous thinking would bring them under the power of sex. And that would ultimately destroy them.

You have to be very careful with this. If you are single and you get involved in sex before you are married, you will only be deceived into thinking that you have something that you really don't have. And, just like the king's subjects that were hungry and didn't follow his instructions to wait for the proper time before indulging, it won't be a blessing for you—all you'll get is garbage. That is because God created sex to be the icing on the cake of a marital union. It is not meant to be enjoyed in a premarital state.

Furthermore, sex is more addictive than crack cocaine because it becomes a stronghold. That is why it is so easy to recall your first sexual encounter; especially if it was pleasurable. You probably remember the person, the place, the time. It may even still make you smile—because of the powerful impression that it left on you. Why do you think there are some women who will allow men to do anything to them that they want? A man can abuse a woman and she will excuse it by saying that he loves her. Some men allow women to dog them out by blindly thinking that the women are actually showing them love. Why is that? Sex has the power given by God to bind one individual to another because that is the purpose of it. When those two individuals are not married, sex has an adverse effect; it will cause them to lose control of their will. It will make them do something they should not do—be bound to someone other than their spouse.

Now, I know what you are probably saying: "I don't understand. Are you trying to tell me that sex outside of marriage is not enjoyable?" Of course, it is enjoyable. You may also be asking, "Are you trying to tell me that sex outside of marriage is not exciting?" No, I'm not telling you that. Here's what I'm telling you. Paul says that all things are lawful but not everything edifies you. You may get excitement from sex outside of marriage, you may get enjoyment, but you don't get enrichment. You don't get the full benefit of what it was designed to do.

2. Sex will pass away

Paul wanted the Corinthian church to see that their argument about food and the stomach could not stand. He was warning them that God will destroy both the meat and the stomach that consumes it. That is what he referred to in verse 13 when he said, *"God will do away with both of them."* The same goes for sex and the body. So, I've got good news and bad news. Sex, my friend, is only for this life. It is for marriage in this life; it is not for the next life. God doesn't want us to put an overemphasis on sex because it is only temporary.

In fact, at some point in our human nature, the desire for sex begins to fade. It seems as though the older you get the less sex you want. Ecclesiastes 12:5 alludes to a time in life when sexual desire begins to wane. That's most likely because when you get old, not having sex is the least of your worries.

Scripture also says there is no sex in heaven. In the book of Matthew chapter 22, Jesus is talking to the Sadducees about the resurrection. They posed a question to Jesus about a man who had seven brothers. The first brother died and had no children. He left his wife to his brother. The second, third, and so on all passed away until the seventh brother died. The woman eventually died also. So, in verse 28 they asked Jesus, *"In the resurrection . . . whose wife . . . will she be? For they all had married her."* Jesus responded to them: *"You are mistaken, not understanding the Scriptures nor the power of God. For in the resurrection they neither marry nor are given in marriage, but are like angels of God in heaven"* (Matthew 22:29–30).

Jesus set them straight. There will be no husband and wife thing in heaven—only angelic-like beings that will enjoy the privilege of worshiping God for eternity. But I do have a hypothesis about sex that I want to share. I don't have chapter and verse, but it is what I personally believe. The mutual expression of orgasm in marriage was given to us by God so that we would have a foretaste of the ecstasy of what it will be like in heaven.

Everything about marriage points to God the Father, God the Son, and God the Holy Spirit. Right? However, ecstasy is not necessary for procreation; we could produce babies without it. So then, why would God make ecstasy a part of having sex? I believe it is because He wants us to enjoy it, to have fun with it while we're here on earth. I could be wrong. I know that experiencing heaven will be far better. Imagine the kind of feeling we will have standing before Jesus in a perfect body and in a perfect place. Doesn't that sound ecstatic to you? I get excited and feel chill bumps just thinking about it.

3. The body belongs to Jesus

Our bodies belong to the Lord and so do our marriages. In fact, everything in this life was made by Him and for Him. And we know that God is the One who made marriage and sex a priority. Because of this, God is looking for us to glorify Him with our bodies and our marriages.

In 1 Corinthians 6:13, Paul also confirms, *"Yet the body is not for immorality, but for the Lord, and the Lord is for the body."* Since God did not create our bodies for immoral purposes, no one has the right to take something that He placed in a position of prominence in the marriage union and put it on the bottom shelf of their relationship. Don't be found guilty of shortchanging your spouse; God is not pleased with that kind of attitude and behavior and neither is your mate.

4. A purpose for God

God gave sex as a marriage partnership seal, and we are also sealed in a relationship with Jesus. Paul asks the question in verse 15, *"Do you not know that your bodies are members of Christ?"* It was his way of reminding the church that their bodies are a part of Christ's body. We are the bride of Christ and members of His church. Our main purpose is to glorify God and be in constant fellowship with Him. To please our Lord, we have to have clean hands and a pure heart. Don't taint yourself by flirting with temptation and end up bringing shame on God and yourself.

This is what I say to fornicators and adulterers: The next time you get into bed and have sex with somebody that is not your spouse, imagine that Jesus is there in the middle of the two of you. He is there anyway; you just need to think about it. Whenever you engage in fornication or adultery you're going to hear the words playing in your mind, *Jesus is right here with me.*

There is a scene in the movie *Mystic Pizza* where the guy was getting ready to get it on and he looked up and there was this bust that was supposed to be an image of Jesus. He said he couldn't go through with it with Jesus looking at him. Jesus is looking at you too! He sees you. He knows what you are doing. He knows what's going on.

5. There are penalties to incur

We are the property of the Holy Spirit who asks, "How can you take that which doesn't belong to you and give it to somebody else?" We belong to God and we will be judged accordingly. That is why the marriage ceremony is performed in the sight of God so that He can acknowledge and ordain the union. God is a part of your marriage whether you recognize that fact or not. Hebrews 13:4 is a clear warning to those who ignore or refuse to accept the truth of God's Word:

> *"Marriage is to be held in honor among all, and the marriage bed is to be undefiled; for fornicators and adulterers God will judge."*

6. Jesus paid the price for you—spirit, soul, and body

Don't take any part of you and give it to anybody that Jesus didn't tell you to give it to. We are no longer slaves to sin because of Him. He is the main reason why you should remain pure and avoid sexual immorality. Jesus is talking to His bride, the church, when He says that friendship with the world is enmity against God. "You're married to Me," He says. "How dare you jump into bed with the world? You are my wife, how dare you uncover yourself for somebody else?"

Finally, allow me to conclude by sounding the alarm: Sex is like fire. In the fireplace, fire is romantic; it is pleasing to the senses and creates an atmosphere of love and warmth. However, fire on the curtains and fire on the couch is destructive and can ultimately burn your house down. People of God, take heed so that you will not be found guilty forfeiting the precious gift of salvation that the Son of God made possible when He took us for His bride. Cherish Him with all your heart, mind, body, and soul.

Making It Happen

We need to protect our marriages by placing hedges around it. To do this, there are principles that will facilitate the priorities of your marriage relationship and keep you accountable to each other.

- Protect your circle of intimacy. A circle of intimacy is the areas of oneness that you exclusively share with your spouse. Certain subjects of conversation and intimate details should never be shared with anyone other than your spouse.

- Be very careful about lunch or dinner occasions with coworkers of the opposite sex. Also avoid counseling sessions or even casual conversations that could form an emotional attachment.

- Don't give your cell number to members of the opposite sex. Have them call your home unless you utilize your cell phone for business purposes. In that case, you should implement an accountability plan with your spouse by showing him, or her, the monthly cell phone bill. Remember the old adage: "An ounce of prevention is worth a pound of cure." I know to some of you this reads like your spouse is checking up on you, but this is important enough for you to set aside your pride. If you know you're going to show it to your spouse it will keep your trust factor high.

I think the following story illustrates my point quite well!

I remember the time when a woman at the health club asked me for my telephone number. She wanted to talk to me about buying some vitamins. I told her, in order to do that, I'd have to ask my wife's permission. She asked me why, as a grown man, I would have to get my wife's permission.

Then she said, "I don't want you, all I want to do is sell some vitamins."

I told her that it had nothing to do with her. My wife and I have made a commitment to each other that we don't give our numbers to anyone without the other's permission.

"Never mind, Bro," she said.

When I arrived home, I recounted the incident to my wife, Leslie. She then told me to tell the woman to call her regarding the vitamins. The next day at the health club I gave the number to this woman whom I will refer to as Debbie. I told her my wife said she could call her and talk about purchasing the vitamins. Debbie did call and my wife purchased over $100 worth of vitamins from her.

Several weeks later, my wife accompanied me to the club to work out with me. She went to change in the locker room and I waited for her. Debbie came over and started talking to me. When my wife came back out, she walked up and said, "Hey, honey." Then she spoke to Debbie and called her by name.

After the conversation was over, I asked my wife had she met Debbie since their phone conversation or did she just happen to recognize her voice. She said that she hadn't met her and didn't really know her voice.

So, I then asked her, "How did you know it was Debbie?"

She explained, "I saw her proximity to you and her body language as she talked to you. I said to myself that she had to be Debbie."

"WOW!" I exclaimed, "Good guess!"

"No," my wife said. "It wasn't just a good guess. And you'd better watch out for her because she is very interested in you!"

I thought to myself, *Jesus, thank You for giving me the wisdom to enter into covenant with my wife on issues that have the potential to destroy the trust in our relationship.* Then I wondered, *What if I had not shared with my wife and she would have seen this woman talking to me.* The situation might have ended quite differently. Like, my wife asking, "Who was that? She was flittering around you like a butterfly." And me responding, "Oh, that was Debbie." There's no telling where it would have gone after that, but thank God we were proactive rather than reactive. Yes, an ounce of prevention is truly worth a pound of cure!

The psalmist leaves us with a fitting sentiment that describes how walking in God's desire for purity will be a blessing worth having:

"The Lord has rewarded me according to my righteousness;
according to the cleanness of my hands He has recompensed me.
For I have kept the ways of the Lord, and have not wickedly
departed from my God. For all His ordinances were before me, and
I did not put away His statutes from me. I was also blameless with
Him, and I kept myself from my iniquity. Therefore the
Lord has recompensed me according to my righteousness,
according to the cleanness of my hands in His eyes."

—PSALM 18:20–24

Reason #7

A Picture of
Christ *and*
His Church
Produces a
Spiritual Reflection

A couple once came to me for counseling. After four sessions of hearing negative talk, I surmised that Michael was not loving his wife, Elaine, with the unconditional love of Christ. I told him that the Bible says we must love our wives like Christ loves the church. I explained to him that the Bible speaks about three different kinds of love: *philos* is affectionate love, *eros* is erotic love, and *agape* is unconditional love.

When I concluded my teaching on love, Michael said to me, "Pastor, I can't love her like that."

I responded to him, "Then, the Bible says to love her like a sister in Christ."

He repeated again, "But, Pastor, I can't love her like that."

So, I said to him, "The Bible says to love her like a friend."

He said to me, "I can't even love her like that."

My response to him was, "Then, love her like an enemy because the Bible tells us to love our enemies."

Surprisingly, to that assertion he replied, "Okay, I'll start there."

But I shocked him when I told him that it didn't matter whether he loved Elaine as Christ loved the church, as a sister, as a friend, or as an enemy.

Even though marriage needs all forms of love to survive, the agape kind of love covers it all. If you love everyone, including your spouse, with the God kind of love, you are taking into consideration everything about that person. It is a selfless love that asks for nothing in return. I guarantee you will be immensely blessed if you read the complete description of agape love that is found in 1 Corinthians chapter 13.

I am glad that Jesus loves us with an unconditional love. Through His love for us we have the assurance that He would never leave us or forsake us. When we do as God commands and love our wives as Christ loves the church, we love each other the way that Jesus loves us.

That is how we become imitators of God!

A Spiritual Reflection

> *"Therefore be imitators of God, as beloved children; and walk in love, just as Christ also loved you and gave Himself up for us, an offering and a sacrifice to God as a fragrant aroma."*
> —EPHESIANS 5:1–2

We began this discussion of the seven reasons why God created marriage with a parallel of a human relationship to the pattern of the Trinity. We end now with the picture of Christ and His relationship with His bride, the church. That means we've come full circle in demonstrating how a marriage partnership is a spiritual reflection of God's Trinity and Christ's relationship with His bride, the church.

God made us in His image. If we are to imitate Him, we must walk in the power and love that He gave us and behave like our Creator God. So, when you look at a husband and wife and the relationship that they build together, that is what you should see—a reflection of God's image. What does that mean? Imagine a portrait of you and your spouse hanging on a wall. That is a picture of your marriage. Now, think about the marriage partnership between Jesus Christ and His church. If you form a picture of that image in your mind and envision it side by side with your marriage portrait, the two pictures should look very similar. When your marriage lines up with God's reasons for marriage, that's what you will see. From God's perspective, if you belong to Him, your life and your marriage are intended to produce a picture of Christ and His church.

Allow me to draw your attention to something quite profound and exciting to discover about this rather complex subject. The spiritual reflection of marriage is most clearly seen in this earthly realm through the tradition of a Jewish wedding. Therefore, the Jewish wedding custom that began in ancient times still holds significance today as it exemplifies the marriage between Christ and His church.

The spiritual picture that was presented when Jesus embraced His bride, the church, follows the steps of the ancient Jewish wedding custom. From the beginning of time, the children of Israel were destined to be God's chosen people. As such, their way of living—their culture and customs—was directly informed by God who is the originator of all life. As you read on, you will discover the fascinating way in which their wedding practices demonstrate the pattern between the dynamics of an earthly human relationship and the divine deity of the Almighty God.

We need to understand this because it has everything to do with how God intends our marriages to mirror the relationship between Christ and His church. The following description summarizes the coming together of a typical Jewish marriage. Although there are many other details of the matrimony process I believe you will be able to see how we connect to the spiritual and natural elements of the following phases.

Phase #1

The *Mohar* or the Bride Price. This stage of the marriage process occurred when the father of the groom and the intended bride's parents held a discussion about a potential marriage. The bride's father asked, "What will you pay for my daughter?" And the groom's father said, "I will pay you whatever you want. What do you want?" Then together they decided on the bride price, which was paid by the father of the groom and symbolically represented the value of the bride. It was intended to provide a measure of compensation to the bride's family for the loss of her contribution to her family's welfare. The price to be paid was also an expression of the groom's love for her in tangible terms.

Phase #2

The *Kiddushin* or Betrothal. In ancient times, this was the engagement process. You will notice there are some stark distinctions between how we go about becoming engaged today. In fact, if you compare couples from the days of old to contemporary couples, I believe that the main difference involves the level of commitment being made or the lack thereof.

Now, check this out. The groom wrote a binding contract that would become a marriage covenant if accepted by the bride and her father. The bride price, the bride's rights, and the promises of the groom were included in this document, called a *Ketubah*. To find out if his proposal was accepted, the groom would pour a cup of wine for him and his bride to be. Then, he waited to see if she would drink from it. If she drank from this common cup, called the cup of acceptance, it signified that she agreed to his proposal, and they would become betrothed, or engaged. Once the covenant was sealed, the young man would offer her gifts symbolizing his love for her and then take his leave. But before he left he would tell his betrothed, "I am going to prepare a place for you, and I will return for you when it is ready."

As she waited in anticipation for his return, the bride would be making her own preparations. His arrival would be unpredictable since he could come on any given day, so she spent her time preparing herself to be pure and beautiful for her new husband. The young lady underwent a purification bath, called a *mikvah*, which was considered to be a necessary sacred ritual. During her time of waiting she would wear a veil whenever she went out into public. This was to symbolize that she had been bought with a price.

Phase #3

The *Huppah* (Hometaking) or Wedding Nuptials. By today's standards, there was a lengthy preparation process that the groom had to complete. After gaining consent from his fiancé, the groom returned to his father's home to prepare a place for her. He would build a honeymoon room, or bridal chamber, referred to as the *huppah*. The bride chamber was a special place that would "cover" the happy couple during their honeymoon as they consummated the marriage.

Another word for the *huppah* is *hometaking* because it represented the time when the groom brought his wife to their new home. Because of its great importance, the huppah would have to meet with his father's approval before the groom could consider it ready for his bride. Therefore, it was the groom's father who determined when his son could return for his bride. While he was assembling the huppah, if anyone asked him about the date of his wedding, he would reply, "Only my father knows."

It could take up to one year for the groom to return for her. She was aware of this and busied herself making all the appropriate arrangements. She faithfully wore her veil and kept her lamp close by. She packed her belongings and set them at her bedside, waiting for him to come for her. When he arrived, it would be around midnight. That's why it was necessary to have her lamp ready. Her bridesmaids waited with her and knew the importance of having an oil supply for their lamps as well. During this lengthy time of waiting, her anticipation continued to build, and it often became a test of the young lady's faith in his promise. It was not uncommon for a young woman to begin to doubt or worry whether he would in fact return.

When the wedding chamber was finally ready, the groom led an entourage with a trumpet player in front of him. When they got close to her house, he signaled for the trumpet, or *shofar*, to blow and his party of followers would all give a shout. She heard the trumpet sound and knew that he was near. With much joy, she immediately proceeded to run and meet her beloved. They would then travel back to his father's house to begin the honeymoon celebration.

The couple went into the wedding chamber, the huppah, to begin a seven-day honeymoon. They placed a cloth, called the garment of virginity, over the bed and consummated the marriage. Her hymen was broken and blood was shed. This represented the blood covenant of the marriage partners.

After the seven days ended, the groom folded the cloth and emerged from the room. He lifted it up in his hands and said, "Huppah," with his bride standing behind him. The cloth was called "the garment of virginity." He then presented it to her father who preserved it in safekeeping. If the groom ever wanted to divorce his daughter, the father could produce the garment of virginity as proof of their blood covenant. This ritual signified proof that she was a virgin when they married and he could not divorce her. The explanation for this is taken from the book of Deuteronomy chapter 22, verses 13–19, which states that a man could divorce his wife if she had not been a virgin when she married him. That's why it was necessary for her father to produce the garment of virginity; it was evidence that the marriage covenant should not be broken.

Finally, before the happy couple joined their guests for the wedding feast to begin, they would dress in fine clothing as a king and queen, complete with crowns on their heads. It was an elaborate and joyous occasion. After the feast ended, the couple lived together as one. As evidenced by this account, God intended the husband to provide for and protect his wife from the very beginning.

The Picture of Christ Revealed

"For God so loved the world, that He gave His only begotten Son, that whoever believes in Him shall not perish, but have eternal life."
—JOHN 3:16

God loved us enough to make a huge sacrifice on our behalf. There is nothing in our human lives that supersedes this truth. And so, we must recognize the significance of the God-ordained practice of matrimony that began so long ago to understand how it directly relates to our lives today. As we search, we will find God's love that is portrayed through the picture of Christ and what He sacrificed for the church. Through the work of Jesus to make salvation a reality for man, we know that God lovingly addressed our need for provision and protection.

When Adam fell into sin, all of mankind fell along with him. But through Jesus Christ, God has given us protection from sin and death. At the same time, He has given us the provision of life in eternity with Him. No doubt about it, if it were not for Jesus Christ, our Lord and Savior, we would be on the road to destruction and there would be no way of avoiding it. But God's generous love and abundant mercy rescued us.

Man's sin and subsequent need for redemption prompted God to provide a salvation plan as the answer for humanity. Two prominent priorities stood out: (1) the Sovereign God showed His boundless love for man; and, (2) as the Savior of man, God would get all the praise. In other words, because of His rescue plan, God receives glory and we receive the benefit of His enduring mercy and love.

So, here is how the plan of salvation goes. God the Father required a blood sacrifice to atone for man's sins. He established what was necessary as a sacrifice on mankind's behalf by saying, *"For the life of the flesh is in the blood, and I have given it to you on the altar to make atonement for your souls; for it is the blood by reason of the life that makes atonement"* (Leviticus 17:11). This Scripture is telling us that, under the old covenant, God accepted animal sacrifices and their shed blood as a means of compensation for man's sins. The only problem was that this form of sacrifice had to be continuously repeated because the blood of animals was a sacrifice of an earthly nature and, therefore, had a limited effect. As a result, it was an insufficient means by which to ultimately satisfy a holy God. The intent was there but each sacrificial act was rendered inadequate by its natural limitations.

Fast forwarding to the New Testament, Jesus changed all of that. Because He is the Son of God, the offering of His own life was a sufficient sacrifice that would allow God to forgive man's sins once and for all. The life that Jesus lived in the flesh held the blood that was necessary for atonement. It was a more excellent sacrifice by which the holy God could forgive a sinful man. What that means is under the new covenant God would accept Jesus' shed blood in exchange for man's forgiveness. The writer of Hebrews explained it this way: *"And according to the Law, one may almost say, all things are cleansed with blood, and without shedding of blood there is no forgiveness"* (Hebrews 9:22).

Out of His love and obedience to the Father, the Son of God agreed to shed His blood and become the Savior of humanity. Here is where the analogy to the ancient wedding custom stands out in remarkable fashion.

The Bride Price

To redeem man, the Son said to the Father, "I will take a bride. She will be called the church. What do you want for her, Father?" The Father asked

Him, "Will you pay the blood as the bride price for the church?" Jesus, the Son of God, said, "Yes, I will." When He accepted the bride price that the Father required, Jesus shed His blood on Calvary's cross and paid the ultimate price for our sins. Scripture explains what took place when the apostle Peter wrote to the early church:

> *"Knowing that you were not redeemed with perishable things like silver or gold from your futile way of life inherited from your forefathers, but with precious blood, as of a lamb unblemished and spotless, the blood of Christ."*
>
> —1 PETER 1:18–19

When our Lord took the church as His bride, He gave His life to redeem us. He became our bride price, our spiritual *mohar*. This is how we became the body of Christ: The wisdom of the Holy Spirit dictated that every one who believes in the redemptive work of Christ would be assembled together as one body and collectively represents the body of Christ. Jesus paid with His very life, which is the highest value that could be demanded of anyone. In doing so, Jesus expressed His supreme love for us and gave us the most priceless gift ever to be received. In His own words, He said, *"Greater love has no one than this, that one lay down his life for his friends"* (John 15:13). You may ask, "What can wash away your sins?" And what can make you whole again? The definitive answer remains—nothing but the blood of Jesus.

We were bought with a price—we belong to Jesus. It is so important to know what the Word of God has to say about who we are. Taking the time to learn God's Word comes down to the difference between success and failure in life. What could possibly be more important than life itself? The apostle Paul reminds the church that we were bought with a price and that we should no longer be slaves to sin. We are married to our Lord Jesus and, therefore, we must not be found guilty of adultery. That is, we must be careful not to get in too close to worldly desires and practices. Yet, it is difficult to remain faithful to God without a steady diet of applying the knowledge and instruction that will help us stay in God's good graces.

The apostle James understood this as a fundamental truth and warned the church. He said to those who had given themselves to Christ and received

Him as their Savior, *"You adulteresses, do you not know that friendship with the world is hostility toward God? Therefore whoever wishes to be a friend of the world makes himself an enemy of God"* (James 4:4). He was talking to the bride of Christ and speaking in defense of our Lord. As children of God, we never want to be found guilty of having Jesus say, "You are married to Me, how dare you jump into bed with the world? You are My wife, how dare you uncover yourself for someone else?" Because we belong to Him, we must take heed to this warning and be careful not to fall prey to the enticements of this world. We have been made free to give God the glory that He deserves and honor Him with our whole heart and soul (see 1 Corinthians 6:19–20).

The blood sacrifice that Jesus made for us was the fulfillment of the will of God. Something very crucial occurred when Jesus set about redeeming man. He separated us from sin and set us apart to Himself. Our sanctification was confirmed in the book of Hebrews: *"By this will we have been sanctified through the offering of the body of Jesus Christ once for all"* (Hebrews 10:10). So, since we have been sanctified, we are also purified by the blood of Christ and the washing of His Word. We would not be worthy of God's forgiveness if it were not for the work of Christ. Listen to how Paul describes it for us:

"But you were washed, but you were sanctified,
but you were justified in the name of the Lord Jesus Christ
and in the Spirit of our God."
—1 Corinthians 6:11

The Betrothal

During the spiritual *kiddushin*, the engagement phase, Jesus wrote out the contract that would obtain His bride and the deal was sealed. That agreement between the Father and Son is recorded in the New Testament. When we accept Christ as our Savior, we are betrothed to our Lord. Jesus gathered His church around Him and offered the cup of communion to symbolize our acceptance of His binding covenant (see Romans 8:1–6). Just as the groom of old offered the cup of acceptance to his bride to be, Jesus wants us to drink of His cup often in remembrance of Him (see Matthew 26:27–28). Because He was willing to pay the price, as His bride, we have been given certain rights and spiritual blessings, even the promise to spend eternal life with Him (see Romans 11; Galatians 3:13–14).

After the cup of acceptance was administered, Jesus went away to His Father's house to prepare a place for His bride. Still, He was following the tradition of the groom of old. However, before He left, He gave His bride, the body of Christ, a comforting promise to hold on to until He returns.

> "Do not let your heart be troubled; believe in God, believe also in Me. In My Father's house are many dwelling places; if it were not so, I would have told you; for I go to prepare a place for you. If I go and prepare a place for you, I will come again and receive you to Myself, that where I am, there you may be also."
> —JOHN 14:1–3

In the meantime while we await His return, we are to remain the faithful bride and live according to the instructions, the Word of God, that will keep us. We are the bride in waiting, and there are preparations for us to make. We are to live pure lives and continue to wash ourselves in the Word of God. We must remember at all times who we belong to because we have been bought with a price.

Even though we have been washed, sanctified, and justified, Jesus knew that we would have some challenging times while we wait for His return. In the meantime, just as the bride of ancient times, our attention is to be focused on preparing for Him to come back for us. Once again, Jesus did not leave us helpless. He knows that life can get extremely hard sometimes, and He sympathizes with our frailties and weaknesses. Jesus was tempted in His own human nature, so, it should bring us comfort to know that we can always go to Him in prayer when we have fallen short and missed the mark.

Yes, the body of Christ has been set apart, sanctified to Christ by our heavenly Father. Even so, the apostle Paul understood this and showed some concern about the faithfulness of the church as they waited in their day for Jesus to return. He spoke to them as their spiritual father: "For I am jealous for you with a godly jealousy; for I betrothed you to one husband, so that to

Christ I might present you as a pure virgin" (2 Corinthians 11:2).

For this reason, Jesus sent us the Holy Spirit to keep us on track while we wait on Him to return. The Spirit of God provides us with comfort and companionship to help us steer clear of the obstacles and hindrances that would otherwise make us forget who we are in Christ. The Holy Spirit has equipped us with the confidence that we need in God to stay away from those who teach false doctrine. There are those who would even tell us that Jesus is not coming back for His bride. You've got to know in your heart and keep your faith built up so that you don't fall for the enemy's lies.

There is a human tendency to do things that we later regret; sometimes we say things in a moment of anger, but later we can't take them back. Moreover, Satan has set clever traps that might appear to be worthy of our attention. There are all kinds of traps; some of them come in the form of people vying for your attention other than your mate. But if you fall for his enticements, it could destroy your life and everything that you stand for.

You have to remember that your commitment is to the Lord. Jesus wants you to be aware because He knows that Satan only wants to do you harm. He warned us accordingly, *"Therefore be on the alert, for you do not know which day your Lord is coming. . . . For this reason you also must be ready; for the Son of Man is coming at an hour when you do not think He will"* (Matthew 24:42, 44). Jesus also said, *"But of that day or hour no one knows, not even the angels in heaven, nor the Son, but the Father alone"* (Mark 13:32).

Even though we have been equipped with the sword of the Spirit, which is the Word of God, the challenge remains while we wait on the Lord. Satan will prey on our vulnerabilities and take advantage of those who are blind to his devices. He will target the thing that your flesh desires, and he knows how your flesh wants to spell relief from the pressures of life. He will offer you a substitute for your real need, which can only be supplied by your heavenly Father.

Scripture warns us to refrain from embracing such things that only serve as a distraction and take our focus away from God. The apostle John cautions us, *"Do not love the world nor the things in the world. If anyone loves the world, the love of the Father is not in him"* (1 John 2:15). And the only sure way to stay away from the temptations of the world is to rely on the power of the Holy Spirit, stay in the Word, study it, and practice it with an earnest desire for the things of God.

Taking Us Home

Then finally the time will come. In the most crucial *huppah*, or home-taking, of all, Jesus will come back for His church. Listen to how Paul describes this most welcome and wonderful event.

> *"For the Lord Himself will descend from heaven with a shout, with*
> *the voice of the archangel and with the trumpet of God, and the*
> *dead in Christ will rise first. Then we who are alive and remain*
> *will be caught up together with them in the clouds to meet*
> *the Lord in the air, and so we shall always be with the Lord.*
> *Therefore comfort one another with these words."*
> —1 THESSALONIANS 4:16–18

Just think of it. We will spend eternity with the Lord. Talk about good news. The covenant promise will be fulfilled in its entirety. Just as there was a seven-day honeymoon, there will be a seven-year marriage supper of the Lamb, seven years of tribulation on earth, and a seven-year marriage feast with the judgment seat of Christ where He will present the garment of virginity. Christ will be able to say that His bride is a chaste bride, without spot of blemish, not because of her own righteousness, but because of the righteousness that is in Christ.

Jesus is our righteousness, and we have new life in Him. The other alternative is to try to be righteous on your own. It's been tried before and, believe me, it just doesn't work. Ask the religious rulers of Jesus' day. In Matthew 5:20, He told them, *"For I say to you that unless your righteousness surpasses that of the scribes and Pharisees, you will not enter the kingdom of heaven."* To walk in wisdom and claim the victory that will allow us to go home with Jesus, we need the righteousness that He gives us. Jesus covered us in it because our own righteousness won't do. But where do we get it? The Word of God has the answer:

"By His doing you are in Christ Jesus, who became to us wisdom
from God, and righteousness and sanctification, and redemption."

—1 CORINTHIANS 1:30

And so it is that the cycle is completed. The sacrificial work of Christ has given us redemption, sanctification, wisdom, and righteousness. These are the promises that are written in our covenant with Him. It is through the life of Christ—the picture we have been given of His life—that we can see how to live. He shows husbands and wives how to conduct our marriages, and He gives us the ability to follow His pattern. The good news is that we don't have to carry out God's wishes in our own strength and power since we can be sure that what God has promised He will deliver.

A Worthy Sacrifice

In the book of Genesis, chapter 22, a profound story of Abraham and his son Isaac is found. It depicts a beautiful picture of the Lord Jesus Christ on His journey to Calvary. Abraham represented God the Father and Isaac represented God the Son. Abraham was well over one hundred years old at the time, and Isaac was a grown man. Under most circumstances, there was no way that an old man could have expected a much younger man to lay down on an altar and be offered as a sacrifice without a great deal of resistance. Yet, in a selfless act of obedience from both of them, a deep love comes shining through.

In this poignant story we find a picture of the voluntary act of submission and the sacrificial work of Jesus Christ made on our behalf. When Abraham told his servants to wait because he and his son were going up the mountain to worship God, he said they would come back again. Now, recall that God had already informed him that He expected Abraham to offer his son as a sacrifice. Abraham knew what God meant by that. So, when he told the men that he and his son would return, Abraham was demonstrating his faith in God. The only way the two men could come back together is if God were to resurrect Isaac from the dead. Abraham was prepared to obey God because he believed God would somehow save his son (see Romans 4; Hebrews 11).

As they traveled up the mountain, Isaac asked his father where the thing was that they would sacrifice. Abraham's response was, "The Lord will provide." When he eventually made it known that Isaac was to lie upon the altar and become the sacrifice, Isaac obediently went along with him. Abraham proceeded to raise his hand to murder his son, and God immediately stopped him. God never intended Abraham to go through with it. He already knew what the outcome would be, but He wanted Abraham to know the depth of his commitment to obey God.

Abraham demonstrated that he was willing to sacrifice the son whom he loved—the son God had given him in his old age—the son that he had waited so long to receive. But he proved that God was more important to him than the gift God had given him. So, when God restrained him from going through with the act, Abraham looked around and saw a bush with a ram caught in its thickets. He knew in his heart that God had provided this "ram in the bush" as a sacrifice for his servant to offer. The ram was God's provision for Abraham. That prompted him to call God by the name Jehovah-jireh, which means "the Lord will provide."

Here is the lesson for us to learn. Abraham had to lift his hand in obedience to God before he saw that the Lord would provide the substitute that would prevent him from taking his son's life. The ram was there all along; he just didn't see it until after he had shown his faith in God to deliver his son. This is a lesson in walking by faith and not by sight, which means that we cannot see the provision that God has in store for us until we raise our hand in obedience to what God requires of us. God asked Abraham to make a sacrifice to Him. That sacrifice happened to be something that Abraham held dearly—his beloved son. When you show God that you have faith in Him, whatever you are believing God for will be there when you need it to be. But know that it comes through a combination of your faith and your willingness to obey God. Like in Abraham's situation, God wants us to know that we can trust Him to bless us beyond our wildest dreams.

Now, what was Abraham looking at when he discovered the substitute for Isaac? Did he see the ram? No, he saw the Lord Jesus Christ. He saw a picture of Christ because the ram represented the Lamb of God, the definitive sacrifice. Jesus was wounded for our transgressions and bruised for our iniquities. Jesus bore our stripes as the punishment that He endured for dealing with our sin (Isaiah 53:5). Not only did He die as a penalty for our sin,

He died to reverse the curse that God had placed on the ground. The earth was cursed as a result of Adam's sin, and the ram's horns caught in the thickets that represented that curse (see Genesis 3:14–19). The thickets on the head of the ram symbolized the crown of thorns around Christ's head. And the crown of thorns jammed into His head represented Jesus bearing our curse.

So, through that experience Abraham saw a picture of the Lamb of God who took away the curse of sin from us. God had given the Lord Jesus Christ as the Lamb that was sacrificed, and Jesus confirmed that Abraham saw it when He attested, *"Your father Abraham rejoiced to see my day: and he saw it, and was glad"* (John 8:56 KJV). When did this happen? Before Adam sinned; before you and I sinned. Before the foundation of the world God placed the Lamb where He would need it and set up the entire sacrifice so that we can enter into salvation by the grace of God. It was the love of God making provision for man before He ever made man—before man ever sinned.

The Trinity of God has shown us a vision of unconditional love—the kind of love that will shine forth regardless of whether you feel that the recipient deserves your love or not. Through offering up His Son for our redemption, we see what it looks like to love someone in spite of the cost. The Holy Spirit then gives us the ability to love others with the same love that God loves us. Jesus has illuminated the way for us by giving us an excellent example to follow. Now, our task is to emulate His actions and follow the pattern of the Trinity's love and forgiveness.

Children of the Light

> *"For you were formerly darkness, but now you are Light in the*
> *Lord; walk as children of Light (for the fruit of the Light consists in*
> *all goodness and righteousness and truth)."*
> —EPHESIANS 5:8–9

So, what does acknowledging the reality of a spiritual reflection do for a husband and wife? It connects what a husband does for his wife with an expression of what Jesus does for us. A man is to anticipate his wife's needs and see that she has access to whatever provision she needs whenever she needs it. On the other hand, a wife is to provide the support that her husband needs in order to do his job as spiritual leader of the home. Moreover, they are to hold each other up in prayer and depend on our Lord to be the equalizing dimension in their relationship. When I counseled Michael and Elaine, I discovered that they were in deep trouble. Michael viewed his wife as his enemy; he did not even begin to know how to love her. He wasn't aware of his responsibility as the provider of unconditional love for his wife. I showed him in the Word that his role as a husband was to love his wife like Christ loves the church. Otherwise, Elaine could not function properly in her role as his helper, the one who was designed to support him with love and affection. They weren't doing their jobs in perfecting each other as a couple.

In case you need to be reminded, as believers in Christ Jesus, you and your mate are no longer walking around in darkness. It's time to allow God to enlighten your walk and direct you in the truth of His Word. So, if you are bashing each other and acting like a dream killer, you need to stop it. Instead, you should be encouraging and promoting the love of your life in every possible way. To bring the goodness of God into your lives, cherish the mate that God has given you. This is what Michael and Elaine needed to learn, and it's what all couples need to know.

The book of Ephesians sheds so much light on what God expects a husband and wife to do. He has deliberately distinguished the roles of the man as the initiator and the woman as the responder. In chapter 5, there are three verses that address the woman and nine verses that are directed to the husband. Paul speaks directly to the wife about submitting to her husband in the same way that she must submit to the Lord (see Ephesians 5:22–24). However, it bears repeating that her act of submission is one that she chooses; it is not to be forced upon her. Remember, she is not in a secondary class with respect to her husband. God assigned her female gender equal status, but He gave her a different position.

Once again, this is truth that points back to the Trinity. Jesus is the second Person in the Godhead, but He is no less God than His Father. Similarly, in a marriage relationship, the wife was created second and given a different role to play. When marriage mirrors the Trinity as God intended, she will respond to her husband favorably because his love and care is genuine and righteous. So, she submits to him as one who is treating her in the same way that Christ treats His bride. She responds to her husband's love because she loves her Creator—the One who designed the marriage covenant that she voluntarily entered into.

On the other hand, the husband is the initiator in the relationship. He was created first and has a great responsibility to love his wife by following Christ's pattern of love. A husband after God's own heart will step up to the challenge and be God's humble vessel. He will be the catalyst by which his wife is blessed. The instructions laid out in verses 25–33 give explicit charges to the husband to serve his wife as Christ serves the church. Christ never shouts at the church. Christ never slaps the church. Christ loves the church and would never slander her. Christ is faithful to the church; He does not commit adultery on His bride. No woman would fail to submit to a man that loves her the way that Christ loves the church.

What's Love Got to Do with It?

So then, we need to know, what are the characteristics of the love that Christ demonstrated for us? He has shown us a sacrificial love and a sanctifying love. Allow me to present them to you here.

Sacrificial Love

> *"Husbands, love your wives, just as Christ also loved the church*
> *and gave Himself up for her."*
> —EPHESIANS 5:25

It has been said that a picture can be worth a thousand words. So, the Word of God details how Christ proved His love for us through His actions. He actually *gave* His life for His church. You know, the old saying, "Actions speak louder than words" is so true. Don't be like the husband whose wife had to ask him if he loved her. His response was very telling when he said, "Woman, when I married you forty years ago, I told you that I loved you. If I ever change my mind, you'll be the first to know." It's so much more than that. You have to show your love to the point that your wife believes that you would give up your very life if it meant saving hers.

Christ incarnated Himself so that He could become a human being and offer the ultimate sacrifice of His very own life. It was a total commitment that was done on behalf of the object of His love—you and me. This kind of love is called agape love. It is taken from the Greek word *agapao* that means unconditional love, the God-kind of love. It means to love someone in spite of how or whether that love is returned to you.

But before you can love like this you have to know one thing. You cannot be deficient in the Word of God if you want to follow God's pattern that has been laid out for us. That was what I discovered to be the brother's problem when I counseled him and his wife. He didn't know that he wasn't coming even close to loving his wife. As a result, they were in counseling trying to get some relief. You cannot expect the right results if you don't follow the recipe for love. So, you have to go to the Source of love to find out how to love God's way. However, when a man has not been sufficiently nourished on God's Word, he just won't understand this and he'll end up missing out on the tremendous blessing God has in store for those who do depend on His counsel. So, it's our responsibility to search the Scriptures and find out what God has to teach us about love and then to rely on the Holy Spirit to make it come alive in us.

I was sharing on this subject once and another brother said to me, "You know, Pastor, I understand what you are saying—" I stopped him at that point and corrected him. I told him, "*I* didn't say it; it's right here in the Bible. So, don't blame me, I'm just the messenger delivering the message. Don't shoot me." He needed to understand that whatever he was about to say, he was saying it to God and not to me. Then he said, "Okay, but I need to say that's not who I am—I've got to be me."

I then suggested to him what Jesus is telling him: "I want you to do for your wife what I did for the church." What He actually means is that you are important, husband. But what I need you to be for your wife is more important. And who I'm going to make you to be for her is most important. That is what Jesus would say based on the kind of love that He demonstrated for us.

Then, I presented him with a hypothetical situation. What if Jesus had said in response to His Father, "That's not who I am. I've got to be me"? When it came time for Him to veil His Deity in humanity and come down here to be a kinsman redeemer, what if Jesus had said, "No. I am a Spirit; I am omnipresent. I will not embody Myself in a human shell. That's not who I am—I have to be Me."

I will tell you what would have happened. We would all die in our sins and be on our way to hell. If Jesus had said, "I don't do earth because heaven is My throne room and earth is My footstool. I will not leave My place in eternity. I am the great I Am and cannot be confined to time and space. I don't do that. I've got to be Me." But He didn't say those things. He knew what we needed Him to do, and He presented Himself in time so that you and I would have a Redeemer that would save us from our sins.

Jesus could have said, "I don't do stables and mangers. I don't have to become a human baby. I am the Ancient of Days, the Alpha and the Omega, the Beginning and the End." But we needed Him to become a child, to be born into poverty. So, He said, "I love you. I will become what you need Me to be so that I can provide what is necessary to bring you to heaven." He didn't say, "I'm not going to let those humans judge Me in so many illegal trials. I am the Judge of all the earth. I am the Creator; I will not allow the creature to judge Me." But He did. Why? Because we needed Him to become all of that for us.

What would we have done if Jesus had said, "I don't do sin; I'm the holy One. I am immutable; I am pure; I am perfect. I will not take your sins upon My sinless being because I've got to be Me." But He bore our sins on Calvary's cross because that's what we needed, a sin bearer. What if Jesus had said, "I don't do tombs because I am the way, the truth, and the life"? Then, we would have no hope of heaven. But He did do a tomb and rose again on the third day. Why? Because that's what we needed for Him to do for us.

Now, brother, take the interpretation of what Jesus did for you and me and apply it to what He wants you to do as a husband. The eternal God did all of that for us, and that is the kind of love He wants us to imitate in our marriages. And He doesn't expect mere human beings to be able to do what He did without first equipping us. That is why He has given us His grace and His power. By His grace, He picked us up. With His Word, He fixed us up. In His church, He cleans us up. With His Spirit, He fills us up. Through His call, He uses us up. At the rapture, He'll take us up. On the way to heaven, He'll change us up. And for all of eternity, He'll love us up.

But you have not yet committed to meeting your wife's needs to the degree that God requires; that is, if you are not ready to make the ultimate sacrifice of dying for her. I'm not even talking about physical death. Remember this is a spiritual reflection so I'm speaking of a spiritual death—dying to yourself. You're never going to be able to pull it off unless you learn to die to yourself. Check out what the Bible has to say about Him.

> *"Who, although He existed in the form of God, did not regard equality with God a thing to be grasped, but emptied Himself, taking the form of a bond-servant, and being made in the likeness of men. Being found in appearance as a man, He humbled Himself by becoming obedient to the point of death, even death on a cross."*
>
> —PHILIPPIANS 2:6–8

I know you're probably saying that this is a tremendous responsibility for a man. If you are saying that, then you're not ready for all of this. Consequently, you're not yet fit to be married—even though you may already be. If you are able to admit it, you've got a lot of work to do on your relationship. And guess what, we'd have far fewer marriages if people realized what this is really all about before they entered into a marital commitment. Jesus put aside His deity and became a mere man—a servant of the people no less. He emptied Himself, meaning that He was a selfless man and not a self-centered one. Can you imagine making the decision to put your physical life on the line because you love someone that much? Well, that's what Jesus did. When He took on a human body, the God of the universe humbled Himself to the point that He could actually die for the cause of love.

A sacrificial love contains two elements: it is a *prioritized* love and a *personal* love. When Paul wrote the phrase *"Husbands, love your wives,"* he used the present tense of the verb. It is a tense of continuous action. In other words, it means "keep on doing it." Husbands, keep on loving your wives. This is your first priority, and it is not a one-shot deal. Rely on the Holy Spirit to help you live sacrificially by being willing to die to yourself and your old ways of doing things. So, when do we do this? When do we sacrifice for her and die to ourselves? The answer is, from day to day because God is speaking in the present tense. So, it means to do it whenever she needs it to be done. It may be a sacrifice; you may feel like you're suffering big time. But don't worry. Jesus has been there, and He'll help you because He wants you to succeed. But know that you must have the faith to believe that it is in every way possible.

On the personal side, Christ "*gave Himself* for the church" (emphasis added). When you give of yourself to promote your wife, it becomes a personal thing because it involves your precious time and undivided attention. That's what love is all about. The truth of the matter is that our wives need us more than they need the things we can provide for them. They need our presence more than fine furniture, fur coats, jewelry, flat-screen TVs, stereos, and even the most up-to-date cell phones. You get the picture. They really need to know that they hold first place in our lives in the way that we hold first place in Jesus' heart. Just as He wants His bride to be all that we should be, we should want the same for the one that we love. And that is what we are to emulate.

Sanctifying Love

> "*So that He might sanctify her, having cleansed her by the washing
> of water with the word, that He might present to Himself the church
> in all her glory, having no spot or wrinkle or any such thing; but
> that she would be holy and blameless.*"
>
> —EPHESIANS 5:26–27

Since the term *sanctify* means to "set apart," it means that we are consecrated and dedicated to Him. He put the church, His bride, on a pedestal in the same way that we are called to put our wives on a pedestal. Although He saved us and forgave us of our sins, God knows that the spots and blemishes in our human nature still exist. So, Jesus went about cleansing the church with the Word of God. And when He finished the work, He said, "*You are already clean because of the word which I have spoken to you*" (John 15:3). But it's so important to know that Jesus sanctified and cleansed the church not just for our benefit, but for the glory of the Father. That is our overarching and ultimate goal in life—that He will receive glory. It is the reason why we sing, "To God be the glory for the things He has done."

Hear me loud and clear, brothers, because you are the initiator in your

relationship and everything begins with you. I want to you start thinking
this way about your wives: you must find the woman that you want in the
woman that you have. Through your role as the thermostat in the relationship, you can go to work on your wife just like Christ did for the church.
And always remember that you can lean on Him. Whatever is missing in
her, you are the catalyst for that thing becoming a part of her life. Just as
Christ brings out the best in the church, you are to bring out the best in
your wife through your physical and spiritual support. Jesus went to work
and provided salvation for us. He works through us to give us sanctification.
He works in us to bring out good works. He did it all so that He could present us to Himself as a body without spot or wrinkle.

What He wants to say to you is, whatever you want your wife to be, be
that to her first. Through times when you are struggling with life's issues
and things start to heat up, remember that *a gentle answer turns away
wrath, but a harsh word stirs up anger*" (Proverbs 15:1). When you model
Christ for her, you are, in turn, allowing her to emulate your example. You
are initiating a Christlike attitude through your behavior, and your relationship will begin to thrive. That is the object. She will eventually pick up
on it and walk in the way of the Lord because you are showing her the way
and giving her the opportunity to do her part.

Don't worry, if you shine the light God has given you, it will illuminate
your way. No one can deny the overwhelming, all-consuming love of God
as He works through you to love her and make her what she needs to be in
Christ's eyes. That is the purpose God has given you as her husband. You
see, she has a purpose to accomplish in life that was given to her by God.
When the two of you hooked up, you agreed to take your place in helping
her to bring that purpose to fruition. But it takes a lot of work to fulfill a destiny, and it is your job to help her make it happen. It is going to require the
kind of submission and sacrifice on both of your parts that can only come
through your obedience to God's commandment to love your wife.

And what will the end result be? You will fulfill your purpose and cause
goodness, righteousness, and truth to shine in your life. God will be satisfied, and you will be given your just reward. You will experience God's pleasure because He will be well pleased with your sacrifice.

Do you realize that for all of eternity Jesus Christ will bear the scars of fulfilling the purpose of giving us salvation? His body is glorified now, but we will know Him when we see Him because He still has the nail prints in His hands and feet. We will see the wound in His side that the spear made. Yet, for all of eternity He will feel God's pleasure because He was obedient to His Father when it came to His purpose of redeeming us from our sins. Jesus has fulfilled His purpose; now is the time that we need to fulfill ours.

Putting the Pieces Together

I know that so many marriages experience brokenness because so often people are broken. But do you know that God is the only One who can make your marriage whole because He can make you whole? There is only one stipulation. You have to give Him the pieces and allow Him to work on you.

Let me give you an example. As the story goes, there was an exquisite mirror in the hallway of a palace in a distant land. A French sculptor was commissioned to create the mirror to the tune of over a million dollars. En route to its destination, the masterpiece was mishandled. When the shipment arrived and was opened, the mirror was lying there in thousands of pieces.

The owners were ready to count it as a loss and were about to throw it away when someone's idea prevented them from doing it. He said that he knew of a man who worked with glass; he was a master craftsman. They decided to bring him in and see what he could do. The master worked on the mirror and put all the pieces back together. However, the finished product was still cracked.

So then, the result was, even though the mirror itself is only one color, when the sunlight beams on it, a spectrum of all the colors of the rainbow is reflected on it. The way that the master repaired it causes a reflection of beautiful colors to complement one another in an exquisite way.

That is the way that God will repair your marriage. It doesn't matter how broken it is. You see, something happened in your relationship. You and your spouse somehow mishandled it, made some costly mistakes, and caused it to be damaged and broken. But we have a Master Craftsman who can take the broken pieces of your marriage and repair it. You must give it to Him so that He can resurrect your dead marriage and make it the masterpiece that it should be. If you submit yourself to Him and line up with His purpose, that is, your reason for living, God will make sure that you have a marriage as He intended it to be—a picture of Christ and His church.

Making It Happen

1. With an open and receptive heart, ask God to help you understand how to apply His reason for creating marriage as a picture of Christ and His church. He will hear your sincere prayers and help you to transform your marriage into a reflection of His image.

2. What does it mean to you when the Bible says that we should be imitators of God? Do you believe that you imitate God in any way? If so, how do you do so? What other ways do you believe you can imitate God?

3. God's love for us is unconditional. Spend some time alone reading and meditating on 1 Corinthians 13:1–8. Then, read it together with your spouse. Share what God has placed in your heart in an answer to your openness to change your behavior toward each other. Talk to each other about what is working for you and where you need improvement. Include these questions: "In what ways have you personally experienced His unconditional love? How do you show unconditional love to your spouse?"

4. Spend some time thinking of ways that you can show a deeper love for your spouse. Reread the descriptions of sacrificial love and sanctifying love, and listen for inspiration and guidance from the Holy Spirit.

5. Sometimes it is helpful to look back and recall how God has helped us in the past when we are faced with a challenge. When Abraham was being put to the test, what was the significance of God allowing him to reach the point of raising his hands to slay his son just before

God provided the ram in the bush? Think about a situation where you remember God's faithfulness to you when He required you to offer up a sacrifice to Him—something that you treasured. What was the ram in the bush that He provided for you? Do you believe that He can provide for you at this time?

Afterword

The seven reasons God created marriage as presented in this book can be summed up in one word: purpose. The main thing that you need to know is that God has a purpose for you and your marriage. Once you discover that purpose, things in your life will become clearer to you. My advice to you is—do not let your life and, therefore, your marriage end without finding the reason why God created you. As you search your heart, you also need to be keenly aware that your purpose as an individual is directly tied to your mate's purpose. Remember, when the two of you exchanged marriage vows you became one flesh in God's sight.

God does not create people or sanction marriages without having a plan. You were born for a specific reason and so was your mate. And somehow the purpose for your individual lives will work together to accomplish God's higher purpose. Therefore, it is no accident that you are who you are. When you know what God created you to do, you will know the purpose that you are to carry out in your marriage.

Furthermore, everyone wasn't created to be a doctor, a scientist, or even a pastor. It may just be that you were made to love your wife or your husband, raise a beautiful family together, and foster the godly care of your children. Or, perhaps God wants you to give guidance to children in need of spiritual direction that will keep their lives on the right path.

Whatever it is, when you have found it you will know it because you will be following God's prescribed reasons for marriage. The Spirit of God will whisper in your ear and say to you, "This is the way; walk in it." And so it is that His guidance will help you reach a level of perfection in your marriage partnership. Then you will feel God's pleasure because the two of you have discovered the purpose for your marriage union. When you reach this point in your lives, you will begin to look like the image of God as stated in God's Word, your life will be pure and blameless before the Lord, and in your marriage others will see a picture of Christ and His church.

Be continually blessed as you endeavor to follow the will of God.

JAMES FORD JR.

Appendix

The Erosion *of* Marriage

So, why is it that something that is supposed to last and fulfill for a lifetime falls into a state of disrepair and decay? We have already discussed that some people get married for the wrong reasons. We know that we need a firm foundation to build a lasting marriage on. So, what happens? I would like to suggest ten possible reasons for the erosion of a marriage.

1. The goal has been attained.

Once the vows have been exchanged we tend to relax. In other words, once we say "I do," we're done. Especially men, because men are generally more goal oriented. The challenge was in the dating and the courtship. We don't work on the marriage as much as we worked to secure the wedding. We fail to realize that the things we did to get to the marriage we have to continue to do if we want to keep the marriage strong.

Marriage should be like a precious jewel; it should appreciate in value not depreciate because of neglect. Jewels are meant to be seen in their best condition. They are put in display cases. Those who have valuable jewels go to great lengths to take care of their prize possessions. They don't want to do anything to diminish the value of them. It actually takes more work to keep the marriage together than it did to get to that point. Tragically, some people put more time and money into their wedding ceremonies than they put into their marriages.

2. We take off our masks.

When we are dating, courting, and getting engaged, we are some of the nicest people you ever want to meet. We are usually very agreeable, considerate, courteous, and excellent models of sensitivity. When you were dating, he didn't raise his voice at you and point his finger at you like a father reprimanding or disciplining his child. He didn't do these things because in all likelihood you would have stopped dating him (at least that's what should happen). She didn't put her hands on her hips and roll her head like it was broken and flip her hands around like she had epilepsy. That attitude started after you got married. (If she did it before and you didn't deal with it then, that's your fault.)

After marriage we take off our masks and let our real selves be known. One man said it this way, "You know that you have become comfortable with each other when both of you are in the bathroom doing different things at the same time."

3. We grow tired of doing what we don't like.

Once people get married they seem to no longer be able to tolerate each other's personal tastes the way they could when they were dating. When a husband and wife used to agree on how they would spend an evening, where they would eat dinner, what movie to see—but they can no longer agree on these kinds of activities—the dating phase of the relationship had ended.

We get tired of doing the things that we pretended to enjoy, and eventually we stop doing them. Men, how many times did she sit with you and watch sports and action movies? She didn't necessarily enjoy them, but she sat there with you. Now, she not only will not sit and watch with you, but she can't understand why you are sitting there "wasting time." The same things she used to do with you are now a "waste of time." How often did you go to the mall with her? You spent half of your day off at the mall with her, carrying her bags and sitting down waiting for her. Now, she knows not to even suggest that you go to a mall with her.

4. We get tired of trying to be who we are not.

Once we are married, we no longer want the roles we played during the dating phase. We conform when we are dating, and keep our real selves hidden. In the dating phase we are like chameleons—we adapt and become whoever we perceive we need to be for as long as we need to be. What happens after marriage? People say "You changed on me." They didn't change; they just camouflaged who they really are. That's how they really were all along, but they hid their true selves. You saw what they wanted you to see to keep the relationship going. Your rose-colored glasses aren't working anymore, and now you are seeing who they really are.

5. Reality sets in.

When the honeymoon is over, the marriage begins. Reality sets in. Honeymoon means "sweet month." That's the honeymoon phase. One person said you find out his breath stinks at 6:00 a.m. and his feet stink at 6:00 p.m. You now realize this is a permanent situation. There is no going back. Now, you realize that he isn't laid back; he's lazy. You thought she had a difficult time dealing with stress, but now you realize she is the cause of the stress. You thought she was sharing things with you, but now you face the reality that she just talks a lot. She even talks about things that should be only between the two of you. Now, you realize that those were not caution lights while you were dating, they were red lights and you ran through them. This is the phase when you realize that those "cute" things he did while you were dating aren't really that cute, now that you realize they are permanently in your face.

6. Now you are living together.

There was a time that when you disagreed about something, you went to your home and he went to his. You didn't have to put up with each other. Now, you are married, living together, and you get to see each other day and night. Regardless of how mad she is, you still sleep in the same bed. It was so much easier when you could go home, but now you are angry and in each other's face. Even when you are not feeling very fond of this person you are married to, you still have to deal with them.

7. We create new issues.

There were some things we didn't think we needed to comment on when we were dating, but now that we are married we point those things out. How many people argue over whether the toilet seat is up or down; and whether the toilet paper faces in or going over. You may think that's small, but you would be surprised at how many arguments begin over something that trivial. Of course, we know that is a sign of deeper issues, but the point is there are some "small" things we never mentioned while dating. When we get married, we let those small things become big issues. When you were dating, you didn't realize that she likes to stay up late reading with the lights and the television on, loudly crunching potato chips. You knew he was an early riser, but you didn't know he expected you to be one as well. These are small issues that become magnified because they were unexpected and we can't get away from them.

8. We are not as attentive to the other person's needs as we used to be.

Men say they don't like to talk. But let's be honest. You had no problem talking on the phone three to four hours before you got married. We had no problem holding hands and spending time together every time we got a chance. You found reasons to touch each other. Now, you go out to dinner together and if anything is said it's more like "Are you ready to order?" or

"Please pass the salt." When you are in a restaurant, you can spot the couples that are dating and those who are newlyweds. They remind you of when you were in that state: touching each other, eating each other's food, sitting in the booth like they are glued at the hip.

It's difficult to understand how we think we can build and maintain a relationship without doing some of the things we did before. After marriage, some of us think as long as we are in the house at the same time, we are spending time together. After marriage some couples act like they are sexual roommates. Each person is living their own separate lives and meeting up with each other in the bedroom.

9. We are not as open to being criticized as we were before marriage.

There were things we could be told then, but not now. It's like the man who said to his wife, "Now that we are married, can I tell you some of the things that I really don't like about you?" She said, "No, because those are the things that kept me from getting a better husband." When you were dating you could tell him that he was driving too fast. Now, if you mention it you are controlling and critical. Before marriage, he could tell you which hairstyle he preferred on you. If he says anything about your hair now (except how nice it looks), he will spend the next three days trying to make up. Before marriage, criticism was corrective or positive or even just a sharing of an opinion. After marriage, criticism is a declaration of war, and each person intends to win it.

10. There were some things about marriage that we just didn't know.

Many of us went into marriage with some expectations that are never going to be met, and because those expectations are not met, we want out of the marriage. There are some things marriage cannot do and was never designed to do. If you were unhappy before you got married, you will be unhappy in the marriage because you don't know how to satisfy yourself and no one else can do that for you.

Some people go into marriage thinking they can live like roommates. They enter marriage with this unrealistic expectation that everything is going to be fifty-fifty and end up in a seemingly unending game of tug of war. They don't understand that the fifty-fifty approach to marriage is a quick route to divorce court. Think about it—that concept does not work in the business world, what makes you think it will work in real life. The reality is that one partner will always bring more of something to the marriage than the other at different times.

Acknowledgments

My heartfelt gratitude to Sister Kathryn Hall who worked so diligently in the preparation of the manuscript for this book. She truly possesses the patience of Job. Thanks to Chris Salley and Pastor Kenny Grant for their invaluable support and scriptural insight. I cherish the input of the members and friends of Christ Bible Church, especially the assistance of Sister Marie Rogers. Finally, I am grateful to Sister Cynthia Ballenger and Sister Roslyn Jordan with Moody Publishers/Lift Every Voice for making my book available to you. The contributions of all my faithful supporters will be forever etched in my heart. Maranatha.

Notes

Chapter 1: Reason 1: The Pattern of the Trinity

1. "40 Days of Prayer Together" Baylor University and Gallop Poll as cited on the Christian Broadcast Network website http://www.cbn.com/special/coupleswhopray/.

2. Charles R. Swindoll, *Strike the Original Match* (Portland, OR: Multnomah Press, 1981), 164.

Chapter 2: Reason 2: A Partnership In God

1. Patricia Dunlavy Valenti, *Sophia Peabody Hawthorne: A Life, Vol. 1, 1809–1847* (Columbia, MO: University of Missouri Press, 2004), 22.

2. "Men Use Only Half Their Brain to Listen—Study," CBC News, http://www.cbc.ca/health/story/2000/11/28/men_hear001128.html.

3. Three Boys Missing, "Sex Crime Stats," http://threeboysmissing.com/Statistics.html.

4. "Homicide Trends in the U.S.," U.S. Department of Justice, Office of Justice Programs, Bureau of Justice, http://www.ojp.usdoj.gov/bjs/homicide/intimates.htm#intimates.

Chapter 3: Reason 3: The Perfecting Reason

1. Louann Brizendine, *The Female Brain* (New York: Broadway Books, 2006), 26.

2. Ibid.

3. Dr. Tony Evans, senior pastor of Oakcliff Bible Fellowship, Dallas, Texas.

Chapter 4: Reason 4: The Procreation Reason

1. Pastor Kenny Grant, Christ Community Church, Savannah, Georgia. Sermon entitled "The Divine Design" taken from Psalm 127:4 and preached at Christ Bible Church in Chicago, Illinois, June 2, 2004.

2. Center for Children's Justice, Inc., "Effects of Fatherlessness (US Data)," http://www.childrensjustice.org/fatherlessness2.htm.

3. U.S. Department of Health and Human Services, "A National Strategy to Prevent Teen Pregnancy: Annual Report, 1999–2000," http://aspe.hhs.gov/hsp/teenp/ann-rpt00/#TOC.

4. Three Boys Missing, "Sex Crime Stats," http://threeboysmissing.com/Statistics.html.

5. Bureau of Justice Statistics, Intimate Partner Violence in the U.S., 2001–2005, http://www.ojp.usdoj.gov/bjs/intimate/victims.htm.

6. Campbell, J. C., D. Webster, J. Koziol-McLain, C. R. Block, D. Campbell, M. A. Curry, F. Gary, J. McFarlane, C. Sachs, P. Sharps, Y. Ulrich, and S.A. Wilt, "Assessing Risk Factors for Intimate Partner Homicide," *NIJ Journal* 250 (November 2003): 14–19, NCJ 196547. Cited by the U.S. Department of Justice, http://www.ojp.usdoj.gov/nij/topics/crime/intimate-partner-violence/extent.htm.

7. Barbara Hart, "Children of Domestic Violence: Risks & Remedies," Minnesota Center Against Violence and Abuse Electronic Clearinghouse, cited by the Violence Prevention Center of Southwestern Illinois, http://www.vpcswi.org/statistics.html.

8. Tjaden, P., and N. Thoennes, "Prevalence, Incidence, and Consequences of Violence Against Women: Findings From the National Violence Against Women Survey," U.S. Department of Justice, National Institute of Justice, and U.S. Department of Health and Human Services, Centers for Disease Control and Prevention, November 2000, NCJ 183781, http://www.ojp.usdoj.gov/nij/pubs-sum/183781.htm.

9. M. Hofford and A. Harrell, *Family Violence Interventions for the Justice System* (Washington, DC: U.S. Bureau of Justice Assistance, 1989), cited by Georgia State University Library, Domestic Violence Statistics, http://www.library.gsu.edu/research/pages.asp?ldID=59&guideID=0&ID=776.

10. K. J. Wilson, *When Violence Begins at Home: A Comprehensive Guide to Understanding and Ending Domestic Abuse* (Alameda, CA: Hunter House, 1997), cited by Georgia State University Library, Domestic Violence Statistics, http://www.library.gsu.edu/research/pages.asp?ldID=59&guideID=0&ID=776.

WHEN A MAN
LOVES A WOMAN

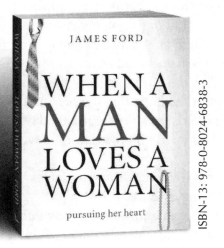

ISBN-13: 978-0-8024-6838-3

Many young people believe Michael Bolton was the first artist to sing "When a Man Loves a Woman" but actually it was written, produced and recorded by two others before Michael was born. Percy Sledge arranged the familiar tune in 1966, but Jacob of the Old Testament penned the first version in Genesis, chapter 29. Everyone knows that Jacob of the Old Testament was a rascal, usurper, and deceiver. But Jacob knew how to do one thing very well . . . Jacob knew how to love a woman. If you want to know if a man really loves a woman, take a close look at what Jacob has to tell us from the passages of Scripture.

www.lifteveryvoicebooks.com
1-800-678-8812 • MOODYPUBLISHERS.COM

Lift Every Voice Books

Lift every voice and sing
Till earth and heaven ring,
Ring with the harmonies of Liberty;
Let our rejoicing rise
High as the listening skies,
Let it resound loud as the rolling sea.
Sing a song full of the faith that the dark past has taught us,
Sing a song full of the hope that the present has brought us,
Facing the rising sun of our new day begun
Let us march on till victory is won.

The Black National Anthem, written by James Weldon Johnson in 1900, captures the essence of Lift Every Voice Books. Lift Every Voice Books is an imprint of Moody Publishers that celebrates a rich culture and great heritage of faith, based on the foundation of eternal truth—God's Word. We endeavor to restore the fabric of the African-American soul and reclaim the indomitable spirit that kept our forefathers true to God in spite of insurmountable odds.

We are Lift Every Voice Books—Christ-centered books and resources for restoring the African-American soul.

For more information on other books and products
written and produced from a biblical perspective, go to
www.lifteveryvoicebooks.com or write to:

Lift Every Voice Books
820 N. LaSalle Boulevard
Chicago, IL 60610
www.lifteveryvoicebooks.com